"Mr. James Gillray. From a Miniature painted by himself & Engraved by Chas. Turner. London. Published April 19, 1819, by G. Humphrey, 27 St. James's Street." The original miniature, given to the Rev. John Sneyd after Hannah Humphrey's death in 1818, is now in the National Portrait Gallery, London.

THE SATIRICAL ETCHINGS OF

JAMES GILLRAY

EDITED BY DRAPER HILL

DOVER PUBLICATIONS, INC. NEW YORK

For Sarah

Published in Canada by General Publishing Company,
Ltd., 30 Lesmill Road, Don Mills, Toronto, Ontario.
Published in the United Kingdom by Constable and Com-
pany, Ltd., 10 Orange Street, London WC 2.

The Satirical Etchings of James Gillray is a new work, first
published by Dover Publications, Inc., in 1976.

International Standard Book Number: 0–486–23340–5
Library of Congress Catalog Card Number: 75–41946

Manufactured in the United States of America
Dover Publications, Inc.
180 Varick Street
New York, N.Y. 10014

ACKNOWLEDGMENTS

For additional biographical and background material, the
reader is referred to my two previous books on Gillray, *Mr.
Gillray The Caricaturist* (1965) and *Fashionable Contrasts:
Caricatures by James Gillray* (1966). Both books are published by Phaidon Press Ltd., 5 Cromwell Place, London
SW7, and Phaidon Publishers Inc., New York (distributors:
Praeger Publishers, 111 Fourth Avenue, New York, N.Y.
10003). The present introduction leans substantially on my
work for Phaidon, and on research originally conducted in
that connection; I am most grateful to them for allowing
me to retrace my tracks.

Portions of the second section of the Introduction draw
on "The School of London," a paper given at the Boston
Public Library in May 1973.

Mr. and Mrs. A. G. Burkhart, Jr. of Memphis have helped
in many ways. Their generous, painstaking aid with the
galley proofs is particularly appreciated.

In addition, I am deeply indebted for assistance and coun-
sel to Mr. Wilmarth Lewis, Mr. Duncan Macpherson, Mr.
Sinclair Hitchings, Miss Catherine Nicholson, Mr. Simon
Haviland, Mr. Dudley Snelgrove, Mr. Andrew Edmunds,
Mr. Stanley Appelbaum, the staff of the Memphis Public
Library and finally—but hardly least—the late Dr. M.
Dorothy George.

D. H.

LIST OF PLATES

A meticulous wood engraving in the manner of Thomas Bewick (1753–1828), probably executed as a tribute to Pitt during his retirement, circa 1803, signed "J. Gillray fec." at bottom center. Seven preliminary drawings are preserved in the New York Public Library Print Room. This design, which appears on the 1847 Bohn title page, was apparently first used on the title page of McLean's folio in 1830.

INTRODUCTION

[I]

THE MAN IN HIS SETTING

It is a positive fact that a degree of levity, and mirth-exciting fancy, plays in Caricatures for the last twenty-five years, which merely dawned in the days of Hogarth, who forces a smile while the moderns excite hearty laughter.
—James P. Malcolm, 1813[1]

SIR,

I greet you as the beginner of a new era in political caricature. There have been artists before you who dabbled in caricature. There have also been caricaturists who dabbled in art. But you, sir, are the first considerable artist who made caricature his full-time occupation. . . . You were the first to realize that the principles of art, selection and emphasis, could be adjusted to a new balance in a new type of draughtsmanship, neither the representation of reality nor mere grotesque invention, but the discriminating exaggeration of what is true. . . . If Hogarth was the grandfather of the modern cartoon, *You* were its father. . . .

—David Low to James Gillray,
As One Caricaturist to Another, 1943[2]

St. James's Street slopes gently down from Piccadilly through the heart of "clubbable" London, past White's, Boodle's and Brooks's, to the squat clocktower portal of St. James's Palace. In the early 1800s, the King's im-mediate neighbors included poet-banker Samuel Rogers; the distinguished printer William Bulmer; Francis Kelsey, dealer in sugar plums; the younger Pitt, betwixt terms as Prime Minister (1801–04); and a "thin, dry, bespectacled man" described by a contemporary German journalist as "the foremost living artist in the whole of Europe."[3]

The recipient of this considerable homage, James Gillray, lived and worked (and occasionally waited on customers) at the shop of his publisher–printseller Hannah Humphrey, halfway down the east side of the street. Her establishment, Number 27, was some 190 yards from George III's doorstep, directly opposite William Pitt's lodgings in Park Place. "Mrs." Humphrey, a maiden lady, operated the city's leading caricature emporium in partnership with her star boarder. (It was alleged in straighter Victorian days that there was a *liaison* between them "not essential to their relation as designer and publisher.")[4] Three decades before cartoons could be served up in magazines or newspapers with any ease or practicality, they supplied an enthusiastic upper-class public with a steady diet of pungent pictorial satire, both political and social. These individual copperplate etchings, available plain or exquisitely colored by hand, were collector's items from the moment of issue. Posted fresh daily for inspection behind the panes of Mrs. Humphrey's capacious bay window, they represent the pre-dawn stirrings of a modern illustrated press.

Tinted impressions of Gillray's "Very Slippy-Weather" (Plate 91) indicate a narrow dark brown house, an orange door framed in yellow, with a delicate fanlight, an imposing lion's-head knocker and the firm name emphatically displayed on the lintel. Inside, the showroom contained two large mahogany counters and a "nest," each fitted with multiple drawers, and a pair of showcases.[5] Mistress Humphrey's drawing room on the floor above was dominated by "a shell work bouquet under a huge glass case." Presumably it also housed a small pedestal bookcase enclosing three of Gillray's original sketches behind a brass grilled door.[6] According to report and tradition, the caricaturist's living quarters and "studio" were in the attic, three stories higher. One pictures a work table before the single dormer, shielded from the direct rays of the afternoon sun by a diffusion screen fixed at an oblique angle to the window frame. Inevitably, the setting would have included a profusion of needles, roulettes and burins, containers of nitric acid and varnish and perhaps a small press for trial proofs. Gillray, like his friend Rowlandson, was an avid collector of old master prints. A special partiality for Rubens might well have been reflected on the walls of his apartment.

The remainder of the domicile and manufactory at Number 27 remains equally conjectural. Mrs. Humphrey employed a shop assistant named Betty (see Plate 38). We know nothing of her colorists; presumably they were teams of extremely accomplished ladies working in relays. It is reasonable to suspect that her basement, or ground floor rear, accommodated two or more large flat-bed presses.

Living in the very bosom of the *beau monde*, petted and patronized by lords and ladies, Gillray and Mrs. Humphrey managed to be *in* society without being *of* it. "There are several people here we know," she wrote him from Brighton on 17 October 1804:

> His Highness of Clarence [later William IV] did me the honour of asking me how I did as we were walking on the Steine [a seafront promenade] tho he had two Noblemen with him. . . . I am sure I was quite surprised as I could not think he would have known me as we were at some distance from Him—but he made me hear whether I would or not and seemed quite pleased He had met somebody he knew.[7]

The house of Humphrey struck outsiders as a singular ménage indeed. Mrs. Humphrey's letters suggest that she was a direct, practical person of limited education; her "likeness" (Plate 38) and other evidence indicate she was some years older than Gillray. The caricaturist was remembered by his acquaintance Henry Angelo as "a man of slouching gait and careless habits":

A careless sort of cynic who neither loved nor hated society. Mrs. Humphreys, and her maid Betty were all the world to him—they saved him the trouble of thinking of household affairs, and, but for that, they might have walked with all the other ghosts in the Red Sea for what he had cared.[8]

The actual situation was probably a bit more complex. A second witness, the German writer cited above, noted that Gillray's motives remained obscure as "He doesn't talk very much at all about things":

> He doesn't explain himself about anything . . . he is of such an exterior, his appearance, manner and conversation are so ordinary and unassuming. . . .

Writing some nine years after Gillray's death, Angelo recalled that the caricaturist seemed "scarcely to think at all and to care no more for the actors in the mighty drama which he depicted, nor for the events which he so wonderfully dramatised, than if he had no participation in the good or evil of his day. Such a character eludes philosophic enquiry. . . ."

In 1798 the "whole of London" was said to regard Gillray with a mixture of approval and fear.[9] By 1803 he was "all over the place, following the troubled elite like the ghost of Hamlet's father."[10] In those hardy prephotographic days, subjects for satire had to be tracked and "taken" on big game safaris in the wilds of Westminster. (Earl Spencer, when warned decades later that there was a caricaturist in the gallery of the House of Lords, shrank on the front bench and "sat huddled-up [with his] face and beard in his knees.")[11] Gillray stalked his prey endlessly, trapping them in sketchbooks or on small bits of pasteboard which he carried around in his pockets. In 1797 the politician J. H. Frere wrote a friend that he had not seen Gillray for days: "The last time was in the gallery of the House of Commons when he was contemplating very seriously and I hope successfully the features of Mr. Nicholl . . ."[12] (see Plate 60). As added inducement to persuade the caricaturist to join her for a week of vacation at Brighton in 1804, Mrs. Humphrey suggested that he might perhaps "pick up a straggler or two on the Steine."[13] In this fashion Gillray went through life, biting, as it were, with needle and *aqua fortis*, the hands that fed him.

A publisher's prospectus of June 1800 described him as "confessedly the first moral satirist since the days of Hogarth."[14] Much of his fascination, then and now, lies in the paradoxical union of intense ethical purpose and outrageous license, of fastidious proportion and grotesque exaggeration. There is no question that he was accepted and celebrated, in a guarded way, by the community he served. It seems less likely that *he* ever accepted *them*. The status of outsider, whether actual or spiritual, is not necessarily a liability to a caricaturist. Some degree of detachment is inevitable—a useful quality, well worth nourishing, cherishing and protecting.

(New Zealander David Low immigrated to Britain in 1919 and established himself in short order as the most influential and respected political cartoonist of the twentieth century; yet 42 years later he could still jerk his thumb at the London outside his studio window and remark to an American visitor: "These Englishmen all went to school together!")

James Gillray's relentless pursuit and classification of the raw material of life shows to advantage in his one surviving sketchbook, leather-bound, four inches by seven, with a delicate, hand-tooled brass clasp.[15] The inside front cover bears signature, address and the date "July 23ᵈ 1801"; the last page carries a rudimentary laundry list: "1 shift, 3 Handke[rchie]fs Pocket" and "1 Pr Stock[in]gs." The interior consists almost entirely of sketches and notes recording a vacation at the fashionable seaside resort town of Margate on the English Channel. From the outset, Gillray must have intended to shape these impressions into a Hogarthian "progress" or series following "John Bull and his family" on their holidays.

The odyssey of some eighty miles commences, in the caricaturist's rough, penciled journal, with reality and black fantasy jockeying one another for position:

Setting of[f] in Post Chaise with Bundles Boxes &c Bills up (1/6 [per] mile pro bono publico) Connections between different Innkeepers on the road . . . Lady dress'd very fine with rings, Medals, bracelets &c . . .

Old post Chaise breaking down. thief cutting off Trunk. Mistaking way on a Common. Blind horse. Wife screaming through broken window. Daughter Fainting. Trunks all scatter'd & in ye Pool. Wrong road to margate. Gibbet over Postilion.

The party finally makes its "Arrival at Margate, quite Fatigued," to be greeted by various notable entrepreneurs, hucksters and gambling-house operators.

Wellcomed by Mitchener, York Hotel, numbers of Bathing Room keepers (Wood Hughes &c) loading them with Cards &c

Bucks in Pantaloons Ladies in Bathing Bonnets People just landed from the [London] Packets fatigued to death —others wrapd up in Great coats with their Baskets of Provisions—Bathing Machines out in High Waves— parties going out fishing—bills stuck up of prices of Provisions

Gillray visits "Mr. Silvertongue's Library," a notorious house of chance, sketches the proprietor (a splendidly unctuous weasel of a man in "Light Coat & Pantaloons") and preserves a snatch of his running patter:

Mr. Silᵉ—give me liberty to mark you down in the shilling list. Chances [are] tis your turn for winning . . . it must be your turn to win the next throw—only 60 names wanting for ye next . . .

Miss—you threw last night within two of the [?] target.

The caricaturist notes with obvious disapproval that this last was delivered to an audience of "very little girls & boys," nor did he see much else that pleased him:

every third house in Margate a Bawdy house Butchers cutting off the meat after bought Fishmongers changing the prices wives & daughters of Citizen debauched & selling themselves for money to gamble with in London a Tradesman is afraid of his reputation being lost if he deals unfairly the modest woman is obligd to take up a Lodging with the Street Walker smuggling shop i.e. Toy Shop on ye Pier opposite the Customs House.

The only breath of relief from this chronicle of depravity is a passing reference to the "High Wind, Blowing up the Petticoats of the Ladies looking over the side of the Pier." Gillray's memoranda are interspersed with sketches of gambling tables, hotel and shop facades, ships and rigging, gigantic accordion-tented, horse-drawn precursors of the Victorian bathing machine, and a variety of local characters. Structure, detail and atmosphere are captured in a dancing, feather-light pencil tracery, flicked occasionally with the barest trace of pen and sepia.

The caricaturist may well have spent his forty-fifth birthday, August 13, at Margate; a reclusive, stooped, balding figure with sad piercing gray-green eyes, prominent brows, a small, purposeful mouth and full lower lip. By then he was troubled by rheumatism, eyestrain and a partiality for drink. At the peak of his powers and his celebrity, he had recently summarized his existence as "a Life made up of hardships & disappointments."[16]

Eventually Gillray rolled and pitched back to London aboard the *Nelson*, a tiny, brightly painted hoy (one of the sturdy, sloop-rigged vessels that served the tourist trade along the Channel coast). He observed his fellow passengers: "some Sick, some Eating & drinking, Tea, Gin &c—Smoking—Cards . . . Crowd in the 5th Cabbin— but few in the for[ward] Gunnel." The *Nelson*'s skipper, Captain Rowe, was carefully preserved in the sketchbook, beefy, jut-jawed and authoritative. "Left Handed" with "Black Hair," a "thin Tail" and "Carroty whiskers," the Captain wore a "Blue Waist[coa]t," a "Black Coat, Shipd Trousers" and "a Blue Great Coat" with "2 Rows of Buttons." Judging from the degree of finish, he rather enjoyed posing for his likeness, and one hopes he was good company on the journey home.

Gillray's working season was pretty much established by the comings and goings of Mrs. Humphrey's eminent clientele, a factor largely determined by the sittings of Parliament. In 1801 the House rose on 2 July and returned on 29 October. The caricaturist's sabbatical appears to have stretched from 13 July to 6 October, judging from publication dates. Back in St. James's Street, Gillray outlined a series of tableaus on "The Journey to Margate." The last scene was to have shown his protagonists

Returning the cheapest way all sick, *Mama Sucking the Brandy Bottle Captain Rowe at helm—Miss Puking up her inside—some eating some smoking some playing at Cards—some singing some drunk—*[17]

He made twelve drawings in this connection[18] but does not appear to have engraved them. To borrow one of his favorite phrases, the caricaturist probably decided that his long, depressing saga would not "come in well."[19]

He might properly have asked himself how many customers would have rushed to invest a considerable sum in so bleak a souvenir of exploitation and misery. (At a minimum price of a half-crown per hand-colored plate, the series could not have sold for less than thirty shillings, about three weeks' wages for most unskilled workers.) It was, after all, a business, and Gillray was a professional in both the higher and lower senses of the world.

[II]

CARICATURE AND THE PRINTSHOP

They walked together, and in all the shops,
    The pictures noted, read th' appended rhyme,
Made in their promenade repeated stops,
    To criticise, applaud, quiz, taking time.
                        —Richard Dagley, 1821[20]

There is a bastard sort of fame,
And *notoriety* [is] its name . . .
To paint a picture with your toes,
Or play the bagpipe with your nose;
To twist, to torture, or to bend,
Things from their proper use and end,
In print shop fame may hand you down
With other blockheads of the town.
                        —Anon., c. 1821[21]

The rise of satirical printmaking as a viable trade during the middle decades of the eighteenth century resulted in large part from the practice and precaution of William Hogarth. There were influential political "emblems" or allegories in the Dutch manner circulated among the English during the early 1600s. Illustrative woodcuts began to crop up in adventurous embryo newspapers after 1638 and in the ribald weeklies which enjoyed a brief period of license at mid-century after the execution of Charles I.

Single-sheet copperplate productions continued to increase in number and quality over the decades which followed, resolutely Dutch in style and often in actual execution. Apart from a shortage of capable draftsmen and engravers, the principal deterrent to the evolution of a native "school" of pictorial satirists was the widespread practice of plagiarism, imitation and forgery among rival printsellers. This situation was modified significantly by Hogarth after he saw a great portion of the anticipated profits from his *Harlot's Progress* (1732) vanish into the pockets of pirates and copyists. At Hogarth's urging, an engraver's copyright act was drafted,

enacted by Parliament and given the King's assent on 15 May 1735, providing:

That from and after the Twenty fourth Day of June, which shall be in the Year of our Lord One thousand seven hundred and thirty five, every Person who shall invent and design, engrave, etch, or . . . from his own Works and Invention, shall cause to be designed and engraved, etched or worked in *Mezzotinto* or *Chiaro Oscuro* . . . shall have the sole Right and Liberty of Printing and Reprinting the same for the Term of Fourteen Years. . . .

Although "Hogarth's Law" was far from watertight, it served generally to legitimatize the calling, enabling engravers and dealers to realize some kind of fair return for original effort. Referred to for convenience as "the Act of Parliament" and before long simply as "the Act," this measure tended to accelerate the production of topical, partisan copperplate prints. Hogarth himself derived no discernible pride or pleasure from the rising taste for visual polemics. In an inscription beneath a famous 1733 tavern scene he absolved himself of any unseemly preoccupation with specifics: "Think not to find one meant Resemblance there / We lash the Vices but the Persons spare."[22] At the end of his life, Hogarth referred to one of his rare exercises in political caricature with apologetic condescension as a "timed thing," to which he had been forced by economic necessity.[23]

In the year that "the Act" came into effect, the satirical output of London printshops reflected by the British Museum's fragmentary catalogue[24] consisted of roughly one hundred items. The overwhelming majority of these were Hogarth's own work, or copies and imitations thereof. There were three, or perhaps four, other publishers recorded as indulging themselves in satire and only six, or perhaps seven, prints which might be termed independent and original. Two decades later, in the military and political trauma of the year 1756, the total production had more than doubled, the "Hogarthian" component was virtually negligible, and a small host of new publishers were pouring forth a steady diet of pertinent impertinencies from a collection of storefront presses. By far the most significant of these was the firm of "Edwards and Darly" or "Darly and Edwards," which issued some 58 designs during the year, most of them of playing-card size, many of them the inventions of 32-year-old Colonel George Townshend (1724–1807), a quarrelsome activist and Member of Parliament for Norfolk. Townshend added two vital new quantities to the existing equation: inside information and personal caricature in the so-called "Italian manner."

The cult of the *caricatura,* or perceptively exaggerated portrait, had long been familiar to young gentlemen of the upper classes completing their education with the prescribed "Grand Tour" of the continent. It was formally introduced to an appreciative English audience by the publication, commencing in 1736, of a series of engravings by Arthur Pond (1705?–58) after drawings by Pierleone Ghezzi and other Italian masters of the quest for a *perfetta deformità* or "perfect deformity." Ghezzi once described a work of his as "a sign with friendly hand" by which the "true image" of the faces could be read "in a flash of lightning."[25] This artful science rested on the broad presumption that the "true image" of a person would serve as a reliable guide to his character. In the late sixteenth century, the classical painter Annibale Carracci of Bologna is supposed to have fostered the practice of intuition, selection and synthesis which we have come to call caricature. As a sort of counterpoint or obbligato to the grander pursuits of the high Renaissance, he laid the foundation for a serious art, frivolously developed, which licensed the projection of inner characteristics, real or imagined, onto outward appearances. In 1586, this approach to investigative portraiture was further stimulated by the publication in Naples of G. B. della Porta's influential treatise *De Humana Physiognomia.* This study suggested a wealth of comparisons which artists might profitably make between men and animals. The owlish person was sure to be wise; the sheep-faced, docile; the aquiline, noble—and so forth. (John Singer Sargent is supposed to have remarked that he saw an animal in every sitter.) Physiognomic considerations played an increasing role in the education of artists through the seventeenth and eighteenth centuries. Gillray's formal training at the Royal Academy Schools (c. 1778–80) evidently included the classification of faces according to a personality spectrum. In a letter to another artist he remarks that the character of an engraved head "seemed to have been that of placid-melancholy."[26] Some sort of simplistic high-water mark was reached in the 1780s by the Swiss J. C. Lavater, who held that beauty was an absolute guide to virtue and ugliness a trustworthy index of vice.

For proof that this sort of inductive daring generated a healthy skepticism from the outset, we need look no

further than Shakespeare. Some fourteen years after della Porta's essay, Viola in *Twelfth Night* addresses Captain Antonio:

> And though that nature with a beauteous wall
> Doth oft close in pollution, yet of thee
> I will believe, thou hast a mind that suits
> With this, thy fair and outward character.

A year or so later, Hamlet declares, "I have that within me which passes show." In *Othello,* staged in 1604, the playwright has Iago gloat that "Knavery's plain face is never seen till used." Even more to the point is Duncan's lament at the commencement of *Macbeth,* written some two years after:

> There's no art
> To find the mind's construction in the face.

Such objections to the validity of the physiognomic approach were augmented over the years by a much more common complaint that *caricatura* drawing was nothing more than a sordid traffic in deformity. In 1712 the *Spectator* printed a letter in defense of "The Dignity of Human Nature" which described "burlesque pictures"

> where the art consists in preserving, amid distorted proportions and aggravated features, some distinguishing likeness of the person, but in such a manner as to transform the most agreeable beauty into the most odious monster.[27]

A generation or so later, the aging Swift paid tribute to Hogarth in his "Legion Club," a savage indictment of the Irish House of Commons:

> Were but you and I acquainted,
> Every Monster should be painted;
> You should try your graving Tools
> On this odious Group of Fools; ...
> Draw them like, for I assure you,
> You will need no Car'catura:
> Draw them so that we may trace
> All the soul in every Face.[28]

Hogarth himself adhered steadfastly to a similarly narrow construction of the word *caricatura,* scorning it in principle and theory while embracing the basic impulse in practice. A 1743 plate, designed to demonstrate the gulf separating his "Characters" from the debased grotesque "Caricaturas" of the Italian school, suggests that the distinction was one of degree rather than substance. A generation later (1763), the Rev. John Clubbe (1703?–73) dedicated a facetious treatise on physiognomy to Hogarth, as one who had "found out the Philosopher's wished for key to every Man's breast" and had brought to publick View the lurking Wickedness of Man's Heart." This said, however, Clubbe went on to question the general reliability of physiognomic perceptions. The artist, he notes, "cannot always be in a fit disposition to make his observations; for, his skill depends on his seeing and feeling, accompanied by a certain happy sagacity arising from both; but if either of these senses fails, the art fails also." Clubbe drily observed that "All seem yellow to the jaundic'd eye; and . . . the severed hand will often mistake the patient's pulse":

> It may then be asked, how came this art into reputation? I answer, by the same means that Urinal Quacks and Conjurers have had a run here in this kingdom; by a difficulty of access and a parade of hard words. . . .[29]

The Rev. Clubbe was concerned primarily with physiognomy in the abstract. Five years earlier, exercised by the great popularity of the caricature vogue, Hogarth came to more of a point in an inscription to his print "The Bench" (September 1758). He argued that the manner "which has, of late Years, got the name of *Caracatura*" must be totally alien to good drawing to realize its purposes; "Lines that are produc'd rather by the hand of chance than of Skill":

> The early Scrawlings of a Child which do but barely hint an Idea of an Human Face, will always be found to be like some Person or other, and will often form such a Comical Resemblance as in all probability the most eminent *Caracaturers* of these times will not be able to equal with Design. . . .

This lecture concerning "the different meaning of the Words *Character, Caracatura* and *Outrè*" was—according to the inscription on a short-lived first state of Hogarth's engraving—"Address'd to the Honble Coll T---s--d."[30]

After a decade in Parliament, George Townshend had returned to active duty in the army. Six months later he would sail for Quebec under Wolfe, as a brigadier general—terminating the first phase of his experience as a "public" caricaturist. There is a certain delicious irony in the fact that the modern editorial cartoon was the creation, or amalgam if you will, of a controversial politician who possessed a thin skin and an extremely low boiling point. Townshend was the elder brother of Charles, the minister who imposed the notorious Townshend decrees on the American colonies. A godson of George I, he commenced in the military as a volunteer in 1743, received his first commission in 1745 shortly before the battle of Fontenoy, and became an aide-de-camp to the Duke of Cumberland the following year. After 1764 he was the fourth Viscount Townshend, after 1786 the first Marquess. As Lord Lieutenant of Ireland between 1767 and 1772 he managed to achieve an unpopularity which would serve as a model for future Anglo-Irish relations.

By his early twenties, George Townshend already had acquired a formidable reputation for frigid wit and sharpness of tongue. (When the head of a nearby comrade and fellow captain was blown to smithereens by cannon fire at the battle of Laffeldt, 1747, Townshend reportedly observed, "I never thought he had so much brains before.")[31] From this time forward, he seems to have made a practice of working out irritations against associates and superiors in caricature, on any scrap or fragment of paper that chanced to be handy. Of the several hundred Townshend vignettes preserved in three surviving scrapbooks and scattered collections, only a handful can be related directly to published satires. His lack of enthusiasm for the Duke of Cumberland, commander in chief of the forces, was registered in savage doodles that reduced his leader to a featureless, posturing blob of flesh. Townshend's bitter criticism of the Duke forced him to retire from the service in 1750. Their continuing feud appears to have revolved around Townshend's efforts to establish a nonprofessional county militia, which Cumberland regarded as anathema. A Townshend militia bill, rejected by the Lords in 1754, was reintroduced by the caricaturist in the House of Commons on 8 December 1755, and energetically promoted by him until it was given a final assent on 28 June 1757. This measure received a first reading on 12 March 1756. Eight days earlier, Horace Walpole noted that

> [George Townshend's] militia bill does not come on till next week: in the meantime he adorns the shutters, walls, and napkins of every tavern in Pall Mall with caricatures of the Duke [of Cumberland] and Sir George Lyttleton, the Duke of Newcastle and Mr. Fox.[32]

Lyttleton was Chancellor of the Exchequer; Newcastle and Fox headed the ministry that was resisting Townshend's bill (notwithstanding the fact that Newcastle was Townshend's uncle).

The resumption of war against France in May heightened the Government's unpopularity and triggered an unprecedented boom in the activity of the printshops. By the middle of August, Townshend's purposeful little public-house *jeux d'esprit* were finding their way, by some unspecified route, into the custody of the publishers Edwards and Darly and thence into the hands of a wider audience. First they took the form of etched cards (approximately 2½ by 4 inches), which were soon followed by collected, bound editions, prefaced by "explanatory keys," which from their variety would appear to have done a brisk business. Walpole (another kinsman—his aunt and godmother was Townshend's grandmother) described the maiden efforts as "the freshest treason" in a letter to George Montagu on August 28.[33] He later credited Townshend with the invention of "a new species of this manufacture [satiric prints] . . . caricaturas on cards. The original one, which had amazing vent, was of Newcastle and Fox, looking at each other, and crying, with Peachum, in the Beggar's Opera, '*Brother, brother, we are both in the wrong.*' "[34] The same writer recorded (about 1762) that Townshend was "famous for his caricaturas":

> the whole mint of which consists in the likeness, for he knows nothing of drawing. Some of them have been engraved. One on a card with the Duke of Newcastle and Mr. Fox gave rise to the fashion of political and satyrical cards.[35]

Walpole, a perennial skeptic in matters of political zeal

and extroversion, was not particularly attracted to Townshend:

> whose proud and sullen and contemptuous temper [Walpole observed] never suffered him to wait for thwarting his superiors till risen to a level with them. He saw everything in an ill-natured and ridiculous light—a sure prevention of ever being seen himself in a great or favourable one. The haughtiness of the Duke of Cumberland, the talents or blemishes of Fox, the ardour of Wolfe, the virtue of Conway, all were alike the objects of Townshend's spleen and contradiction. . . .[36]

These endearing traits have helped to insulate Townshend from prospective biographers for two centuries. We are still waiting for a thorough appraisal of his contribution to the art of the cartoon. In view of his political involvements and of family connections to a number of his targets, it is not surprising that Townshend's relations with the publisher were conducted with considerable discretion. Anthologies of the political cards were promoted as having been "Drawn and Etch'd by some of the most eminent Parties interested therein." In 1762 a tiny "how to do it" caricatura manual by Mary Darly proudly claimed that "Some of our Nobility & Gentry do equal if not excel any thing of the kind that ever has been done in any other country. . . ." Townshend's anonymity and pseudonymity (he was fond of "Leonardo da Vinci"), as well as the adulterating hands of journeymen engravers, make it difficult to uncover his tracks. On stylistic grounds, he appears to have been wholly or partially responsible for some thirty published satires in 1756 and 1757, and probably for two or three more in 1760 after his return from Quebec.

There is much work still to be done on the caricatures of the climactic third quarter of the eighteenth century, and particularly on Townshend and the crucible summer of 1756. His wit, instinct for the jugular, and amateur's economy of line exerted an influence on succeeeding generations which approaches that of the professional Hogarth, his polar opposite. Both would leave indelible marks on the work of Thomas Rowlandson and James Gillray. The latter's homage to Townshend is especially evident in numerous echoes and conscious borrowings as the younger man came to grips with another Fox, another Pitt and yet another war with the French. (At the end of his career, Gillray etched some social plates after drawings by Townshend's son Edward; the aged Marquess himself may have supplied the inspiration for a political satire in 1799, judging from a preliminary sketch "suggestion" in the British Museum print room.) By extraordinary coincidence, Townshend's printshop debut must have occurred within days of Gillray's birth on 13 August 1756.

In the early sixties, Mat Darly—drawing-master, designer of chinoiserie, and entrepreneur—became sole proprietor of London's leading caricatura printshop. This establishment was identified by the sign of a golden acorn (appropriately enough, considering its germinal role in the history of graphic satire) and was located at Number 39, Strand, across from the site now occupied by Charing Cross Station. Darly and his caricaturist wife Mary, who operated the family's second outlet in Ryder's Court, Leicester Fields, were the great innovators and marketers of the popular print. They followed the successful propagation of Townshend with a shrewd cultivation of the wider amateur field. A title-page note on one collection of caricatura cards reminds prospective clients that any "Sketches, or Hints, sent Post paid, will have due Honour shewn them." Mary Darly produced the instruction booklet mentioned above. Mat undertook to reproduce designs for private amusement "at the most reasonable rates." Abandoning controversy for comedy after 1766, he advertised that descriptive hints of a nonpolitical nature would "be immediately Drawn and Executed. . . ." "Gentlemen and Ladies" were assured that they might "have Copper plates prepared and Varnished for etching." Members of the gentler sex "to whom the fumes of the Aqua Fortis are Noxious" could have their plates bitten for them, be "attended to" at home and receive "ev'ry necessary instruction."

Original drawings by amateur clients were kept available for inspection, "to prevent Piracies and Impositions," a practice which evolved by 1773 into the first organized public exhibition of caricatures, consisting of 233 items (presumably original drawings) catalogued anonymously as the work of "a Gentleman," "a Lady" or "an Artist."[37] The amateur involvement became increasingly significant after 1770, providing both an inexhaustible source of supply and a ready, affluent market. Drawing was a natural part of any "proper" upper-class education and there was no shortage of sophisticated dilettantes anxious to make a hit with their friends. Publishers continued to attract contributions with the promise of free engraving service and one liked to boast that he had acquired much of his stock "for the price of the copper." There is some indication that the plentiful supply of talent was used by printsellers to keep their professional caricaturists in line and underpaid. However, late in life, George Cruikshank remarked that the most profitable work of his career, and of Gillray's and Rowlandson's, had been etching the work of fashionable amateurs, a pastime he described as "washing other people's dirty linen."[38] The professionals were also available to execute special commissions for nonartistic customers. Gillray penned a straight-faced note to one correspondent explaining difficulties posed by a suggested satire on pension abuse which involved a tree laden with upwards of a thousand apples, each to contain a name, title, place and income. The artist partiently computed the space required "merely for apples" at five to eight feet square and concluded drily that this was "a size far too great to be printed by any press from copper."[39] Public-spirited citizens, and others with axes to grind, supplied a continuing flow of gratuitous hints and tips, the greater portion of which appear to have been utterly useless (as, for example, the scrawled note which was dropped unceremoniously into the areaway in front of the Humphrey window in St. James's Street: "A noted long Nosd jew Looking wretch about 40 attends this Picture Shop every afternoon for hours. Mark him Out—he is known on the town."[40]

The Darlys continued to dominate their field through the seventies, briefly employing the young Gillray at the very beginning of his career in 1779 and 1780. As they yielded ascendency to the Humphrey family, William, George and Hannah, the caricature printshop was well on its way to becoming a social institution of recognized importance in the daily routine of a man of fashion. By 1790, overseas visitors alighting from the Paris coach could cross Piccadilly to S. W. Fores's "Grand Caricatura Exhibition" and purchase a copy of his *New Guide For Foreigners* complete with advertisement for "the most complete collection of Humorous, Political, and Satirical Prints and Drawings ever exposed to view in this Kingdom." The following year, William Holland in Oxford Street was challenging Fores with "the largest collection of caricatures in Europe," also for an admission charge of one shilling.

The 33-year span which separates the end of the American Revolution from the Battle of Waterloo is correctly described as the "golden age" of English caricature. During the 1780s, the cards of the fifties and sixties and the magazine format of the seventies (determined by a page size of about six inches by nine) were supplanted by larger compositions expressly designed to be fully and vividly colored by hand. Most of the Gillray satires reproduced in this book were executed on the order of ten inches by fourteen, although many are considerably larger. (Plate 55 is reduced from an original size of 16½ x 20⅛; Plate 62 from a copper 16¾ x 21⅞. It is worth noting that Gillray had to work to exact size, and that it was necessary to letter all titles and legends in reverse.)

According to the tally provided by the British Museum's catalogue of satires, roughly 8000 plates were published between 1770 and 1815, nearly tripling the number of English caricatures known to have been issued up to that time. At the turn of the century a Mr. Johnes of Hafod, Cardiganshire, ordered the printseller Fores to supply him with "all the caricature prints that had ever been published." By June 1800, when the shipment was dispatched along with a bill for £137.10s, the Museum inventory suggests that a comprehensive collection of English pictorial satires would have exceeded 9500 (a figure roughly equal to the output of a single newspaper cartoonist who turns out six drawings a week for three decades). Johnes refused to accept or pay, on the grounds that the collection included obscene and immoral subjects, as well as duplicates. A court battle followed, culminating in the balanced judgement that Fores was entitled to recover for "prints whose objects are general satire or ridicule of prevailing fashions or manners" but not for those "whose tendency is immoral or obscene;

nor for such as are libels on individuals and for which the Plaintiff might have been criminally answerable for libel."[41] The significant phrase is "might have been," as M. D. George points out.[42] Through the days of their wildest license, caricaturists and their publishers enjoyed a conspicuous immunity from prosecutions for personal malice. William Cobbett was apparently voicing a prevailing viewpoint when he argued in 1808 that caricatures did not "constitute a branch of sober criticism . . .":

. . . caricatures are things to laugh at. They break no bones. I for instance, have been represented as a bull-dog, as a porcupine, as a wolf, as a sansculotte, as a nightmare, as a bear, as a kite, as a cur, and in America, as hanging upon a gallows. Yet, here I am, just as sound as if no misrepresentation of me had ever been made. The fact is, that caricatures are nothing more than figures of rhetoric proceeding from the pencil; and as the inimitable Gillray is not in the habit of making sentences, I see no reason why he should not ridicule what he deems to be the follies and vices of the times, or of particular persons, with his pencil.[43]

The print industry was an intensely competitive one, particularly during the lean depression days of the 1790s. Through this time there were some 71 shops or related merchandising operations attempting to do business in London, with another thirteen imprints recorded elsewhere in Britain and Ireland. From his "Repository of Arts" in the Strand, Rudolph Ackerman issued some two hundred feet of hand-tinted "comic strips" intended as wallpaper or, strictly speaking, as decorative borders for doorways, wainscoting and screens. He also operated a drawing school on the side, exhibited patriotic and satirical gas-illuminated "transparencies" in his window, developed a parachute for the aerial distribution of broadsides and advertised his emporium as "the morning's best lounge." Nearby, in Brydges Street, Covent Garden, Richard Newton operated an "Original Print Warehouse," supplementing his income from satire by taking "warranted strong likenesses for half a guinea in miniature on ivory [f]or a locket or framing."[44] In the City proper, the long-established concerns of Bowles & Carver and Laurie & Whittle were primarily occupied with noncontroversial social humor and whimsy.

In 1788 Francis Grose produced the first attempt at a systematic instruction book, *Rules for Drawing Caricaturas*, which was popular enough to go into a second edition in 1791. At about the same time, Robert Wilkinson, publisher of a number of early, "serious" works by Gillray, brought out a new, revised edition of Mary Darly's 1762 guide. Across the Channel, an impetuous Royalist editor rushed into print the following year (1792) with the first of a projected four-volume *Histoire des Caricatures de la Révolte des Français.* (This work was dedicated to the notion that caricatures were the "thermometer of public opinion" and that the present, rather than the past or the future, was the proper concern of the historian. Its author, one Boyer de Nîmes, was guillotined one-third of the way through Volume Three.)

Back in London, caricature transparencies formed the basis for popular public lectures and theatrical presentations. On the side, printshops traded in illustrated books, playing cards, (comic?) teapots and special folios of prints which could be rented out for short periods to entertain dinner or weekend guests. William Makepeace Thackeray fondly recalled memories of his youth, when grandfathers' country libraries would always contain "two or three old mottled portfolios, or great swollen scrapbooks of blue paper, full of the comic prints." Born in 1811, Thackeray remembered finding "in some other apartments of the house, where the caricatures used to be pasted in those days [evidently the latrines] . . . things quite beyond our comprehension."[45] The *Morning Chronicle* remarked, on 1 August 1796, "The taste of the day leans entirely to caricature"; and in retrospect it is difficult to disagree.

[III]

LIFE AND CAREER

Gillray . . . acquired the use of the graving tool under the celebrated Ashby, who then resided at the foot of Holborn-Hill. Many a choice specimen of penmanship was copied by young Gillray, in sweeping flourishes, on the copper. . . . This wag used to say that the early part of his life might be compared to a spider's, busied in the spinning of lines.

—Henry Angelo, 1824[46]

Silent and reserved he was, till he discovered that his companions upon any given occasion were frank and liberal. His own patriotism and free principles then began to peer forth, and occasionally rose to enthusiastic fervor. . . . Gillray [displayed] no deficiency either of good sense, benevolent feeling or gentlemanly propriety of conduct; yet there was an eccentricity about him. . . .

—John Landseer, 1831[47]

He is very well informed, an extremely literate man who reads a lot, a pleasant popular fellow in society, a fountain overflowing with joke. . . . You should also understand that Gillray is a simple, honest man, an exceptionally good son who helped his old father in every possible way.

—Anonymous German correspondent, 1798[48]

James Gillray was born on 13 August 1756 at the Thames-side village of Chelsea, about three miles southwest of central London. According to contemporary ratebooks, the family then resided in a tiny cottage at the north end of Robinson's Lane, next door to the Robin Hood Tavern, two hundred feet perhaps from the village docks. The future caricaturist was the third child and second son of James Gillray, sexton of Chelsea's Moravian community, and of the former Jane Coleman of Long Hope, Gloucestershire. He was the only one of their five children who was to survive to maturity.

The senior Gillray had been born in 1720, in the Lanarkshire hamlet of Culter, 29 miles south of Edinburgh. An Andrew Gilry appears in ecclesiastical records at nearby Biggar in 1638, and the name occurs again in the adjacent Walston parish during the 1660s. (However, the surname originated in the Highlands as a nickname for "ruddy-faced.") The caricaturist's grandfather, blacksmith John Gilry or Gilray (c. 1698–1778), married Lillias Penman at Culter in November 1719. Their eldest son, James, the caricaturist's father, was born the following September. He seems to have been one of at least four sons raised in the piety and strictness of the Scottish Calvinist Church. However, only the birth record of a younger sister, Isobel, in 1739, survives in the (interrupted) register of Culter Kirk. After some experience as a blacksmith in his father's shop at an adjacent cluster of dwellings known as Culter Park, James enlisted at age 22 as a private in the Royal cavalry. Two years later, he was a member of the "Queen's Dragoons" led into battle against the French at Fontenoy (11 May 1745) and lost his right arm in the bloody Allied defeat which followed. (The commander in chief on this occasion was the Duke of Cumberland; an amateur caricaturist from Norfolk named George Townshend had just became a captain in the regiment led by Lord Dunmore.)

Light horseman Gillray (as the family elected to spell it by mid-century) next figures as an applicant for admission to Chelsea Royal Hospital the following March. His name is first recorded on the muster roll of inpensioners in 1748, and continues there until May 1753. In February 1754 he received permission to swap his bed and board for another man's daily out-pension allowance of ninepence. Gillray then formally resigned his place, terminating a military career of ten years at the age of 33.[49] Five years earlier, he became a member of the

Moravian Brotherhood, a long-persecuted, fiercely evangelical Protestant sect that had transferred its base of operations from Silesia to London in the 1730s and 40s. They based their religion on a belief in the fundamental depravity of man, the total worthlessness of human life and the anticipation of death as a glorious deliverance from terrestrial bondage. This sober philosophy must have struck a responsive chord in the God-fearing Scots temperament. James Gillray the elder was followed into the United Brethren by an Arnold Gillray and a Robert Gillray, brothers (or possibly cousins) who elected to leave Lanarkshire and settle in Chelsea. The caricaturist's father withdrew from the Brethren at the time of his marriage in 1751, but was readmitted some two years later with his bride, after she had accepted instruction in the faith. Soon afterward, James Gillray was named sexton of the new chapel and burial ground which the Moravians were establishing to serve the needs of a planned community and manufacturing center on Chelsea's western edge. In spite of his war disability, Gillray must have been a singularly industrious and dedicated person. He had to be nudged into retirement at the age of 77 and apparently was still in demand as a house painter at that time.

One can only guess at the effect which the intense, emotional, soul-searing theology of the Moravians might have had on his son. (A manual of that faith, formally inscribed "Js Gillray Sept. 1781" in his best student hand, and a clothes brush appear to have been the only personal effects preserved in the family after his death.)[50] Hoping to protect the lambs of their flock from secular contamination, the Brethren set up schools of their own shortly after coming to England. In the early 1760s, by any standard of the day, these were offering an unusually broad curriculum to pupils of both sexes. However, the plan called for separating children from their families at the age of five, the regimen was spartan and the atmosphere tended to be chillingly introspective. It was a steady diet of milk-soup, bread, brimstone and contrition. A nineteenth-century Moravian historian recalled: "Through the faithfulness of the teachers . . . the deadness of the children to spiritual things was removed, the Holy Ghost produced true repentance among them, and a sighing and crying to their Saviour for mercy ensued. . . ."[51] Students were encouraged to stand and declare, individually, "how they stood with their Saviour," to take comfort and delight in funerals, and to see the bright side of *not* recovering from illnesses. In the words of a second Moravian archivist, it was a program "more fitted for hermits and fakirs than for English boys and girls."[52]

The Gillrays' daughter Mary died in December 1756, just before her fourth birthday. In the summer of 1760 they placed their eldest son, Johnny, aged five and one-half, in the Moravian academy at Bedford, some 46 miles to the north. In all probability, his younger brother, James, joined him there when he reached the same age

nineteen months later. Johnny Gillray's health began to fail during his second year at Bedford, and on at least three occasions his parents journeyed there to visit him and hear him affirm that "he had fixed his mind upon going over to the Saviour."[53] In July he informed his mother that "he would rather go to our Saviour than go home with her if he was even sure he sho'd thereby recover his health." At his death in September 1762

All the children surrounding his bed kept him a Liturgy. . . . he begged his coffin might be brought and soon after Said "Pray dont keep me. O let me go, I must go—" which were his last words. . . . The Brethren had very happy feeling of the Nearness of our Saviour during his last hours and his corps retained such pleasant look as rejoiced all who saw him.

The end came eleven weeks before his eighth birthday. Burial was at Bedford. The family would face this kind of tragedy twice again—in November 1766 with a seven-year-old daughter, Hannah, and in March 1770 with a nine-year-old daughter, Anna Johanna Lilly. James was six when his brother died, ten and thirteen respectively at the deaths of his younger sisters. The future caricaturist continued his education at Bedford until December 1764, when the school was disbanded for financial reasons. The *Diary of the Moravian Congregation at Bedford* noted the closing of the boys' dormitory and the departure of the last of the nonlocal students:

Brother Gottwalt set out for London with the three Boys, George & Robert Hinz & James Gillray, who are to go to their Parents. They had last night very movingly taken leave from the Rest of the Children; with Tears on all sides.

Gillray was then eight and one-half. Although it seems probable that he continued to receive some manner of instruction over the next five or six years, no record of any such training has been found. Although there was a boys' school in Chelsea open to sons of Royal Hospital pensioners, the Moravian community would probably have taken a dim view of it.

Nor do we have any clear notion of when, or how, Sexton Gillray's son first acquired an interest in drawing. The earliest surviving sketch—a watercolor portrait of a bright-eyed goldfinch—is preserved in the British Museum. Perhaps the work of a precocious, self-assured boy of twelve or thirteen, it is sharply observed and cleanly rendered. A proud caption, "James Gillray the First Bird he did Draw & Paint," has been added above in a delicate, controlled hand embellished with large, flowering capitals. Probably dating from the years 1767–9, it is scarcely a beginner's effort. On the strength of this sort of performance, the young draftsman was apprenticed about 1770 or 1771 to Harry Ashby (1744–1818), a prosperous London writing engraver and publisher of fancy scripts, maxims, maps and banknotes.

Ashby, like Gillray's mother, was from a tiny village in Gloucestershire, and this might have been a factor in the arrangement. Gillray's tenure with Ashby, like the rest of his early life, is largely a matter of conjecture. He may have boarded with his master in the house and workshop at the bottom of Holborn Hill, close by the north end of the busy Fleet Market. He could well have stayed with Moravian friends in the Brethren's Fetter Lane settlement, a few short blocks up the way. Presumably this experience occupied him for much of the early seventies. Henry Angelo recalled in 1824 that "many a choice specimen of penmanship was copied by young Gillray, in sweeping flourishes, on the copper, from the incomparable pen of Tomkins of Sermon-Lane."[54] Angelo added the somewhat improbable tidbit that, as in the case of the student Hogarth, the boy's originality "displayed itself in humorous borders of the examples of round hand and text."[55]

Ashby appears, from an engraved portrait, to have been an astute, practical, no-nonsense sort of fellow, and it is somewhat unlikely that he put up with much self-expression of this kind. His forte lay in simplicity and elegance of style. He was much praised for having helped to eliminate an earlier addiction to decorative knots, sprigs and other irrelevant embellishments. From him Gillray was able to acquire the sort of skill and facility which Hogarth had yearned for and despaired of during his apprentice years as a silver-plate engraver a half-century before. (At the end of his life, Hogarth remembered that at age twenty, engraving on copper had been his utmost ambition, but that the "bad habits" of his "former business" and his own impatience prevented him from "attaining that beautifull stroke on copper which has often been [learned ?] by early habits and great care. . . ."[56] Ashby also did a considerable business in aquatinted maps, and it is reasonable to suppose that Gillray had an opportunity to familiarize himself with this exacting new French technique for simulating wash effects on copper.

Apart from his remark about "the spinning of lines," Gillray's only recorded comment on his experience with Ashby was that "he didn't like it." In 1798, he told a German journalist that he deserted, along with a group of fellow apprentices, joined a company of strolling players, and spent some time in the country.[57] This tale was sufficient to confirm one of his Victorian biographers in the belief that Gillray began adult life as an avowed bohemian, early acquiring "an antagonism to restraint which coloured his principles to the end."[58]

By the autumn of 1775, this sowing of thespian wild oats would seem to have been completed, and Gillray, aged nineteen, appears to have been back in London trying to make a place for himself as a professional engraver. Indications of his earliest manner can be found in "Six-Pence a Day," an anonymous print issued on 25 October 1775 by William Humphrey of Gerrard Street, Soho. Humphrey's younger sister Hannah had made her publishing debut with a pair of prints the previous year, but she did not commence in earnest until 1779. The first product of her long association with Gillray seems to have been "A Tip Top Adjutant," etched after an amateur sketch and issued on 11 February of that year.

Between 1775 and 1779, Gillray's evolving style can be spotted on some 25 plates produced for a number of competing shops. After 1776 he was increasingly influenced by the distinctive, wiry etching manner of John Hamilton Mortimer (1741–79), but the greatest advance in his draftsmanship and composition is traceable to his admission to the schools of the Royal Academy in April 1778. Accepted for study as an engraver, Gillray came under the direction of Francesco Bartolozzi, one of the Academy's founding members. Bartolozzi (1728–1815) excelled at insipid, super-soft, exquisitely modeled stipple engravings. Gillray's aptitude was demonstrated by the publication in the summer of 1780 of two small oval illustrations to Fielding's *Tom Jones* which rival the master at his own game. Over the following decade, the caricaturist lived two professional lives, ranging between the polar extremes of "serious," highly polished sentiment and outrageous, often obscene satire. The two strains came together, after a fashion, in 1792 when he began regularly to combine the finesse of the stipple discipline with the biting caricature of his "popular" manner. One cannot escape the suspicion that the virulence of his caricature was a kind of revenge upon the prevailing academic milieu of saccharine grace and moral uplift in which he tried, and failed, to make his mark as a reproductive engraver of "quality" subjects.

Gillray's association with the schools of the Royal Academy probably lasted two or three years, overlapping that of William Blake, who entered in October 1779. Once admitted, a student was entitled to make whatever use he chose of casts, models and instruction without charge for up to six years. No record was kept of comings and goings. Gillray's published work during this period reflects a deep interest and a corresponding improvement in the handling of muscular and skeletal detail; this probably indicates that he was regular in his attendance at the anatomy lectures and dissections of Dr. William Hunter (1718–83, pioneer of scientific surgery). According to the German correspondent cited above, Gillray "worked very hard" and "received acclaim" for many things he engraved, etched and painted at Somerset House.[59] Unfortunately, that is the extent of our knowledge on the subject.

The foundation of the Academy in 1768 provided a great stimulus to British art in general, and to engraving and satirical draftsmanship in particular. Writing of the pictorial humor of earlier days, historian J. P. Malcolm remarked in 1813 that "there is nothing in all the preceding descriptions that applies to caricaturing as it is now used":

The satirists carefully avoided offending the ruling powers; and they had not [in the sixteenth century] the means of multiplication by engraving, as at present. Painting had met with little encouragement in England;

consequently, those who had a genius for drawing, possessed not the means to expand their ideas.[60]

Although there were some earlier eighteenth-century attempts, this situation was not really rectified until Joshua Reynolds' fledgling institution, under generous royal patronage, made a comprehensive art education available to applicants of limited or nonexistent means. It is both interesting and significant that Thomas Rowlandson, son of a bankrupt wool merchant, and James Gillray, offspring of a sexton-painter, would emerge as conspicuous beneficiaries of the Academy schools during their first decade.

Several other factors were converging to set the stage for the lively days ahead. Daily papers were demonstrating a new vitality and independence from government influence—ironically enough, as a result of increasing advertising revenues. From 1767 to 1772, the pseudonymous letters of "Junius"[61] in the *Public Advertiser* lanced politicians with a murderous mixture of eloquence, ruthless logic and inside dope. Six years before the Declaration of Independence, "Junius" addressed an open letter to George III that undertook to lecture the monarch for public and private shortcomings as though he were a misguided, dimwitted schoolboy, reminding him finally that his crown, acquired by one revolution, could be lost by another. In the government prosecution which followed this challenge, a jury refused to return a directed verdict against the publisher—thereby supporting and extending both the freedom to record and comment on public affairs, and the freedom of juries to resist dictation from the bench.

Of similar importance to the rising generation of caricaturists was John Wilkes's successful defiance in 1771 of the traditional ban on newspaper reports of the proceedings of Parliament. After an extended war of nerves between Alderman Wilkes (1727–97) and his City mob on one side, and the legislature on the other, journalists were in effect conceded the privilege of access to the gallery of the House of Commons, and the implied right to transcribe and publish debates. Technically the prohibition remained in force, but a generation later, when Gillray and his colleagues were making regular use of this perch to mark out their targets, a two-shilling tip to the doorkeeper was the customary prerequisite for admission.

A third development of great importance, related to the first two, was the developing respect entertained by politicians for the power of public opinion. Looking back, once again from the vantage point of 1813, J. P. Malcolm noted:

> The administration of Lord North [1770–82] gave fresh vigour to the Caricaturists; and the manner in which the different ruling parties appear to have viewed their labours, encouraged them to proceed, till they became a kind of allegorical history of public events, which is continued with unabated zeal to the present moment.[62]

By the time of the notorious Westminster elections of 1784 and 1788 (see the note to Plate 17), this "encouragement" was taking the form of subsidies and bribes.

Stimulated by the internal ferment which accompanied the closing months of the American Revolution and sundry other foreign crises, Gillray's satirical output leaped to more than seventy recorded items for 1782 and the first half of 1783. At 26 he was already the best draftsman among the city's political printmakers. However, his evolution as a physiognomical caricaturist was stimulated by the example of James Sayers (1748–1823), attorney, light poet and propagandist, who began to produce small full-figure *portraits chargés* in 1781 and witty, pertinent Parliamentary satires the following year. Sayers' draftsmanship was amateurish and his etching technique was rudimentary, but he recognized the value of establishing immediate, easily repeated recipes for individual faces. He helped to supplant the old emblematic tradition with a fresh, highly personal, "reportorial" approach, evidently based on close firsthand observation from the gallery of the Commons. Gillray's rapid progress in the same direction can be seen by contrasting Plate 2 with the four that follow it. In 1787 and 1788 Gillray parodied Sayers (Plates 9, 13a and 13b), mocking his defense of Warren Hastings and his situation as a dedicated (and well-paid) supporter of Pitt. Three months later, Gillray was briefly on the same payroll himself (Plate 17).

From the outset, Gillray seems to have cultivated the image of a detached, cynical "hired gun," concealing any actual political convictions beneath a veil of ambivalence and irony. It is probable that he began by regarding his caricature work as a revenue-producing activity incidental to his quest for recognition as a reproductive engraver. Unlike Sayers, who made a practice of initialing his prints from 1781 on, Gillray did not drop the traditional anonymity of the popular field until 1789, and did not start to sign his satires on a regular basis until 1792, when he had all but abandoned his "serious" aspirations. Commencing in November 1781, Gillray's stipple engravings were issued at irregular intervals by Robert Wilkinson of 58, Cornhill, an arrangement that continued until 1794. As distinct from his early caricatures, these were published with full credit to the artist.[63] The particular care shown in this regard underscores the obvious fact that caricature was anything but a gentleman's game.

During 1783 Gillray started a sabbatical from the production of satires which lasted (with an occasional interruption like Plate 6) for more than two and one-half years. During this time, his efforts for Wilkinson ranged from nostalgic pastoral illustrations to "eyewitness" reconstructions of celebrated marine disasters. Gillray tried, without success, to secure commissions from the painter Benjamin West and the entrepreneur printseller John Boydell, self-styled patron saint of British engraving. These and other prospective clients might have been put off by Gillray's reputation as a caricaturist, but a constitutional inability to copy anything without adding a special touch of his own probably did not help matters. The existence of an elegant business card

Gillray
Portrait Painter
No. 7 Little Newport Street.
Leicester Fields

suggests that he diversified his activities even further.[64] The Victorian illustrator Robert William Buss (1804–75) understood that Gillray "made some progress as a miniature painter."[65]

In mid-1786 Gillray returned to the ranks of the professional satirist a sadder, wiser man with a dazzling new command of the tricks of the etcher's trade. His feeling for stipple, aquatint, sinuous baroque outline and meticulous contour modeling was transferred to the popular field, where it constituted a distinct novelty. Working primarily for the publishers Holland and Fores over the next three years, Gillray produced some of his finest and most beautiful work (see Plates 7–12).

In the autumn of 1791, at 35, he concluded a freelance vagabondage of some fifteen years and settled down to etch more or less exclusively for Hannah Humphrey, the younger sister of his first publisher. This practical, square-faced maiden lady of forty or so (who preferred to be called "Mrs.") brought a measure of order to both his life and his art. Up to this time, Gillray's satires for a disparate group of publishers had reflected a variety of viewpoints and assessments of public mood, but very little underlying conviction or philosophy. The new partnership must have increased his freedom of action. It appears highly unlikely that Mrs. Humphrey made any real effort to influence the choice of subjects, and in fact Gillray may have taken more of a hand in the financial management than she did in the creative. By early 1793, when he took up lodgings over her shop at 18 Old Bond Street, they had secured the first position among the printsellers of the West End. He accompanied her the next year to 37 New Bond Street, and in the spring of 1797 to 27 St. James's Street, where he lived to the end of his life. The relationship seems to have ripened steadily from 1793, when the caricaturist inscribed a gift firescreen to "his old friend and Publisher . . . as a mark of respect and esteem." Unfortunately, none of his letters to her survive, but by 1804 hers to him began "Dear Gilly" and concluded "your affectionate friend." Surviving scraps of correspondence and receipts in his handwriting indicate that Gillray operated the store when Mrs. Humphrey and her assistant Betty were both out of town ("I hope you take care of the Cat," Mrs. Humphrey reminded him in a letter of October 1804).[66] A formal acknowledgment, dated the twenty-first of the following February, notes his acceptance from her of the very considerable sum "of Five Hundred Pounds, being in full of all demands, for every Engraving executed by me up to this time—& all accounts Settled."[67] At his death, he is supposed to have left an estate of one thousand guineas.[68]

Gillray's plates long continued as a major source of revenue; in 1823, eight years after his death and five years after that of Mrs. Humphrey, her nephew and heir was using printed receipts identifying himself as "Publisher of Gillray's Satirical Prints &c. Being the proprietor of his original works."[69]

In addition to unspecified domestic comforts, the alliance with Hannah Humphrey seems to have brought Gillray a new sense of purpose and regularity. Although he observed no pattern or schedule, thereafter his political commentaries appeared every week or ten days, on the average, during the months that Parliament was in session. He was inclined to take extended summer holidays from publication (if not from production) balanced by turbulent periods like November 1795, which saw the release of eight political plates and one social subject.

During the early nineties Gillray finally decided to devote himself fully to the profession of caricature. Until this time, he still reserved his highest degree of finish and technical expertise for the "straight" tableaux that he continued to engrave for Wilkinson. By contrast, many of the satires appear to have been drawn with great haste directly on the copper. Plate 16 must have been, Plate 19 seems to have been; and Gillray's preliminary outline is clearly visible throughout Plate 20—particularly on the right leg and on a false start for the hands and tape measure. Over the preceding decade the caricaturist had become conversant with the elevated eclecticism of Sir Joshua Reynolds' pretentious, didactic "Grand Manner," with the school of reportage or narrative "history painting" (popularized by Benjamin West's 1770 *Death of Wolfe*) and with the esoteric Romantic nightmares of Henry Fuseli. Now Gillray brought these strains to the service of pictorial satire. (In 1800, Gillray would write of "the use to be made of" Fuseli and of his "Mock Sublime 'Mad Taste.' ") On 23 December 1791, he "respectfully" dedicated an "attempt in the Caricatura-Sublime" to Fuseli, with whom he had obviously been spending some time (see Plate 22 and the accompanying note). Thereafter, he returned repeatedly to this genre (Plates 35 and 55), employing it simultaneously to ridicule the mechanisms and clichés of the emblematic tradition and to sublimate his obvious enthusiasm for the high baroque.

By June and July 1792, when he produced his celebrated tributes to the royal family (Plates 28, II and III), Gillray's new commitment to style and craftsmanship were apparent. From this time, important works were customarily signed, generally "Js Gy design et fecit," or some variant thereof. (In December 1795, he began to use the abbreviation "d: et f:" to denote a work based on a sketch or suggestion from someone else [for example, Plates 40 and 43]. After September 1796, his own ideas are inscribed "inv: et fect" and those of others scrupulously marked "des & fect.")

Gillray's ideological progress is much harder to graph, for reasons already suggested. After 1793, his published work falls increasingly into line with the prevailing negative Tory attitude toward the French Revolution, "Democracy" in the abstract and the radical idealism of Charles James Fox. The indications are that he joined in the first euphoric expressions of optimism which greeted the fall of the Bastille, but that the Reign of Terror cured him of any lingering sympathy for "French principles." In 1831, John Landseer believed that Gillray's heart had always been "on the side of whiggism and liberty" but that he was pressed into government service by "an unfortunate concurrence of circumstances."[70] Landseer remembered a meeting attended by Gillray, presumably c. 1792–94, "to form a fund and institute a society for the relief of decayed artists":

> After business and supper were concluded, we drank toasts; and when it came to his turn to name a public character, the Juvenal of caricature surprised those who knew him but superficially by proposing that we should drink DAVID! (the French painter). [Gillray] was by this time a little elated, having become pleased with his associates, and having drowned his reserve in the flow of soul, and kneeling reverentially on his chair as he pronounced the name of the (*supposed*) first painter and patriot in Europe, he expressed a wish that the rest of our company would do the same.

It was Landseer's understanding, quite possibly fostered by the enigmatic Gillray himself, that the caricaturist

> had unluckily got himself into the Ecclesiastical Court for producing a politico-scriptural caricature . . . and while threatened on the one hand with pains and penalties he was bribed by the Pitt party on the other with the offer of a pension, to be accompanied by absolution and remission of sins both political and religious and by the cessation of the pending prosecution. Thus situated he found, or fancied himself obliged to capitulate.

It is true that Gillray was brought before a Bow Street magistrate in January 1796, charged with selling an objectionable print, and that the matter never seems to have been tried. It is also true that this incident coincided precisely with Gillray's introduction to George Canning (1770–1827, newly appointed by Pitt as an under-secretary in the Foreign Office) and that this connection led to an annual pension of £200 for Gillray by the end of 1797.[71] Landseer's disclosure prompted Thackeray to speculate in 1840 "that Gillray would have been far more successful and more powerful but for that unhappy bribe, which turned the whole of his art into an unnatural channel."[72]

In fact, the question of party alignment probably had been determined for Gillray by the disintegration of the Opposition, and by their general unpopularity. During the depression days of 1795–96, the printsellers needed to be particularly sensitive to public mood. The frequency and intensity of Gillray's attacks on the Foxites increased, but he was hardly guilty of rushing to idealize Pitt (see Plate 50 of 9 March 1797). Asked about this changing

emphasis in 1798, the caricaturist remarked, "Now the Opposition are poor, they do not buy my prints and I must draw on the purses of the larger parties."[73]

Gillray was pulled gradually into the orbit of the Canning "circle" of brilliant young Tories as the result of his acquaintance with the Rev. John Sneyd (1763–1835), Rector of Elford and an active amateur caricaturist (see Plates 36 and 91). There is reason to believe that Gillray visited Sneyd's home in Staffordshire in 1794. In 1795 Sneyd and Canning embarked on a lengthy campaign to convince him that Canning's arrival on the political scene should be "noticed" in caricature. (On 9 August the future Foreign Secretary and Prime Minister, then 25, noted in his diary: "Sneyd tells me that Mr. Gillray the caricaturist has been much solicited to publish a caricature of me and intends doing so. A great point to have a good one.") Gillray resisted this pursuit for fourteen months; Canning finally appeared in a print of 20 October 1796, a peripheral figure hanging from a lamp bracket. Three months later he was shown as a pygmy kissing Pitt's colossal toe. In November 1797, Canning and his friends commenced to write, edit and publish a weekly satirical paper, *The Anti-Jacobin*, designed to marshal public opinion against the French and their sympathizers (see note to Plate 54). At this point they resolved to secure Gillray's collateral support and his loyalty with the government stipend mentioned above. The caricaturist must have agreed to avoid direct attacks on Pitt and on the King and Queen. On 14 November, Canningite J. H. Frere wrote to ask Sneyd's help with the drawing and composition of "The Friend of Humanity" (Plate 54), adding: "Gillray is to be here to-morrow, and Canning is to have his will of him." The chase was over. Shortly thereafter, Gillray himself reported to Sneyd that he had received a pension and that he looked forward to "skirmishing against the common enemy."

Gillray's association with the editors of *The Anti-Jacobin*, evidently a close one during the eight-month duration of the paper (see Plates 55 and 56), continued erratically for the rest of his career (Plates 62, 72, 89 and possibly 80 and 90). The pension seems to have been discontinued when Pitt left office in March 1801 and reinstituted, in a casual fashion, after 1804. William Cobbett later asserted that Gillray had told him "Canning and Frere and George Ellis and William Gifford and even Pitt himself" had assisted in suggesting subjects.[74] The arrangement resulted in a number of the caricaturist's better satires, and probably helps to explain a rapid growth in his political awareness from this time forward, particularly in regard to foreign affairs. The pension never reduced Gillray to hireling status, although in 1800 Canning did use it as leverage to persuade him to discard six months of work on an illustrated edition of the *Poetry of The Anti-Jacobin* which Canning regarded as a potential embarrassment.[75]

Inevitably, Gillray's government ties were the object of speculation. In March 1798 the *Morning Herald* referred derisively to "the *Loyal Labours* of his pencil." A few weeks later the Weimar periodical *London und Paris* reproduced a singularly savage satire against Fox with the observation that Gillray did not sign it "for good reason" as he was speaking for the Ministry "in as satisfying and complete a way as you can expect from an honest follower of the governing and paying party."[76] The next year the same paper remarked on an apparent anti-government slant and wondered if Gillray could "really be serving the Ministerial party only for money, as was suggested."[77] Seven years later, in 1806, *London und Paris* was still trying to figure it out:

> [Gillray's] enemies are saying that he got a pension from the last Ministry, but this is not proved and Pitt had too much courage and too much pride to appease his enemies. Probably Gillray had patriotic motives for his political actions. He saw the influence of his pictures and he thought he could keep the Anti-Gallic ghost alive, with his works, among his countrymen. If Gillray received a pension from the Ministry why did he keep following them after the death of Pitt?[78]

With the exception of a thirteen-month respite in 1802–03, Britain was at war with France from February 1793 until after Gillray's death. The security of John Bull and the salvation of "the Roast Beef of Old England" had been a dominant theme of his work for almost five years before the pension began. The notion that he was helping in the defense of the land must have been a comforting rationale. When the authors of *The Anti-Jacobin* opposed his illustrated edition of their verse, the caricaturist's defense, not without its irony, was that he felt "no uneasiness whatever from what may be the results of ridiculing the Abettors of Vice and French Principles."[79] In offering or relaying suggestions, John Sneyd took continuing pains to assure Gillray that the nation was obligated to him "for great and good exertions" or that a proposed satire would afford him pleasure "in promoting and encouraging good English feelings."[80]

Gillray kept in touch with Sneyd during his final working decade, although as time passed he declared his independence from Canning's influence on several occasions, notably the "Phaeton alarm'd!" (Plate VIII) of 22 March 1808. The caricaturist continued to dominate his profession, and while devoting more time to social comedy than previously, he picked his political shots with devastating accuracy. Commenting on Gillray's influence in 1806, *London und Paris* observed:

> Everyone can see that [rival caricaturists] are unable to fill his shoes. . . . Paris has good men in this field, but they look pale in relation to Gillray. If you examine the work of his contemporaries you discover immediately that they went to him for training . . . even if they disagreed with him . . . they took many things to which Gillray had accustomed the public. . . .[81]

In June 1809, John Sneyd informed Gillray: "I should be glad to hear that you have been benefited . . . by the endeavours I have been making in your favour. Mr. Bagot [Charles Bagot (1781–1843), Canning's under-secretary at the Foreign Office] promised that he would see you often and inform you what was going on before it was known to the publick at large, and I have pledged myself that you will never mention his name, which in these times of enquiry seems to frighten all publick men"[82] (a reference to the Wardle-Clark scandal; see Plate 94). However, by now the caricaturist's capacity for original work was all but exhausted. His health began to fail in 1807, followed before long by his reason. As early as 1795, when Gillray was 39, Sneyd wrote expressing the hope that his arm had been "released from the *jaws* of rheumatism" as "it must sadly interrupt your ingenious labours."[83] By 1807 Gillray was troubled by poor eyesight, a concern which may well have grown into an obsession. Although there is little to support the Victorian myth that he was a lifelong alcoholic, he probably drank excessively, particularly under tension. Henry Angelo remembered him as "always hypped,"[84] that is morbidly depressed or affected with hypochondria, and to all indications the introverted, highly-strung caricaturist was subject to the soarings and plummetings of moods which we have come to describe as manic-depressive. Gillray's production continued to decline in 1808; he placed more reliance on preliminary work, required additional time to complete his assignments for amateur patrons and tended to wield the burin in a choppier, more aggressive manner. On the whole his touch was becoming less sure. He used the signature "Inv^t & Fec^t" for the last time in September 1809;[85] thereafter, his total output consisted of two political designs and twenty-odd miscellaneous social subjects, all based on outside hints or drawings. This sporadic activity came to an end in the late spring or summer of 1810, when he lapsed into a state of insanity that continued, with lucid intervals, until his death on the first of June 1815 (see the note to Plate 96).

Mrs. Humphrey was "unremitting in her care of him":

> Though insane, it was but seldom that his paroxysms were very violent, consequently he was allowed to wander at pleasure over the house. . . . It was only during his aberrations from his right mind that he was kept close in an upper room. . . .[86]

Accounts differ as to the dénouement. There are three instances recorded of apparent suicide attempts. A paragraph in *The Examiner* of 21 July 1811 is the most poignant:

> On Wednesday afternoon Mr. Gillray the Caricaturist who resides at Mrs. Humphrey's, the caricature shop in St. James's Street, attempted to throw himself out of the window of the attic story. There being iron bars his head got jammed and being perceived by one of the chairmen who waits at White's [Club] and who instantly went up to give assistance, the unfortunate man was extricated. . . .

According to the undocumented testimony of the anecdotal writer John Timbs (1801–75), first aired in

1866, Gillray finally succeeded in an effort of this sort and died from the injuries he received.[87] We can only be sure of the fact that he expired on a Thursday, some sixteen days before the Battle of Waterloo. The next week Hannah Humphrey, his "old friend," and George Cruikshank, his heir apparent, saw him to a final resting place in the churchyard of St. James's Piccadilly. Presumably it was at her direction that the spot was marked with a flat stone bearing the simple inscription:

In Memory of Mr. James Gillray
THE CARICATURIST
Who departed this life 1st June 1815,
Aged 58 years.

[IV]

THE PRINTMAKER

Dear Gilly. What think ye of one week at Brighton after your Fatigue, Aquafortis &c. it would certainly do you a great deal of good....
—Hannah Humphrey, letter of 17 October 1804[88]

Will you be good enough to send me down a couple of needles and some wax, the same that you etch with yourself—and tell me how to lay it on . . . I have sent up by the Mail Coach of Tonight a Copper Plate that has a very bad etching on it . . . Now I want you to cover the Plate with a wax that you can see the lines thro and touch it up for me. . . .
—Note from an amateur patron, 18 November 1799[89]

It is a pity that Gillray's response to the latter communication, if in fact he made one, does not appear to have survived. During a professional career of some 35 years his total output of prints approached an even thousand, all but a tiny fraction of which were copperplate etchings. Unlike his contemporaries and successors, Gillray never regarded the etching process as merely an instrument of multiplication. Working in an era of great innovation and restless experimentation, he was one of the most inventive technicians and painstaking craftsmen that the medium has ever known. A.M. Hind's standard 1908 *History of Engraving and Etching* observes simply that he was "a far poorer artist than either Hogarth or Rowlandson" but that "as political satire of almost incomparable licence his work has a considerable historic value."[90] This sort of evaluation reflects the tunnel vision of most Victorian experts on the subject, although it is only fair to add that Gillray's virtuosity is easier to appreciate in uncolored impressions, to which the exposure of connoisseurs could have been limited.

Strictly speaking, most of Gillray's satires are neither etchings nor engravings, but a judicious mixture of the two disciplines with a variety of refinements added here and there for good measure. His original training as a

letter engraver consisted of pushing or plowing, with square or lozenge-shaped burins, formal "v"-shaped trenches directly into the surface of the metal, sufficiently deep to hold enough ink to print from. Later he learned to etch, that is to draw lightly and freely with a needle on copper that was "grounded" or shielded with a thinly spread compound of wax and pitch. It was possible to operate on this surface with mechanical roulettes and rollers, simulating the effect of a chalk line or stroke (Plates 28, II and III). Gillray's master, Bartolozzi, is known to have employed roulette devices with as many as six separate wheels or heads and a variety of tooth sizes. After such a design had been completed to satisfaction, or carried to a point where a trial proof was thought necessary, it was immersed in a mordant solution, commonly nitric acid or *aqua fortis* (literally "strong water"), which etched, or ate, away the bared metal to a depth that would hold the desired amount of ink.

In addition, Gillray developed a special facility for aquatint, an auxiliary etching technique invented in France about 1750 and increasingly popular after 1762 as a means of approximating watercolor washes and other tonal effects. This involved the laying of a second "imperfect" or porous ground after the linework had been completed and the initial ground removed. Resin powder of a selected degree of fineness or coarseness was dusted onto the plate, or floated on in a spirit solution, and permitted to dry. Once this pebbled veneer had been heated and thereby bonded to the metal, the precisely timed application of a mordant could be used to lay an even network of pockmarks or microscopic ravines. (In the final inking and printing, these indentations would transmit monochrome tones of varying intensity to the dampened paper, which was forced into them under great pressure.) Any area which the artist wanted to leave untouched had to be protected at the outset with a varnish or "resist." After the lightest passages of tone had been given a proportionately brief exposure to the acid, they too were covered. The stopping-out process continued through however many gradations were needed, with the darkest shadows naturally receiving the longest, deepest "bite." Gillray's procedure may be followed on Plate 17, where he used two tints, or on Plate 22, where he used three—in each case after painting out his highlights. On Plates 47, 60 and 61, he can be seen drawing directly on the aquatint ground with brush and resist.

Although the caricaturist made more use of sketches and working drawings than has been traditionally asserted, he saved the greater portion of the creative process for the copperplate itself. As alternatives to aquatint, he used a variety of methods to establish background grains and patterns. On Plate I the tones appear to have been raked in with double- and quadruple-pointed burins and modulated during biting with stopping-out varnish, as if they were aquatint. Plate 35, executed the following month, is an incredibly controlled blend of drypoint, etching and stipple (both hand and mechanical) in the light and middle areas, with the heavy darks handled with needle, multiple burin and drypoint accents. In both plates, the inscriptions are laid in by needle, their serifs and miscellaneous extremities touched up with a burin. (Under magnification the former lines are easily identified by their blunt terminations, in marked contrast to the crisp dagger point of the burin thrust.)

Gillray had some means of combing minute parallel lines into what would otherwise seem a conventional aquatint ground—note the left half of Plate 34 as distinct from the right. A result of this sort might have been obtained by using an abrasive, or by applying a grooved, flat-bellied instrument called a threading-tool, normally used by engravers to rule a series of regular lines directly into the metal. In this instance the light sky mass behind and above the moon has been stippled in with a mechanical roulette wheel, a probable indication that the caricaturist had lost control of the situation during the biting, burnished that corner smooth and tried again.

To lend a faint, allover grain to the huge "Apotheosis of Hoche" (Plate 55), Gillray appears to have run his grounded copper through the press, sandwiched against a fine sandpaper or other abrasive surface. The drawing here is primarily executed with a needle; the remainder of the tones are drypoint. (I am strongly inclined to agree with Mr. Duncan Macpherson[91] that many of Gillray's special effects could not have been produced by the customary immersion of the plate in a pan of acid. Macpherson suggests that Gillray avoided this sort of guesswork by feathering, pressing, flicking, sponging or dribbling his mordants onto the surface of the metal.)

In 1798 and 1799, Gillray flirted briefly with softground etching, notably for Plates 59 and 64. This process was primarily intended for the approximation of crayon textures. It involved drawing with pencil on paper fastened over a copperplate which had been prepared with a sticky ground of wax, pitch and tallow. When the paper was lifted off, lines were left bare on the metal which reflected the grain of the paper and some of the quality of the pencil. In the examples reproduced, Gillray strengthened his designs with stipple and drypoint.

Each major project seems to have had its own battle plan. A trial proof for an abandoned satire of 1793 shows the aquatint tones fully blocked out and bitten before the addition of line.[92] In November 1792, Gillray developed a plate in aquatint, saw it completed and published, evidently concluded that it was an aesthetic failure and spent another two weeks reworking it as a line etching with drypoint.[93] From the late nineties on, he was apt increasingly to make more and bolder use of a burin to supply his final accents after the plate had been bitten (compare Plates 62, VI and 96). At the end he was assaulting the copperplate with an intensity which inspired the reminiscence that "he worked furiously, without stopping to remove the burr thrown up by the etching needle [more probably the drypoint]; consequently his fingers often bled from being cut by it."[94]

Gillray's technical ingenuity and curiosity deserve more consideration than possible at present. With patience and a good magnifying glass his tracks can be retraced, one plate at a time. The more close attention is paid to the adventurous years of his prime, roughly 1795–1803, the more remarkable this blend of daring and diligence becomes. Gillray seemed to thrive on the union of spontaneity and control implicit in his particular wedding of etching and engraving. To attain the swelling, undulating character of many of his principal outlines, the caricaturist must have relied on a tool like the etcher's oval-tipped échoppe, slicing through the ground and into the metal with a bravura roll of the wrist. This illusion of ease and elegance—paradoxically achieved with the expenditure of extraordinary discipline—appears to symbolize a larger truth. Given the introspective, hesitant character revealed in the deletions and revisions of the initial drafts for his letters,[95] it is perhaps fair to suggest that Gillray's astonishing devotion to process represented a retreat from some of the realities and contradictions of his political, social and professional situation.

As previously stated, his compositions were designed to be tinted by hand. There is evidence that Mrs. Humphrey's stable of colorists worked from a master proof prepared by the caricaturist. The color frequently strengthens and completes the design; here and there it even adds ironic or symbolic content, as in the case of a rubicund nose or a partisan insignia. (In 1793–96 the hues of the prints often correspond to those of Gillray's surviving drawings from the same period.) He must have worked with the awareness and intention that much of his most delicate aquatint shading would be muted by the addition of watercolor washes.

The completed copperplates had to be heated, dabbed over with a thin, oily ink, and wiped absolutely clean every time an impression was to be taken from them. The printer used a damp, high-quality rag paper. Probably working steadily with a team of at least four men, and keeping two plates in continuous rotation, it seems to have been possible to produce a quality print in less than four minutes. (A modern printer will insist that the operation cannot be properly performed in less than ten minutes. On the one occasion when the present writer watched an experienced printer ink and pull one of the five known surviving Gillray copperplates, it took a great deal longer than that to get the job done.)

The freshly inked sheets were carefully stacked up to dry, one on top of another. Occasionally the "ghost" of a second composition on the back indicates that a print wound up on the wrong pile. Afterwards, they were colored, placed in the shop, displayed in the front window and distributed wholesale to other dealers. The logistics of manufacture make it unlikely that more than a few hundred copies of any satire could have been available during the month of its initial publication. However, plates were customarily hammered to increase their surface toughness, and were capable of supplying excellent impressions for years. After the 1780s Mrs. Humphrey tended to avoid paper with watermarks, which makes it almost impossible to distinguish those first issued from the firm's later strikes.

Gillray carried his experimentation into wood engraving, turning out a highly finished salute to Pitt circa 1803 (page vii), very much in the manner of Thomas Bewick. At about the same time he executed a single venture in the infant medium of lithography, then being aggressively promoted in London under the name "polyautography." A small grotesque sketch of "A Musical Family," singing from Haydn to flute and piano accompaniment, seems to have been drawn in pen and ink.[96]

[V]

GILLRAY'S LEGACY

> English art collectors are already putting Gillray's originals alongside the best . . . their worth will grow with time.
>
> —Anonymous German correspondent, 1806[97]

Gillray's reputation continued to rise during the decade which followed his retirement from the field. In 1818 John Miller, William Blackwood and two others commenced the serial publication of *The Caricatures of Gillray*. This set of reduced copies with explanatory text appears to have extended into nine parts, and to have been remaindered in 1824 as a single volume costing ten shillings and sixpence. A oblong quarto with hand-colored plates averaging six inches by eight, it probably qualifies as the earliest anthology of one cartoonist's work. Despite the obvious existence of a continuing market, the editor observed:

> It is a scandal upon all the cold-hearted scribblers in the land to allow such a genius as Gillray to go to the grave unnoticed; and a burning shame that so many of his works should have become ambiguous for want of a commentator. The political squibs have already lost half their point for want of a Glossary and many of the humorous traits of private life so characteristic of men and manners are become oblivious to ninety-nine hundredths of those who perambulate the streets of this mighty town.[98]

After Hannah Humphrey's death, which must have occurred in the late winter or early spring of 1818,[99] the shop in St. James's Street was taken over by her nephew George. Although George Humphrey played a leading role in the virulent campaign against Queen Caroline (1820–21), he lost ground rapidly thereafter to his competitors. By 1828 a lion's share of the trade had been captured by Thomas McLean's new establishment at 26 Haymarket, which dealt in lithographs and woodcuts, as well as in the traditional etchings. During the late twenties, when Humphrey's fortunes were in reversal, he joined in partnership with McLean to produce a subscription series of Gillray satires from the original plates in his possession. Separate wrappers for numbers 10 and 12 of this undertaking, both dated 1827, are preserved in the print room of the Victoria & Albert Museum. These bear the announcement: "To be continued every Fortnight till completed," and a note: "Price One Guinea & a Half, / or to Subscribers to the whole work, price One Guinea." The inside front covers carry a prospectus, dated "London, April 6th, 1827," explaining that each part would contain seven, "or not less than six sheets . . ." and that the whole would consist of "from Twenty to Twenty-five Parts." "Where the humour will be considered too broad for general Inspection," it continues, "those plates will be reserved till the end of the Work, when, if the profits of the Publication should enable the Publishers to do so, they will be presented to the Subscribers in a Supplement, gratis." It seems logical to suppose that this project fared poorly, and that George Humphrey's physical indisposition or death left McLean with a large quantity of unsold sheets, some of which he colored to enhance their attractiveness.[100]

The "House of Humphrey" was managed by George, and then by his widow until her retirement in 1835. According to a catalogue published by E. Foster and Son of 54 Pall Mall, the public had an opportunity to purchase her entire stock at auction from 13 to 16 July 1835. The title page drew special attention to "Gillray's Drawings, Prints and Copper Plates," and to the "many thousand caricatures, Coloured and Plain, and the Shop Fixtures." An advertisement in the *Morning Post* of 16 July stated that Mrs. Humphrey "was obliged to quit the premises" and that the final day's sale would include "760 copper plates, original drawings and sketches, & [Charles James] Fox's personal collection of caricatures in several volumes." A copy of the catalogue in the library of the Victoria and Albert Museum, to which the sale prices have been added, indicates that almost 20,000 caricature prints were disposed of at an average of a penny each. Some 600 Gillray drawings and sketches brought between one and five shillings apiece. There are a number of tantalizing bargains: "Portraits on cards taken at public meetings" (two lots of 75 each), "A Portfolio with a Parcel of Drawings &c." (knocked down at thirteen shillings) and "A Bundle of Gillray's Sketchbooks" (a decent buy at one pound, fifteen shillings). The key item was brought up on the fourth day. Lot 1061 consisted of "Gillray's Works—610 Plates . . . (in an excellent state of preservation)." The auctioneers apologized for "taking the liberty" to "suggest the great advantage that may be derived from publishing these plates in numbers, in a cheap and popular form." There were no buyers adventurous enough to meet Mrs. Humphrey's reserve price, which must have been at least one thousand pounds.

In the words of H. G. Bohn, the man who finally acquired and republished them, the history of the Gillray copperplates "affords a remarkable instance of the vicissitudes of literary property."[101] Bohn's recollection was that the plates were valued at "several thousand pounds" when "the trade in them began somewhat to decline," presumably about 1825. (John Timbs stated in 1866 that the metal was "estimated to be worth 7000 pounds" at the period of the artist's death.)[102] According to Bohn, Mrs. [George] Humphrey "had occasion to raise money, and obtained a loan of upwards of a thousand pounds upon a deposit of the coppers." Thomas McLean seems to have been at work on a volume of explanatory text in 1827, and he might conceivably have entered into a loan agreement which entitled him to bring out a limited Gillray edition of his own. Mrs. Humphrey's financial arrangement could have been concluded with another party after the publication of McLean's album. In any case, the latter's handsome *Genuine Works of Mr. James Gillray* appeared early in 1830; it gathered 584 satires on 304 "folio" sheets. In a preface to his gilt-edged 400-page "Illustrative Description," McLean noted that the project had been accomplished under the patronage of "the highest noblemen and statesmen of our times," men "well known to be the very first to laugh at the freedom with which their own personal likenesses are introduced, and their features humorously exaggerated." The rarity of McLean's *Gillray* was underscored by the auctioneer's call five years later for a "cheap and popular" edition, as well as by an apologetic "Note" pasted in early copies of the descriptive guide:

> Lest the price of this Key to the Works of Gillray should be thought too high, the Publisher deems it right to state in explanation, that there have been only One Hundred copies of that Work printed for sale—that the KEY has been composed at great expense of time and research, expressly for the occasion, and that the price charged for it is scarcely adequate to the heavy expenditure incurred by the Proprietor for the composition and printing.[103]

At the Humphrey auction in 1835, a copy of McLean's plate volume with its accompanying key brought £15/4/6—a sum roughly equal to the amount realized from the first twenty lots of Gillray drawings, consisting of more than 200 original items.

When Mrs. George Humphrey put the plates up for auction she was still trying to recover enough to discharge her debt. The situation had clearly engaged the interest of Henry G. Bohn (1796–1884), an enterprising and extremely acute 39-year-old bookseller of York Street, Covent Garden. On the third day of the sale he acquired Lots 837–839, scrapbooks containing some 552 "caricatures" by Gillray and others. On the fourth day he bought nothing. "Subsequently," notes Bohn, Mrs. Humphrey offered the copperplates to him "with the consent of the lien-holder . . . for eight hundred pounds, and actually refused five hundred":

> After the lapse of about three years [Bohn continues] she would have accepted the five hundred, or even less, but the time having then passed for expensive publications as a judicious investment, the Publisher [Bohn himself] declined any further negociation, and the coppers remained *in statu quo* till the day of her death. The executors, probably not aware of what had passed, and unable to meet with a purchaser at the value of engravings, sold them for old copper, that is, for about as many shillings as Mrs. Humphrey had once refused pounds. By mere accident the Publisher heard of this transaction just in time to rescue them from the melting pot, and the public in consequence are now presented, for a few guineas, with a volume, which under ordinary circumstances, would have cost four or five times as much.[104]

In these remarks, Bohn was speaking (1851) of his own massive atlas folio *The Works of James Gillray, from the Original Plates*, which seems to have been in preparation by 1845 or 1846. The time required for production must have been considerable; this work united 588 satires between marbled boards measuring 20 inches by 26. It was gilt-edged, and bound in half-morocco with elaborate gold tooling. Together with a matching companion folio of 45 "Suppressed Plates," it weighed more than forty pounds. A new "Historical and Descriptive Account" running to some 500 pages was assembled for Bohn by Thomas Wright and R. H. Evans. This appeared in 1851—the date customarily assigned to the entire project—and according to Bohn's preface, had been commenced in 1848 after Wright completed his caricature history of *England, under the House of Hanover.* (Some copies of the larger folio bear the date 1847 on the title page, stamped rather than imprinted. A facetious proposal in *Punch* concerning a pretentious resuscitation of cheap, popular illustrations might indicate that copies of the Bohn collection were circulating by January 1848.)[105]

Although he has been largely forgotten, H. G. Bohn is one of the most resourceful and innovative figures in the history of book publishing. After making a debut as a dealer in the old and rare, between 1840 and 1846 he carried the commerce in other publishers' "remainders" to new heights. In 1846 Bohn began to devote his principal energies to the inexpensive reissue of classics, anticipating the bounties of the Modern Library and the paperback abundancies of the present day. In rapid order, "Bohn's Standard Library" was followed by his "Classical Library," his "British Classics," his "Antiquarian Library," his "European Library," his "Illustrated Library," his "Ecclesiastical Library," his "Scientific Library," his "Philosophical Library" and a number of others. The library series alone ran to more than 600 titles, and represented only a portion of his activity, which extended deeply into writing, editing and collecting. Bohn's enthusiasm must have been supported by his friendship with George Cruikshank, who was four years his senior. In 1842 Bohn brought out an edition of the *Humorous Sketches* of Robert Seymour (1800?–1836) which served as a sort of practice run for his Gillray, presumably at about the time of the fortuitous acquisition of the Humphrey copperplates.

> Upon obtaining possession of these coppers [Bohn's preface continues], the Publisher made diligent search for those which he found to be missing, and discovered a considerable number in different places, but principally with Mr. Fores of Piccadilly.

This would have been a son and heir of Gillray's old partner Samuel William Fores (1761–1838), for whom Gillray etched some of his most important work between 1787 and 1791 (see Plates 10–12, 13B–16 and 21).

A prominent line on the title page of Bohn's folio refers proudly to "The Addition of Many Subjects Not Before Collected," and indeed this work was to provide an invaluable cornerstone for the later study, collection and appreciation of the caricaturist's achievement. Bohn was able to locate 46 satires absent from McLean's album. Conversely, eighteen plates present in McLean's publication were missing by 1851, including "Sir Sidney Smith" (Plate 67) and "The Keenest Sportsman in Broomswell

Camp" (Plate 79). The upward march of Victorian sensibility was reflected by the fact that Bohn chose to group among his "Suppressed Plates" (because of their actual or presumed indecency) twelve satires which had been routinely handled by McLean. On the other hand, McLean had declined to catalogue the more offensive attacks on the former Prince of Wales while he was still on the throne, and probably omitted "Fashionable Contrasts" (Plate 24) out of respect to the Duke of York, who died in 1827. In the present selection, Plates 6, 18, 19, 24, 29, 33, 41, 48 and 82 have been reproduced from Bohn's "Suppressed Plates." This special offering was intended by Bohn for the perusal of gentlemen only—at least one horrified customer barricaded his copy with ribbon and sealing wax to guard the innocents of his family from contamination.[106]

It is to H. G. Bohn that we are indebted for the existence of an extensive, easily accessible set of uncolored impressions containing almost all of Gillray's major efforts. About two-thirds of the satires in the present book are reproduced from Bohn, as indicated by the presence of his catalogue number in the upper right-hand corner of the plate. (The remainder are from the author's collection, including the items from the "Suppressed Plates," which have separate engraved numbers at the *lower* right.) Bohn's three volumes sold for ten guineas, and were still in print a quarter-century later. There is no clue as to the final disposition of the copperplates. Only five plates etched by Gillray are still known to exist.[107] One of these is an unfinished social subject of the mid-nineties; the rest date from the early eighties and are not to be found in McLean or Bohn. Until the happy day when Gillray's oeuvre is discovered sheathing a roof in Shoreditch or Wapping, it seems realistic to assume that the bulk of his coppers were dispatched to the Mint, pressed into military service, or otherwise reconsigned to the melting pot from which Bohn had rescued them.

The perceptive English cartoonist and critic Osbert Lancaster has argued persuasively that James Gillray can be regarded as the last great exponent of the baroque. At the same time, Mrs. Humphrey's dour lodger occupies a special place in that earthquake of the spirit which we have come to call the Romantic Rebellion. His influence on the subsequent growth and development of his profession has been emphatic. Phil May (1864–1903), perhaps the leading British cartoonist of the nineties, surprised an interviewer with the strength of his enthusiasm at a time when Gillray was rather out of fashion. "There is nobody to-day to touch him," said May. "Look at his sweep of line and his astonishing mastery over the grotesque and ridiculous. There are pictures so extraordinarily funny that you can't laugh. . . ."[108]

During the past decade, Gillray's "worth" from the collector's standpoint has come into its own with a vengeance. This writer purchased his copy of the Bohn folio in September 1960 for $24. The same item has since brought as much as $800 at auction and a recent London exhibition consisted entirely of individual uncoloured pages from it offered for an average of $75 apiece. While the success of this singular venture is not known, an original-issue, hand-colored impression of Gillray's "A Voluptuary under the Horrors of Digestion" (Plate II) realized approximately $300 in April 1973,[109] and would almost surely do rather better now. Where an "average" original-issue, hand-colored Gillray satire in good condition might have fetched between $3 and $12 in London in 1965, the current price on the London market would be between $60 and $140. A portfolio of five Gillray "classics" reproduced in color by *The Sunday Times* of London in an edition of 2500 was an almost immediate sell-out at five guineas per set (August 1969). Since that time, the caricaturist's work has been laminated onto placemats, used on postcards and Christmas greetings, has figured more frequently as illustrative matter in historical works, and has even been recaptioned to form a running commentary on Watergate in the catalogue of one enterprising New York publisher.

In his authoritative and highly readable study of *Victorian Novelists and Their Illustrators*, John Harvey has examined the fundamental impact which Gillray's manner and imagination exerted on pictorial satire, and then on book illustration, in succeeding generations.[110] Referring to echoes of the senior man's touch in the works of such artists as George and Robert Cruikshank, William and Henry Heath, Robert Seymour and C. J. Grant, Harvey suggests that "for the world of lusty comic entertainment, primarily visual, amid which the young Dickens grew up, Gillray was *the* formative genius."[111] As Harvey goes on to suggest, the heritage of Hogarth, Gillray and Rowlandson had an unmistakable effect in shaping the author's vision. This influence by caricaturists was recognized by a reviewer of Dickens' early *Sketches by Boz* (1836) who described him as "the CRUIKSHANK of writers."[112] According to Buss, Dickens "thoroughly understood and appreciated the great power of James Gillray as a caricaturist."[113] (Dickens possessed a copy of Bohn's Gillray in his library at Gadshill. An estate appraisal in 1870 speaks of "fine early impressions," gives the publication date as 1850 and values it at £6.10s.)[114] Unfortunately, Dickens' only recorded mention of Gillray is a negative response to "vast amounts of personal ugliness," apparently written off the top of his head in the course of a tribute proclaiming John Leech (1817–64) as "the very first English caricaturist . . . who has considered beauty as being perfectly compatible with his art."[115] Presumably the novelist did not base his objection on any systematic review of Gill-

ray's work. The lone example cited is a late social satire pointedly inscribed "Drawn by an Amateur—Etch'd by Js. Gillray."[116] Despite Thackeray's evident familiarity with Gillray's prints, and notwithstanding the deep impression that they must have made on his imagination,[117] the author of *Vanity Fair* seems never to have ventured a serious appraisal.

The lack of critical enthusiasm for Gillray among the Victorians is hardly surprising. An age which had attuned itself to the grace and humor of Leech and to the allusive Olympian dignity of John Tenniel could scarcely cherish the memory of the man who perfected caricature as an instrument of public aggression. The scattered appreciations tended to dwell on Gillray's uninhibited ferocity, audacity, exuberance and "hireling" status, rather than on his subtlety, frequent delicacy and the control with which superb technique was subordinated to content. Over the years, the diatribes range from a description of him as a "caterpillar on the green leaf of reputation" (1831)[118] to an expressed conviction that "from first to last his drawings impress one as emanating from a mind not only unclean, but unbalanced as well. . . ."

> There is an element of monstrosity about all his figures, distorted and repellent. Foul, bloated faces; twisted, swollen limbs; unshapely figures whose protuberant flesh suggests a tumefied and fungoid growth—such is the brood begotten by Gillray's pencil, like the malignant spawn of some forgotten circle of the lower inferno (1904).[119]

On the opposite side of the ledger, in 1865 Thomas Wright drew attention to "a distinguishing characteristic of Gillray's style":

> . . . the wonderful tact with which he seizes upon the points in his subject open to ridicule, and the force with with he brings those points out. In the fineness of his design, and in his grouping and drawing, he excels all the other caricaturists. He was, indeed, born with all the talents of a great historical painter. . . .[120]

Perhaps the most remarkable early homage to Gillray and his art had been delivered almost three decades before—in 1837, the year of Victoria's ascension. The *London and Westminster Review* noted the caricaturist's fall into obscurity with regret and compassion, recalled that Gillray had employed "the whole resources of the ridiculous" and concluded: "He shows us that the ludicrous is not divided by a step from the sublime, but blended with it and twined round it."[121] One has difficulty imagining an epitaph that might have pleased him more.

NOTES

1. James P. Malcolm, *An Historical Sketch of the Art of Caricaturing*, London, 1813, p. 157.

2. David Low, "An Imaginary Interview" written for the British Broadcasting Corporation, reprinted in *The Listener*, 2 December 1943, p. 635.

3. *London und Paris*, Weimar, 1806, vol. xviii, p. 7.

4. George Stanley, *Bryan's Dictionary of Painters and Engravers*, 1849, p. 283.

5. *Foster's Sale Catalogue . . . of the Entire Stock of Mrs. Humphrey*, 13–16 July 1835, in the library of the Victoria and Albert Museum, London.

6. Josceline Bagot, *George Canning and His Friends*, London, 1909, vol. 1, p. 55; and the catalogue of Sotheby's sale (18 November 1927) of the estate of Ralph Sneyd of Keele Hall, Staffs.

7. British Museum Department of Manuscripts, Add. MSS. 27,337, f. 103.

8. *Somerset House Gazette*, 3 April 1824, p. 410.

9. *London und Paris*, 1798, vol. i, p. 196.

10. *Ibid.*, 1803, vol. xi, p. 158.

11. Harry Furniss, *Furniss At Home*, London, 1904, p. 56.

12. Bagot, *op. cit.*, vol. i, p. 143. The reference is to John Nicholls, M.P. for Tregony.

13. B.M. Add. MSS. 27,337, f. 103.

14. *Ibid.*, f. 57, promoting the abortive *Poetry of The Anti-Jacobin*.

15. Author's collection.

16. B.M. Add. MSS. 27,337, f. 74.

17. *Ibid.*, f. 201, and D. Hill, *Mr. Gillray The Caricaturist*, London, 1965, pp. 136–37.

18. *Foster's Sale Catalogue. . . .*

19. B.M. Add. MSS. 28,833. George Canning to J. H. Frere, 6 October 1806: "The enclosed . . . I should think would 'come in well' as Gillray says. . . ."

20. *Takings*, London, 1821, p. 96.

21. Quoted without attribution by Richard Dagley, *ibid.*, p. 171.

22. "A Midnight Modern Conversation" of March 1732/3.

23. "The Times," Plate I, of 7 September 1762.

24. The first five volumes of the catalogue, down to the year 1770, compiled c. 1870–83, is useful but chronologically capricious and far from complete.

25. Frontispiece, *Raccolta di XXVI Caricature . . .*, Dresden, 1750, author's collection. Ghezzi lived from 1674 to 1755.

26. Letter to James Northcote, c. 1786, collection of Keith Mackenzie, London.

27. John Hughes (1677–1720), in the *Spectator* of 14 November 1712.

28. Lines 219–30, published in June 1736.

29. John Clubbe, *Physiognomy*, c. Dec. 1763/Jan. 1764, London, p. 7.

30. "The Bench," dated 4 September 1758. On 11 January 1759, Townshend's friend William Windham II wrote

Garrick that he had seen Hogarth's print and "could not make any meaning out of [it]." "[Hogarth] is an ignorant conceited puppy, nor has no sure idea of a car*i*cature, which the blockhead writes car*a*cature, not knowing it comes from *caricare*, to overload any part or *outrer* any feature . . . ," R. W. Ketton-Kremer, *Felbrigg: Story of a House*, London, 1962, p. 150.

31. C. V. F. Townshend, *The Military Life of Field-Marshal George First Marquess Townshend*, London, 1901, p. 113.

32. Letter to H. S. Conway, 4 March 1756; W. S. Lewis, ed., *Yale Edition of Horace Walpole's Correspondence*, New Haven, 1937– , vol. xxxvii, p. 444.

33. *Ibid.*, vol. ix, p. 95.

34. *Memoirs of the Reign of George II*, London, 1822, vol. ii, p. 68.

35. From H. Walpole's manuscript *Book of Materials*, c. 1762, collection of W. S. Lewis, Farmington, Conn.

36. *Memoirs and Portraits*, ed. Matthew Hodgart, London, 1963, p. 85. Henry Seymour Conway, Field Marshal (1721–95), was Walpole's cousin.

37. See M. D. George, *English Political Caricature*, Oxford, 1959, vol. i, pp. 147–48.

38. William Bates, *George Cruikshank*, Birmingham, 1879, p. 83.

39. BM. Add. MSS. 27,337, f. 162.

40. *Ibid.*, f. 158; dated 19 April 1823 by George Humphrey, Jr.

41. *London Chronicle*, 17 February 1802; cited by M. D. George, *Catalogue of Political and Personal Satires*, London, 1942, vol. vii, p. xvii.

42. *Ibid.*

43. *Cobbett's Political Register*, 20 August 1808, pp. 269–70.

44. A window-card lettered on the back of British Museum print 9177, of 26 February 1798. Newton, an extraordinarily original and "modern" humorist, died on 9 December 1798, aged 21.

45. "Pictures of Life and Character," *Quarterly Review*, December 1854, p. 78.

46. *Somerset House Gazette*, 3 April 1824, p. 409. Angelo (1760–1839) was a fencing master, gossip and friend of both Gillray and Rowlandson.

47. *The Athenaeum*, 15 October 1831, p. 667. Landseer (1769–1852), painter, engraver, author and father of Sir Edwin.

48. *London und Paris*, 1798, vol. i, p. 196.

49. D. Hill, *Mr. Gillray The Caricaturist*, London, 1965, pp. 7–8. This work may be consulted for additional background concerning the caricaturist, his family and career. I am indebted to Brian Lambie of the Gladstone Court Museum, Biggar, for newly researched information on the family origins.

50. In the possession of Mrs. Ann (Carrick) Scott, Melrose, Roxburghshire.

51. Daniel Benham, *A Short Sketch of the Origin and*

History of the Schools of the London Congregation of the Brethren, London, 1853, p. 2.

52. W. T. Waugh, *A History of Fulneck School*, Leeds, 1909, p. 27.

53. According to a memorandum written by a schoolmaster, one of the few surviving family papers preserved by the caricaturist. Add. MSS. 27,337, f. 7.

54. Thomas Tomkins (1743–1816), master calligrapher, frequent collaborator of Ashby's, known for his ability to swing a perfect freehand circle.

55. *Somerset House Gazette, loc. cit.*

56. *The Analysis of Beauty*, autobiographical notes, Joseph Burke, ed., Oxford, 1955, pp. 201–02.

57. *London und Paris*, 1798, vol. i, p. 196.

58. Joseph Grego, *The Works of James Gillray, the Caricaturist*, London, 1873, p. 9.

59. *London und Paris, loc. cit.*

60. J. P. Malcolm, *op. cit.*, p. 18.

61. Thought to have been Philip Francis (1740–1818).

62. J. P. Malcolm, *op. cit.*, p. 101.

63. Two surviving copperplates (10 April 1783 and 3 June 1783, author's possession and private collection in Scotland) bear the inscription "J. Gillray fecit," as if he might have attempted to follow Sayers' example and take credit for a satire against the prevailing custom. These etched lines do not appear on contemporary impressions. They could have been temporarily filled in, but it seems more probable that they are posthumous additions.

64. Heal Bequest of Trade Cards, Department of Prints and Drawings, The British Museum, London.

65. R. W. Buss, *English Graphic Satire*, London, 1874, p. 114, based on lectures delivered 1853–54.

66. B.M. Add. MSS. 27,337, f. 103.

67. MS. in the collection of Charles Hamilton, New York.

68. R. W. Buss, *op. cit.*, p. 129.

69. B.M. Add. MSS. 27,337, f. 152.

70. *The Athenaeum*, 15 October 1831, p. 667.

71. See D. Hill, *Mr. Gillray The Caricaturist*, pp. 56–72.

72. *The Westminster Review*, June 1840, p. 421.

73. *London und Paris*, 1798, vol. i, p. 196.

74. *Cobbett's Political Register*, 30 May 1818, p. 625. Cobbett (1762–1835) was a radical writer and politician; J. H. Frere (1769–1835) and George Ellis (1751–1815) were regular contributors to *The Anti-Jacobin*; William Gifford (1756–1826) was the editor.

75. D. Hill, *Mr. Gillray The Caricaturist*, pp. 88–101.

76. *London und Paris*, 1798, vol. i, p. 292, in reference to "Shrine at St Ann's Hill" of 26 May 1798.

77. *Ibid.*, 1799, vol. iii, p. 355. Ironically, the satires in question were, like Plate 62, "intercepted French drawings," almost surely based on Canningite suggestions.

78. *Ibid.*, 1806, vol. xviii, p. 7.

79. B.M. Add. MSS. 27,337, f. 73.

80. D. Hill, *Mr. Gillray The Caricaturist*, pp. 106–08.

81. *London und Paris*, vol. xviii, p. 7.

82. Bagot, *op. cit.*, vol. i, pp. 307–08.

83. *Ibid.*, p. 57.

84. *Somerset House Gazette, loc. cit.*

85. On five of the eight plates in the series *The Life of William Cobbett*, published 29 September 1809.

86. R. W. Buss, *op. cit.*, p. 128.

87. John Timbs, *English Eccentrics and Eccentricities*, London, 1866, p. 334.

88. B.M. Add. MSS. 27,337, f. 103.

89. *Ibid.*, f. 53.

90. Page 236 in the revised (third) edition, Boston, 1923 (Dover reprint, 1963).

91. I am indebted to Mr. Macpherson of Toronto (perhaps the only master cartoonist of our day with extensive training in etching and lithography) for much useful counsel.

92. ["England and France Contrasted"], British Museum Satire 8301.

93. "Tom Paine's Nightly Pest" (not reproduced), published 26 November and 10 December 1792.

94. R. W. Buss., *op. cit.*, p. 129, probably on the authority of Cruikshank.

95. Add. MSS. 27,337.

96. British Museum Satire 10,308. Lithography was invented in Munich (1796–98) by Alois Senefelder, who in 1800 and 1801 was a London resident, kept under close wraps by greedy and jealous partners in a cul-de-sac just north of the Tower of London.

97. *London und Paris*, 1806, vol. xviii, p. 7.

98. Page 20.

99. A letter of John Sneyd's to Charles Bagot fixes the date within a few weeks of an April 1 assassination attempt on Lord Palmerston. Bagot, *op. cit.*, vol. i, pp. 55–56.

100. I am grateful to Mr. Andrew Edmunds of London for much useful counsel concerning the joint enterprise of Humphrey and McLean.

101. Preface to Thomas Wright and R. H. Evans, *Historical and Descriptive Account of the Caricatures of James Gillray*, London, 1851, p. xiii.

102. Timbs, *op. cit.*, p. 337.

103. Initial copies bore the words "Gillray's Works / Letterpress Description" on the spine; collection of Mr. and Mrs. A. G. Burkhart, Jr., Memphis. This soon was changed to "Gillray's Genuine Works / Illustrative Description," perhaps to draw a sharper contrast with the Miller and Blackwood publication of 1824.

104. Wright and Evans, *op. cit.*, pp. xiii–xiv.

105. "The Catnach Collection," *Punch*, 29 January 1848; a short article pretending to subject the penny ballads, broadsides and chapbooks of James Catnach (1792–1841) to art criticism in the grand manner.

106. Collection of Mr. and Mrs. A. G. Burkhart, Jr., Memphis.

107. In the possession of the Victoria and Albert Museum, the London Museum, Mr. Andrew Edmunds of London, a private collector in Scotland, and the author.

108. "The Best Comic Pictures," *The Strand Magazine*, London, April 1904, p. 395.

109. At Sotheby's Belgravia, London, 25 April 1973.

110. London, 1970; particularly Chapter 2.

111. *Ibid.*, p. 30.

112. *The Spectator*, 26 December 1836; cited by Harvey, *ibid.*, p. 33.

113. Buss, *op. cit.*, p. 171.

114. J. H. Stonehouse, *Catalogue of the Library of Charles Dickens*, London, 1935, p. 50.

115. A review of Leech's "The Rising Generation," *The Examiner*, 30 December 1848, p. 838.

116. "Farmer Giles & his Wife shewing off their daughter Betty . . ." (1 January 1809). Dickens contends that "to represent what is being satirized as necessarily ugly . . . is but the resource of an angry child or a jealous woman—it serves no purpose but to produce a disagreeable result. There is no reason why the farmer's daughter in the old caricature who is squalling at the harpsichord . . . should be squat and hideous. The satire on the manner of her education, should there be any in the thing at all, would be just as good if she were pretty. Mr. Leech would have made her so." *Ibid.*, p. 838.

117. See his review of Leech's *Pictures of Life and Character* in *The Quarterly Review* [December 1854], pp. 75–86. As Harvey points out, all the Georgian caricatures to which Thackeray makes specific reference, apparently from memory, seem to have been by Gillray.

118. *The Athenaeum*, 1 October 1831, pp. 623–33.

119. A. B. Maurice and F. T. Cooper, *The History of the Nineteenth Century in Caricature*, New York, 1904, pp. 21–22.

120. Thomas Wright, *A History of Caricature and Grotesque in Literature and Art*, London, 1865, p. 465. Wright skirted critical evaluation in his two earlier works on the subject of caricature, *England, under the House of Hanover* and the *Historical and Descriptive Account* of Gillray's works for Bohn.

121. *The London and Westminster Review*, vol. vi, London, 1837, p. 261.

I. [2 March 1795] An imaginary, reconstituted "republican" House of Commons tries Prime Minister Pitt for his crimes against the "new order."

A *VOLUPTUARY under the horrors of Digestion.*

II. [2 July 1792] "The Good Life" as exemplified by the Prince of Wales's establishment at Carlton House.

III. [28 July 1792] Contrasted with the Prince's life is the somewhat more severe regimen observed by his royal parents at Windsor.

Pub⁴ Jan⁵ 5ᵗʰ 1803 by J.Gillray, 27 S⁴ James's Street.

A PHANTASMAGORIA ;—Scene—Conjuring up an Armed-Skeleton.

IV. [5 January 1803] *Macbeth's* witches—Prime Minister Addington, Hawkesbury and Fox— summon up a frightful vision of Britannia at peace, debilitated by concessions to the French.

L'ASSEMBLEE NATIONALE; — or — *Grand Cooperative Meeting at S[t]. Ann's Hill.* — *Respectfully Dedicated to the admirers of a "Broad-Bottom'd Administration."*

V. [18 June 1804] St. Anne's Hill, Fox's estate near Chertsey in Surrey, provides the locale for a Whig reception in the french manner which appears to follow, or anticipate, the establishment of a regency under the Prince of Wales.

VI. [7 August 1804] In a boisterous Hogarthian setting, various Opposition leaders (wearing proletarian dress) celebrate and assist the anticipated return of Sir Francis Burdett as Member of Parliament for Middlesex.

VII. [23 January 1806] Napoleon at the apex of his power, seven weeks after the French triumph at Austerlitz, confirms the new Imperial ascendancy over Bavaria, Württemberg and Baden by converting their electors into satellite monarchs. He is assisted by his foreign minister, the club-footed Talleyrand. Tiddy-Dol Ford (d. 1752) was a colorful Mayfair pitchman memorialized by Hogarth in the eleventh plate of *Industry and Idleness* (1747).

London Published March 22 1808 by H Humphrey 27 S' James's Street

PHAETON alarm'd! — {
"Now all the horrors of the heav'ng he spies,
And monstrous shadows of prodigious size,
That deck'd with stars, lie scatter'd o'er the skies.

"Th' astonish'd youth, where e'er his eyes could turn.
"Beheld the universe around him burn:
"The world was in a blaze!" ——— *Vid. Ovid: Metamorphoses*
}

VIII. [22 March 1808] Foreign Secretary George Canning struggles to guide the sun of his mentor, Apollo-Pitt, through the menacing skies of parti-san opposition. A sequel to the "Light Expelling Darkness" of 1795 (Plate 35).

THE CHURCH MILITANT.

1. [5 September 1779] The Church of England is criticized for its energetic support of the unpopular war with the American colonies.

ARGUS.

2. [15 May 1780] While Britannia grieves and the British lion slumbers in chains, the dozing King is surrounded by schemers.

S.ᵗ GEORGE & the Dragon.

Pub.ᵈ June 13.ᵗʰ 1782. by H. Humphrey New Bond Street.

3. [13 June 1782] Charles James Fox rushes to "reward" Admiral George Rodney
for his services against the French.

A New ADMINISTRATION, or — The State Quacks ADMINISTRING.

Pub.ᵈ April 16ᵗʰ 1783, by W.Humphrey, Nᵒ 227 Strand.

4. [1 April 1783] After years of contentious rivalry, Lord North and Charles James Fox joined forces in February 1783 to "serve Britannia" in a notorious, short-lived coalition.

The LORD of the VINEYARD.

Says the Badger to Fox,
We're in the right Box.
   These Grapes are most charming & fine;

Dear Badger you're right,
Hold them fast squeeze them tight,
   And we'll drink of Political Wine.

5. [3 April 1783] The new government formed on 2 April under the nominal leadership of the Duke of Portland was marked by a struggle for ascendancy between Fox and North. From the outset, Fox appeared to dominate.

WESTMINSTER SCHOOL.

or — Dr Busby settling accounts with Master Billy and his Playmates.

"Illustrious Bums, might merit more regard;
Ah! Bums too tender for a stroke so hard."
Vide Rolliad.

Pub.d Feb.y 4th 1785. by J. Ridgeway. Piccadilly

9

6. [4 February 1785] Schoolmaster Fox teaches the 25-year-old Prime Minister
Pitt a thing or two about government.

Designed by Heliogabalus.   *A new way to pay the NATIONAL-DEBT*,   *Dedicated to Mons.r Necker.*

Executed by Sejanus.
Pub.d April 21. 1786 by Wm. Sutherland N.o. Boggs.

7. [21 April 1786] King George and Queen Charlotte enjoy the bounty of their
grateful land; a vision of royal avarice inspired by the King's disinclination to
pay off the debts of his prodigal eldest son.

Published 1788 by W. Holland, N.º 50 Oxford St. **The POLITICAL-BANDITTI** *assailing the SAVIOUR of INDIA.*

8. [First published 11 May 1786] Warren Hastings, Governor-General of British India (1773–85), is menaced by

Opposition leaders Burke, North and Fox, who seek his impeachment on grounds of cruelty and corruption.

9. [20 March 1787] Under the direction of Pitt's crony Henry Dundas, government management of East India Company affairs is seen to have a Scottish bias.

A MONSTROUS CRAMS, at a New Coalition Feast.

Pub.⁵ May 29ᵗʰ 1787, by S. W.Fores, Piccadilly.

10. [29 May 1787] Gillray commemorates a reconciliation of sorts between the Prince of Wales and his royal parents. On 21 May the King supported Pitt in a move to authorize discharge of the Prince's debts out of public funds.

A MARCH to the BANK. Vide. The Strand, Fleet Street, Cheapside &c. Morning & Evening.

Pub^d Augt 23^d 1787 by S. W. Fores, Piccadilly.

11. [22 August 1787] The regular transit each evening and morning of a detachment of guards to and from the Bank of England was widely regarded as a nuisance to pedestrians.

The MORNING after MARRIAGE —— or —— A scene on the Continent   *Pompho Gorgy Feat*

12. [5 April 1788] A "nostalgic" and totally fanciful reconstruction of the notorious secret marriage of the Prince of Wales and Mrs. Maria Anne Fitzherbert, which actually took place at the bride's lodgings in Park Lane on 15 December 1785.

The Princess's Bow alias the Bow Begum.

13A. [1 May 1788] Rival caricaturist James Sayers rises to the defense of Hastings, ridiculing the emotional testimony of the Begum of Oude, the deference of Fox, Burke and Sheridan and the conspiratorial influence of Philip Francis (beneath the bench).

The Bow to the Throne, – alias – The Begging Bow.

13B. [6 May 1788] In Gillray's close parody, complete with "JS" monogram, Sayers' loyal jibe is twisted into a vicious indictment of the manner in which Hastings was thought to be enlisting the aid of Lord Chancellor Thurlow, Pitt, Queen Charlotte and the King (lower left).

'Every Man has his Price.' — Sir R.¹ Walpole. **MARKET-DAY.** 'Sic itur ad astra.'

Pub.ᵈ May 2.1788.by S. W. Fores. N.º 3 Piccadilly.

14. [2 May 1788] In a pungent comment on the supposed venality of public men, Gillray shows leading members of the House of Lords placidly awaiting the pleasure of the highest bidder in the cattle pens at Smithfield.

STATE-JUGGLERS,

"Who wrought such wonders as might make
Egyptian sorcerers forsake
Their baffled mockeries, & own
The vain of magick ours alone." *Church*.

15. [16 May 1788] Pitt (producing decorations and honors), Hastings (vomiting gold) and Thurlow (exploding bombast) are represented as mountebank entertainers, practicing their impostures on an audience of grasping politicians.

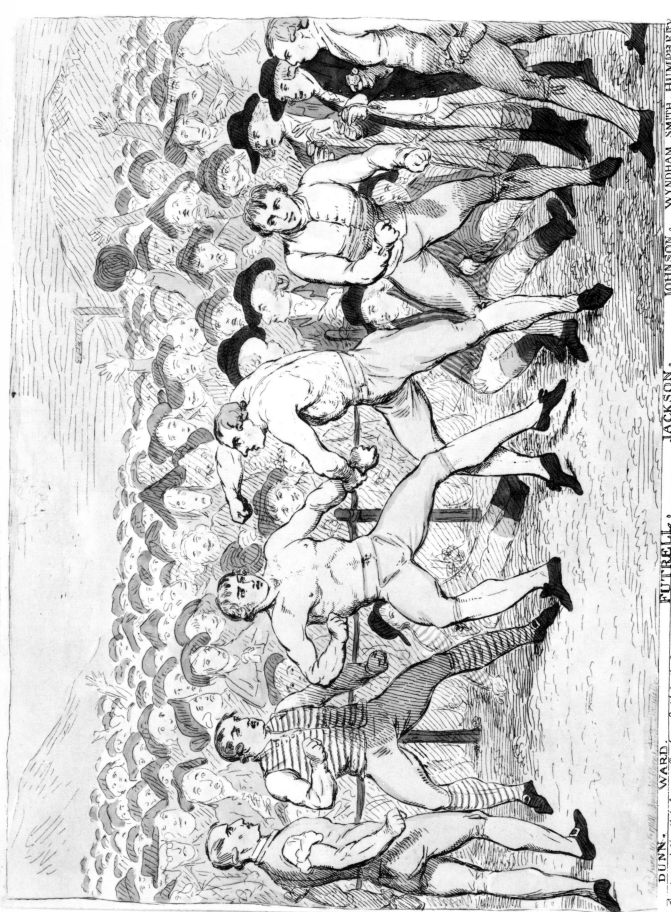

16. [10 June 1788] "Gentleman" John Jackson (1768–1845), future champion
of England, celebrates his ring debut by trouncing the favored Thomas Fewtrell
on 9 June 1788.

The BUBBLES of OPPOSITION.

Pub.d July 19.th 1788.

Price 1.s

17. [19 July 1788] Charles James Fox attempts to float a new "opposition bubble," Lord John Town- shend, his candidate for Parliament in a special Westminster election.

Pub.d May 10th 1790. by H.Humphrey No 8. Old Bond 1t.

The MONSTER going to take his Afternoons Luncheon.

18. [10 May 1790] Public attention was drawn to the exploits of an unknown knife fanatic, the "Cutting Monster," wanted for several attacks on young women in the West End of London.

The BALANCE of POWER

— or — "The Posterity of the Immortal CHATHAM, turn'd Posture Master." — vide Sherridans Speech —

19. [21 April 1791] The (celibate) Prime Minister Pitt attempts to impose an equilibrium on hostile relations between Turkish Sultan Selim III and Catherine the Great of Russia.

Humbly dedicated to the Jacobine Clubs of France & England!!! or Common Sense
"These are your Gods, O, Israel!"
54
Pubᵈ May 23ᵗʰ 1791, by H. Humphrey No. 18, Old Bond Street
"Fathom & a half! Fathom & a half! Poor Tom!"
ah! mercy upon me! that's more by half than my poor Measure will ever be able to reach! – Lord! Lord! I wish I had a bit of the Stay-tape or Buckram which I yous't to Cabbage when I was prentice, to lengthen it out; – well, well, who could ever have thought it, that I, who have served Seven Years as an Apprentice, & afterwards worked Four Years as a Journeyman to a Master Taylor, then follow'd the business of an Exciseman as much longer, should not be able to take the dimensions of this Bauble!" for what is a Crown but a Bauble? which we may see in the Tower for Six-pence a piece? – well, altho' it may be too large for a Taylor to take Measure of, there's one Comfort, he may make mouths at it, & call it as many names as he pleases! – and yet, Lord, Lord, I should like to make it a Yankee doodle Night-Cap & Breeches, if it was not not so damn'd large, or I had stuff enough Ah! if I could once do that, I would soon stitch up the mouth of that Barnacled Edmund from making of any more Reflections upon the Flints – & so Flints & Liberty for ever – & damn the Dungs
Vive la Liberté
"THE RIGHTS OF MAN; – or TOMMY PAINE, the little American Taylor, taking the Measure of the CROWN, for a new Pair of Revolution-Breeches.

20. [23 May 1791] The first part of Paine's *Rights of Man* was published 13 March 1791, dedicated to George Washington, in response to Edmund Burke's *Reflections on the Revolution in France* of the preceding November.

The HOPES of the PARTY, prior to July 14th. ——— "*From such wicked CROWN & ANCHOR-Dreams, good Lord, deliver us.*"

Pub. July 19 & 1791. by S. W. Fores N°3, Piccadilly.

21. [19 July 1791] Charles James Fox presides over the public execution of George III, assisted by Opposition allies Horne Tooke, Sheridan and Sir Cecil Wray. Behind Sheridan,

Joseph Priestly—controversial theologian and scientist—offers words of comfort.

To H.Fuzelli Esq.r this attempt in the Caricatura-Sublime, is respectfully dedicated.

Pub.d Dec.r 23.d 1791.
by H.Humphrey N.o 18. Old Bond Str...

WIERD-SISTERS; MINISTERS of DARKNESS; MINIONS of the MOON."
— "They should be Women! — and yet their beards forbid us to interpret. — that they are so." —

22. [23 December 1791] Continuing concern for the King's sanity is expressed in a haunting visual metaphor of lunacy. Anxious ministers Dundas, Pitt and Thurlow study the ascendant crescent profile of Queen Charlotte and the slumbering shadow of her royal husband.

Pub.d Jan.y 3.d 1792 By H Humphrey N.18 Old Bond Street

A SPHERE, projecting against a PLANE.

Definitions from Euclid.

Def: 1.st B:4.th A Sphere, is a Figure bounded by a Convex surface; it is the most perfect of all forms; its Properties are generated from its Centre; and it possesses a larger Area than any other Figure.— Def: 2.d B: 1.st A PLANE, is a perfectly even & regular Surface; it is the most Simple of all Figures; it has neither the Properties of Length or of Breadth; and when applied ever so closely to a SPHERE, can only touch its Superfices, without being able to enter it.— Vide. Euclid, illustrated, by the Hon.ble M.rs Circumference.

23. [3 January 1792] A tangential encounter between Prime Minister Pitt and Mrs. Albinia Hobart, substantial lady of fashion.

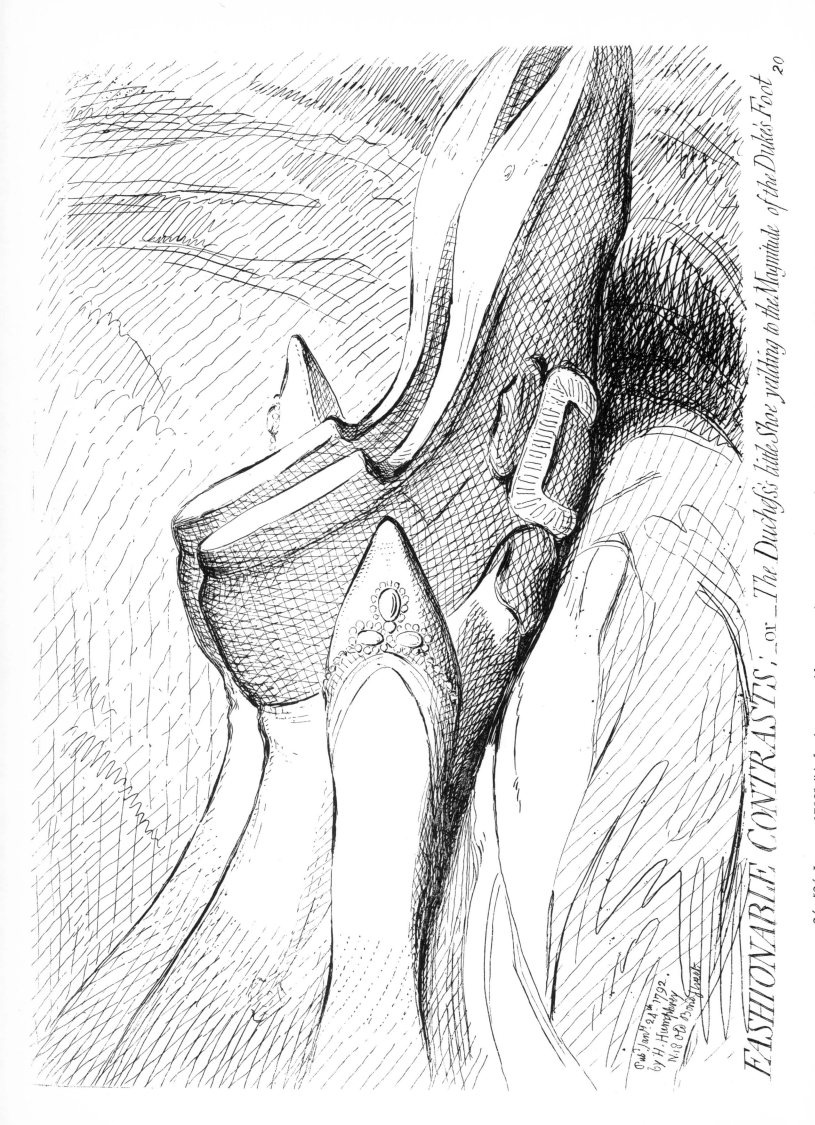

FASHIONABLE CONTRASTS; _or — *The Duchefs's little Shoe yeilding to the Magnitude of the Duke's Foot*

24. [24 January 1792] "A foreigner would suppose that several of our flimsy prints [newspapers] were conducted by

shoe-makers . . . so much have they said about the Duchess
of York's slipper" (*Morning Post,* 7 January 1792).

ANTI-SACCHARRITES, — or — JOHN BULL and his Family leaving off the use of SUGAR.

To the Masters & Mistryses of Families in Great Britain, this Noble Example of ECONOMY, is respectfully submitted.

O my dear Creatures, do but Taste it! you can't think how nice it is without Sugar; and then consider how much Work you'll save the poor Black-moors by leaving off the use of it, and above all, remember how much expence it will save your poor Papa! — O its charming cooling Drink your

O delicious! delicious!

Pub. March 27ᵗʰ 1792 by H. Humphrey, Nᵒ 18 Old Bond Street

25. [27 March 1792] Gillray visualizes teatime at St. James's Palace. A proposed sugar boycott (to encourage the abolition of slavery in the West Indies) receives support at the highest level.

Pub.d May 17.th 1792. by H. Humphrey N.o 18 Old Bond Street.

A SPENCER & a THREADPAPER.

26. [17 May 1792] The "lateral component" of this fashion plate is George, second Earl Spencer (1758–1834), who had wagered successfully that he could create a new style by chopping the skirts from his overcoat. According to one legend, the project was inspired by a riding accident which unceremoniously de-tailed his lordship's coat. A thread-paper was a pleated card used to divide skeins of thread; the phrase was popularly applied to slender individuals.

The Royal Sovereign, was formerly to be seen by all admirers of Natural Curiosities

Nell H—t—n, weighs rather under Thirty Stone; & in the absence of the Great Man, his

as Subsistance for Head, it is reported to weigh near Forty Stone —

place is agreeably filled by T—W—d, the celebrated collector on the Highway —

Pub.d May 1792. by H.Humphrey N.o 18 Old Bond Street

Le Cochon et ses deux petits — or — Rich pickings for a Noble appetite. vide. Strand Lane.; Temple Barr.; &c &c &c

27. [May 1792] Charles Howard, 11th Duke of Norfolk, Earl Marshal of England, appears in the company of a pair of courtesans (introduced after the fashion of sideshow curiosities).

Pub.d June.18.th 1792. by H.Humphrey N.º.18. Old Bond Street.   J.Gᴿ. del.et fecit.ad.vivam.

A CONNOISSEUR examining a COOPER.

28. [18 June 1792] In a time of increasing revolutionary tension, George III takes a close look at the regicide "Protector," Oliver Cromwell, nemesis of King Charles I.

The Zenith of French Glory; ⸞ The Pinnacle of Liberty.
Religion, Justice, Loyalty, & all the Bugbears of Unenlighten'd Minds, Farewell!

29. [12 February 1793] The execution of Louis XVI in Paris on 21 January was
followed on 1 February by a declaration of war against England.

DUMOURIER dining in State at St. James's, on the 15th of May, 1793. Vide his own Declaration, as printed by the Anti-levelling Societies.

LIBERTAS

J.G. delin et fec: pro bono publico.

Pub.d March 30.th 1793, by H. Humphrey N.o 18 Old Bond Street —

To the worthy Members of that Society at the CROWN & ANCHOR, this Print, illustrative of Treasons in Embryo (by them hunted out & exposed) is submitted, by an admirer of their Loyal principals & truly Classic publications.

30. [30 March 1793] Sketchy reports concerning a French invasion of Holland, led by General Dumouriez, contributed to speculation about his subsequent objectives. Priestly, Fox and Sheridan welcome their sansculotte visitor to London with a feast of ecclesiastical pudding, roast Pitt and stewed crown, liberally garnished with frogs.

JOHN BULL, going to the WARS.

JOHN BULL, Happy.

J^sG^y Jas. et fecit.

JOHN BULL'S Property in danger.

JOHN BULL'S glorious Return.

Pub^d June 3^d 1793, by H.Humphrey N° 18 Old Bond Street

JOHN BULL'S PROGRESS

31. [3 June 1793] Patriotic John, aroused from idyllic complacency by duty's call, returns to his destitute family as a
gaunt, one-eyed cripple. A "moral history" after the fashion, but not the spirit, of Hogarth's celebrated "progresses"
of sixty years before.

FLANNEL-ARMOUR: FEMALE-PATRIOTISM. — or — Modern Heroes accoutred for the Wars —

To the Benevolent Ladies of Great Britain, who have so liberally supported the new system of Military Cloathing, this Print is dedicated

Pub.ʰ Nov.ʳ 18ᵗʰ 1793 by H. Humphrey N.º 18. Old Bond Street

J.ˢ G.ʸ des.ⁿ et fec.ᵗ

32. [18 November 1793] With allied forces in disarray, and winter coming on, the proprietor of the *Sun* announced, on 1 November, that he was collecting flannel waistcoats for "our gallant Soldiers fighting in Flanders." The cam- paign was quickly taken up by other newspapers. By 6 November wagonloads of underwear were pouring into London.

Presentation of the Mahometan Credentials — or — The final resource of French Atheists.

33. [26 December 1793] The Turkish plenipotentiary, a sort of playboy of the eastern world, advances on George III with an ambiguous proposal labeled "Powers for a new Connexion between the Port, England & France." His retinue of "French atheists" includes Sheridan, Fox and Priestly. A tricolor flag, "Vive la Republique," supports the notion of a Parisian plot.

A FRENCH-TELEGRAPH making SIGNALS in the Dark.

34. [26 January 1795] Charles James Fox's continued opposition to the war is seen as a treasonous assertion of British weakness.

James Gillray, des. et fec.   *LIGHT expelling DARKNESS, — Evaporation of Stygian Exhalations, — or — The SUN of the CONSTITUTION, rising superior to the Clouds of OPPOSITION.*   *Pub.d April 30.t 1795, by H.Humphrey, N.º 37.New Bond Street.*

35. [30 April 1795] William Pitt, a serene Phoebus Apollo, guides the British sun through the perilous night of Whiggish obstruction, "French principles" and revolution.

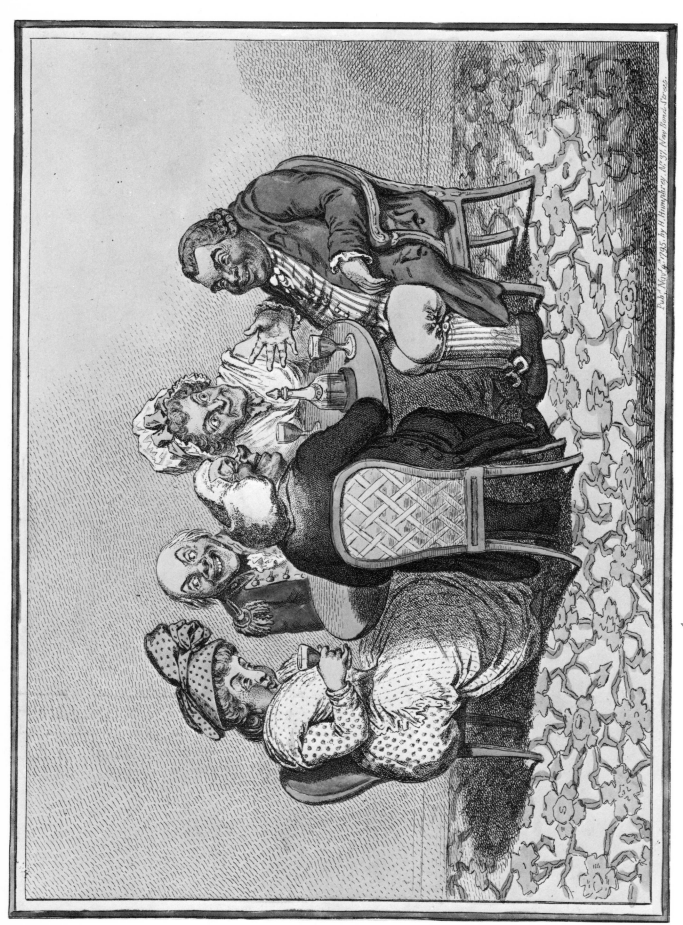

A DECENT STORY.

Pub.^d Novr 4th 1795, by H. Humphrey, N.º 37, New Bond Street.

36. [4 November 1795] Port and good company, etched after an amateur.

154

Pub. Nov.r 16.th 1795. by H. Humphrey, New Bond Street.

COPENHAGEN HOUSE. ["and turn it, and set a new Nap upon it," *Shakspeare.*

["I tell you, Citizens, we mean to new-dress the Constitution"

37. [16 November 1795] "Eyewitness account" of a mass meeting held on 26 October on the outskirts of London. Principal harangues were delivered by radical speakers

John Thelwall (1764–1834, right), John Gale Jones (1769–1838, left) and William Hodgson (1745–1851, distant center).

J. Gillray ad viv^m fec—

Pub.d Jan.y 11th 1796, by H.Humphrey New Bond street.

TWO-PENNY WHIST.

38. [11 January 1796] Gillray's publisher, "Mistress" Hannah Humphrey, and her shop assistant, Betty, have some neighbors in for a friendly game.

MATERNAL LOVE.

The Fashionable Mamma, — or — The Convenience of Modern Dress. Vide. The Pocket Hole, &c.

39. [15 February 1796] The free-flowing, classical "new look" introduced by Lady Charlotte Campbell in 1793 is associated with an offhand approach to *beau-monde* motherhood.

410

Pub. March 12, 1796, by H. Humphrey New Bond Street.

J. G. Rowl. F.

Lady Godina's Rout; — or — Peeping-Tom spying out Pope-Joan. Vide *Fashionable Modesty.*

40. [12 March 1796] Lady Georgiana Gordon, clad in the very latest transparency, puts a roving eye to the test.

FASHIONABLE-JOCKEYSHIP.

41. [1 June 1796] The Prince of Wales, resplendent in his uniform as an officer of the "English Light Horse," employs the good offices of Lord Jersey to pay a social call on Lady Jersey.

42. [1 October 1796] A bellicose Lord Camelford menaces his former commander, the explorer George Vancouver, during a chance encounter in Mayfair.

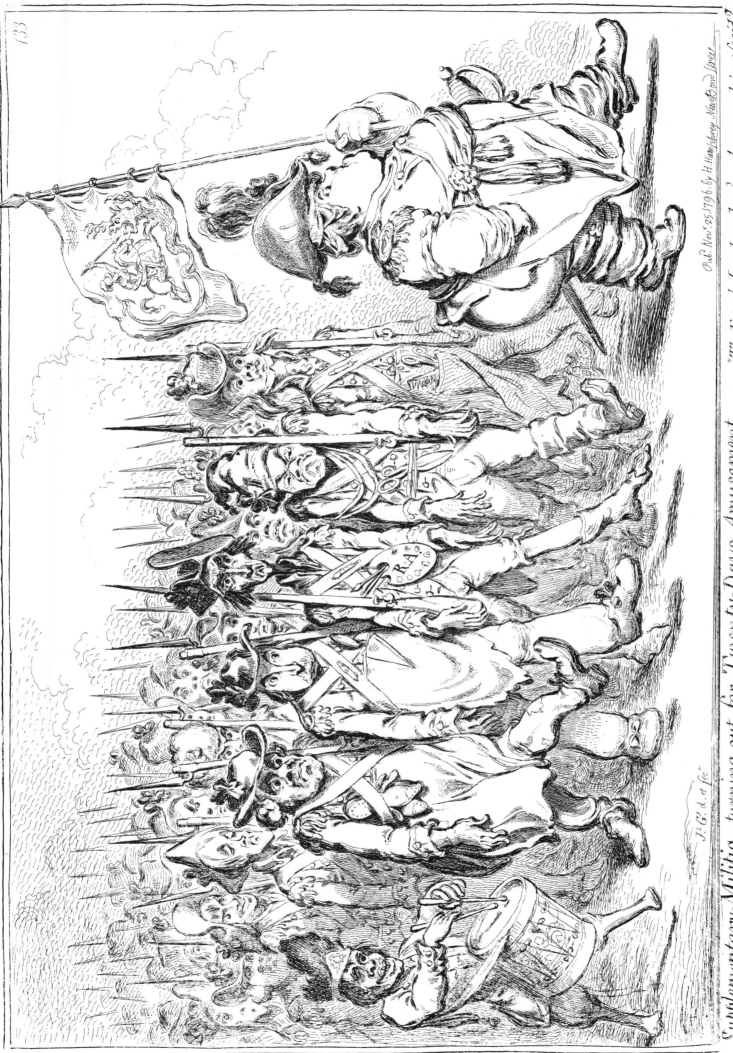

J.S.G. d. d. fec.

Pub. Nov. 25, 1796, by H. Humphrey, New Bond Street

Supplementary-Militia, turning-out for Twenty-Days Amusement. — "The French Invade us, hay? — damme, whose afraid?"

43. [25 November 1796] One mixed company of patriots responds to Prime Minister Pitt's proposal of 18 October for a supplementary militia of sixty thousand men.

JJ.

Charité bien ordonnée commence par soi-même.

HET COMMITTÈ VAN NOODLYDENDE.

44. [Summer 1796] "Charity begins at home": The "Committee of Public Assistance" in the new Batavian Republic gets down to business. A propaganda print commissioned for distribution in the Netherlands.

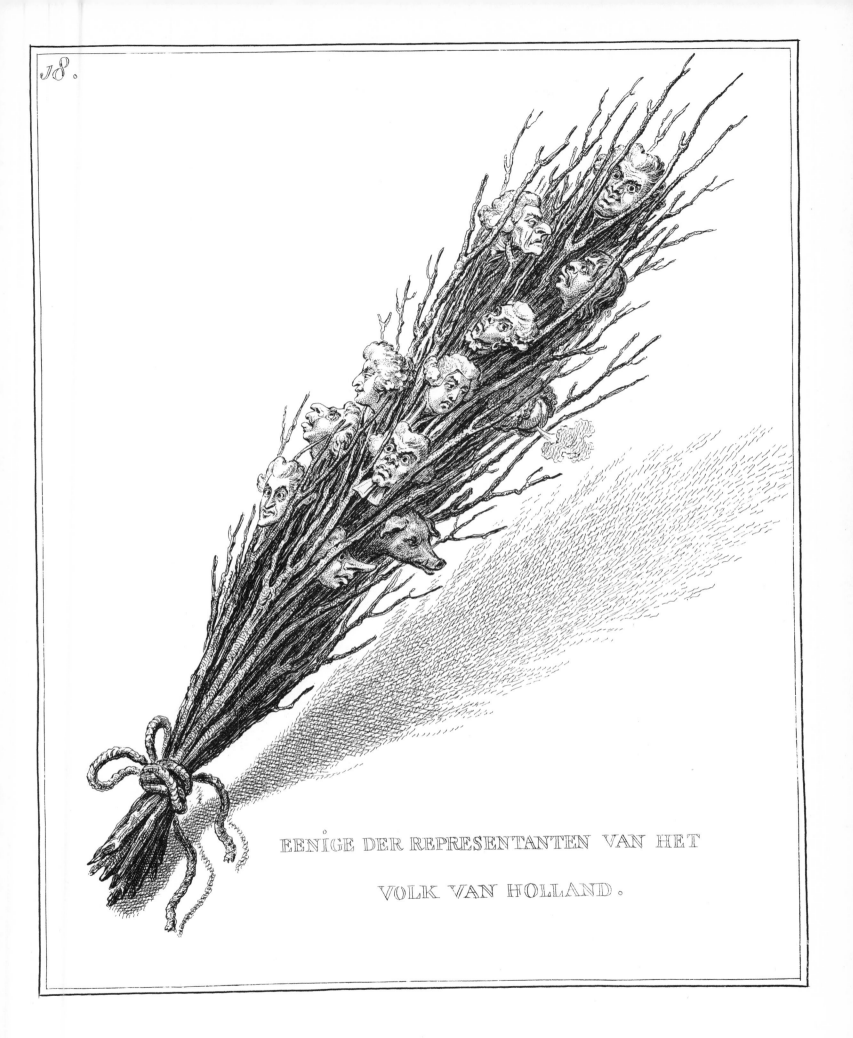

EENIGE DER REPRESENTANTEN VAN HET

VOLK VAN HOLLAND.

45. [Summer 1796] A birch rod or scourge labeled "Some of the Representatives of the People of Holland." Another subsidized gesture at the overthrow of the Batavian Republic, strikingly modern in conception.

Here they are my Lord, here's the slunk Calves, by Gxx
_no allusion, dxmme,! _ almost forgot you was a North Countrey-
-Man! _ Runt carries weight well,! _ no less than Thirteen
dxmme ! _ come push about the Bottle, & Ill tell you
the Story; ____ In Scotland they eat no Veal,
no Veal, by Gxx! nothing but Staggering-Bobs, _ by Gxx!
on my Honor & Soul I mean no insult,! _ but Tattersal he
swore, d_n me, if he didn't, _ that on a small Scotch Runt
he saw, Gxx dxxn my blood, _ how many d'ye think he saw?
("Saw what, Georgey?") _ why Calves! Staggering-Bobs
to-be-sure! _ why d'ye think he saw Seventeen? _ no!
but dxx me, by Gxx, he saw Thirteen!!! _ & all just
upon such another little Cock-Horse as my own!!!!

Pub Decr 1st 1796. by H Humphrey New Bond

STAGGERING-BOBS, a Tale for Scotchmen, _ or _ MUNCHAUSEN driving his Calves to Market
This Print is dedicated to Lord Exxl, his Party, & the Frequenters of Steevens's in general _

46. [1 December 1796] Colonel George Hanger (man-about-town, eccentric and sometimes crony of the Prince of Wales) defends the prowess of his low-slung pony.

Pub.d Jan.y 20.th 1797, by H. Humphrey, New Bond Street.

End of the Irish Invasion:— or — The Destruction of the French Armada.

47. [20 January 1797] A disastrous day for the Opposition in the House of Commons (30 December 1796) coincides with a gale at Bantry Bay (27 December) that confounded a major French naval assault on southwest Ireland.

"The Feast of Reason, & the Flow of Soul." — i.e: — The Wits of the Age, setting the Table in a roar.

48. [4 February 1797] The air is heavy with *bons mots, jeux d'esprit* and rib-tickling rejoinders as Opposition wags enjoy a wild night at their tavern club.

160

Billy in the Devils claws .   { THE TABLES TURND . }   Billy, sending the Devil packing;

J. G.x. y   Pub.d March 4.th 1797. by H. Humphrey. New Bond Sheet

49. [4 March 1797] Left: Billy Pitt in the claws of Devil Fox   Billy confounds his old Devil with news of the defeat
as 1400 French terrorists land in South Wales. Right: of the Spanish fleet at Cape St. Vincent.

MIDAS, Transmuting all into GOLD PAPER.

History of Midas, ___ The great Midas having dedicated himself to Bacchus, obtained from that Deity, the Power of changing all he Touched
Apollo fixed Asses Ears upon his head, for his Ignorance ___ & although he tried to hide his disgrace with a Regal Cap, yet the very Sedges which grew
from the Mud of the Pactolus, whisper'd out his Infamy, whenever they were agitated by the Wind from the opposite Shore ___ Vide Ovids Metamorphosis

50. [9 March 1797] A financial panic triggered by Tate's landing in Wales forced
the Bank of England to suspend gold payments on 26 February.

Le Baiser a la Wirtembourg.

"Heav'n grant their Happiness complete,
And may they make **both Ends to meet**; *in these hard times*.

51. [15 April 1797] Prince Frederick of Württemberg greets his bride-to-be, Princess Charlotte, eldest daughter of the King. Published to mark the arrival in London of the "Great Bellygerent" for his marriage on 17 May.

J^S G^y ad vivam fec^t.

La Promenade en Famille. — a Sketch from Life.

Pub^d April 23^d 1797, by H Humphrey New Bond St James's Street.

52. [23 April 1797] The Duke of Clarence (1765–1837, later King William IV) takes a Sunday stroll with his great and good friend Dorothea Jordan and their three children.

A Corner, near the Bank, — or — *An Example for Fathers.*

53. [26 September 1797] A pair of "trawlers" catch the fancy of an adventurous
soul.

The FRIEND of HUMANITY and the KNIFE-GRINDER, _ Scene. The Borough, in Imitation of Mr Southey's Sapphics. _ Vide. Anti-Jacobin. p. 15.

54. [4 December 1797] Gillray illustrates a poem from the new Pittite satirical weekly, *The Anti-Jacobin*. The verses ridicule "bleeding-heart liberals" in the abstract; the caricaturist zeroes in on George Tierney, parsimonious Whig M.P. for the Borough of Southwark, leading Opposition spokesman after the "secession" of Fox in May.

The Apotheosis of HOCHE.

55. [11 January 1798] The late Lazare Hoche, fire-breathing French general and Anglophobe, rises from his blood-stained country into an extraordinary sansculotte heaven. Probably the most elaborate political "cartoon" ever published.

The Tree of LIBERTY, — with, the Devil tempting John Bull.

56. [23 May 1798] Pockets bulging with the (golden) pippins of constitutional monarchy, John Bull declines the rotten fruit of "Reform" dangled before him by Charles James Fox.

United Irishmen in Training

United Irishmen upon Duty.

57. [12 & 13 June 1798] Deprived of leadership and denied French support, radical peasant factions of the "United Irishmen" commenced a month-long rampage on 23 May.

58. [24 October 1798] Horatio Nelson and his fellow admirals serve up a victory feast of French "Frigasees," guaranteed to tickle the national tastebuds.

J. Gillray inv. & fec.

DOUBLURES of Characters; — or — striking Resemblances in Physiognomy. — "If you would know Mens Hearts, look in their Faces." — *Lavater.*

I. The Patron of Liberty. II. A Friend to his Country. III. Character of High Birth. IV. A Faithful Patriot. V. Arbiter Elegantiarum. VI. Strong-Sense, VII. A Pillar of the State. Doub.ˢ Judas selling his Master. Doub.ˢ The Arch-Fiend. Doub.ˢ Silenus debauching. Doub.ˢ Sixteen-string-Jack. Doub.ˢ A Baboon. Doub.ˢ A Newmarket Jockey.

Pub.ᵈ ⸝ Nov.ʳ 1.ˢᵗ 1798. by J. Wright, Piccadilly. — for the Anti-Jacobin Review.

59. [1 November 1798] A short course in the art of caricature, "dedicated" to the celebrated Swiss physiognomist Johann Kaspar Lavater. Gillray's "Characters" are Fox, Sheridan, Norfolk, Tierney, Sir Francis Burdett, Derby and Bedford, all prominent Opposition leaders.

Stealing off: — or — prudent Secesion: — "courageous Chief!" N.B. The back ground contains; a corner of the House next Session; with the Persons
"The first in Flight!" for Secession: — also, a democratic Byeaunt: — (i.e. Opposition Leaking up their Win...

60. [6 November 1798] Charles James Fox quits the House of
Commons in terror as his cringing colleagues eat their
"disloyal" words. William Pitt, offstage, confronts them

with an inventory of governmental triumphs and accomplishments in one hand, and "proof" of their treason in
the other.

Js Gillray inv & ft.

Pubᵈ Novʳ 20ᵗʰ 1798. by H Humphrey
Sᵗ James's Street.

Fighting for the DUNGHILL; — or — Jack Tar settling BUONAPARTE.

61. [20 November 1798] Another patriotic spin-off of Nelson's August victory in the Battle of the Nile: John Bull's seagoing alter ego sends the French menace reeling.

SIEGE DE LA COLONNE DE POMPÉE. *Etched by J.^s Gillray, from the Original Intercepted Drawing.* SCIENCE IN THE PILLORY.

London, Published March 6th 1799 by H. Humphrey, 27 St James's Street.

It appears by an Intercepted Letter from General Kleber, dated "Alexandria, 5 Frimaire, 7.th Year of the Republic", that, when his Garrison was obliged to retire into the New Town at the approach of the Turkish Army under the Pacha of Rhodes, a Party of the Scavans, who had ascended Pompey's Pillar for Scientific Purposes, was cut off by a Band of Bedouin Arabs,

who, having made a large Pile of Straw and dry Reeds at the foot of the Pillar, set Fire to it, and rendered unavailing the gallant Defence of the learned Garrison, of whose Catastrophe the above Design is intended to convey an Idea.

*To study Alexandria's store
Of Science, Amru deem'd a bore;
And, briefly, set it burning.
The Man was Ignorant, 'tis true,
So sought one comprehensive view
Of the Light shed by Learning.*

*Your modern Arabs, grown more wise,
French vagrant-Science duly prize;
They've fairly bit the biters.
They've learnt the style of Hebert's Jokes;
Amru to Books confin'd his Hoax,
These Bedouins roast the Writers.*

62. [6 March 1799] Personal letters from disgruntled French officers in Bonaparte's Egyptian command had been intercepted by the British Navy and published in London. Gillray offered this vision of French "savants" in difficulties with the natives, assuring his audience that it had been etched "from the Original Intercepted Drawing."

The Twin Stars, CASTOR & POLLUX.

63. [7 May 1799] George Barclay and Charles Sturt, concurrent Members of Parliament for the town of Bridport, Dorset, are cast as the inseparable twin brothers of Greek mythology.

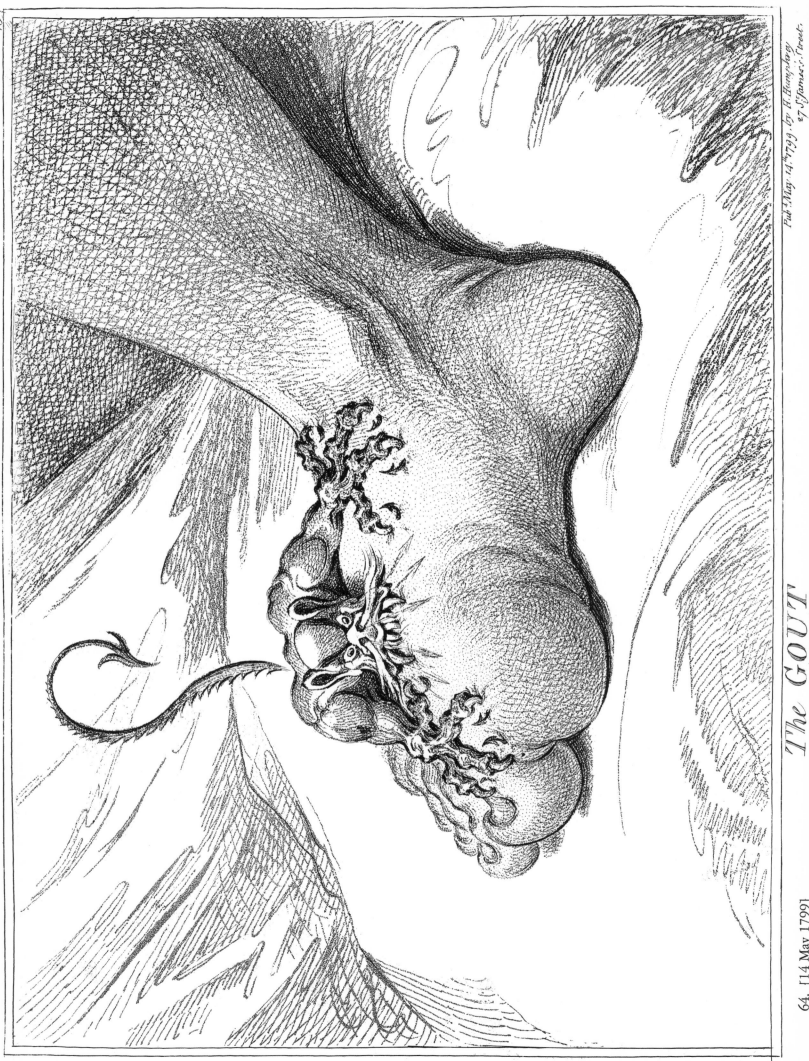

The GOUT

Pub. May. 14. 1799 by H. Humphrey 27 S. James's Street.

64. [14 May 1799]

The State of the WAR — or — the Monkey-Race in danger.

65. [20 May 1799] Armies of the Second Coalition (Great Britain, Russia, Turkey and Austria) inflicted a series of defeats and reversals on French forces in Europe and the Mideast during the spring of 1799.

ALLIED-POWERS, UN-BOOTING EGALITÉ.

66. [1 September 1799] The powers of the Second Coalition gang up on France (personified by Bonaparte), depriving him of his ill-gotten Italian "boot" and booty.

SIR SIDNEY SMITH,

67. [10 November 1799] British hero of the siege of   up Gillray's singular incapacity for flattery.
Acre: a "straight" ceremonial portrait which points

French-Taylor, fitting JOHN BULL with a "Jean de Bry".

68. [18 November 1799] The latest Parisian monstrosity is tried and found wanting:
a satire on sartorial and political "freedom" under the Directory.

DEMOCRATIC RELIGION.

Buonaparte turning Turk at Cairo for Interest, after swearing on the Sacrament to support ye Catholic Faith.—

DEMOCRATIC CONSOLATIONS.

Buonaparte on his Couch, surrounded by the Ghosts of the Murder'd,—& ye Dangers which threaten his Usurpation, and all the Horrors of Final Retribution.—

DEMOCRATIC GRATITUDE.

Buonaparte, heading the Regicide-Banditti which had dethron'd & Murder'd the Monarch, whose bounty had foster'd him.—

DEMOCRATIC GLORY.

Buonaparte, as Grand Consul of France, receiving the adulations of Jacobin Sycophants & Parasites.—

DEMOCRATIC HUMILITY.

Buonaparte, when a boy, receiv'd thro' the King's bounty into the Ecole Militaire at Paris.—

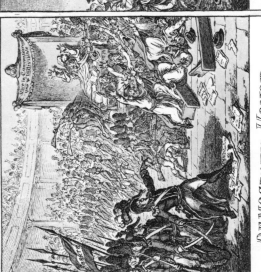

DEMOCRATIC HONOR.

Buonaparte, overturning the French Republic which had employ'd him, & intrusted him with the chief Command.—

DEMOCRATIC INNOCENCE.

The young Buonaparte, & his wretched Relatives, in their native Poverty, while Free Booters on the Island of Corsica.—

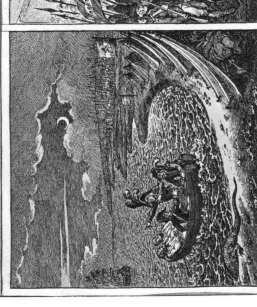

DEMOCRATIC COURAGE.

Buonaparte deserting his Army in Egypt, for fear of ye Turks; after hoping that he would extirpate them all—

J. Gillray, inv. & fec. Pub'd May 12th 1800. by H. Humphrey. No 27 St James's Street London.

DEMOCRACY; — or — a Sketch of the Life of BUONAPARTE.

69. [12 May 1800] In February 1800, Bonaparte's takeover as First Consul was confirmed by plebiscite and he moved into the royal palace, Les Tuileries, as virtual monarch. Gillray travesties his rise as a "mushroom" of the French Revolution.

70. [6 February 1801] Emma, Lady Hamilton, turns from a slumbering spouse to lament the departure of her "Aeneas"—Lord Nelson.

A COGNOCENTI contemplating ye̱ Beauties of ye̱ Antique.

71. [11 February 1801] Connoisseur Sir William Hamilton rivets his gaze on a damaged bust of Lais, celebrated mistress of an ancient philosopher. His other "treasures" are equally pertinent to the highly public affair between his wife and Lord Nelson.

72. [28 May 1801] After seventeen years as First Lord of the Treasury, William Pitt stepped down on 7 March as the result of a disagreement with the King regarding political concessions for Roman Catholics. A new Tory administration formed by Pitt's close friend Henry Addington is welcomed by Gillray in the spirit of Jonathan Swift.

"Whilst, snug in our Club-room, we jovially 'twine — The myrtle of Wenus with Bacchus's wine".
505
ANACREON
J. Gillray inv. & fec.
London. Publish'd Dec. 1st 1801. by H. Humphrey. 27. St. James's Street.
ANACREONTICK'S in full Song.

73. [1 December 1801] As the hour approaches four in the morning, a tavern club raises its collective voice in the "Anacreontic Anthem," a melody applied some thirteen years later to Francis Scott Key's "Star Spangled Banner."

Publish'd Jan.r 16.th 1802, by H. Humphrey, 27 St. James's Street.

Ah, here's your sort! here's your Nice fine Fat, my boys! O how he will cut up! (as my old friend Burke said) how he will Tallow in the cawl, & on the Kidneys—

To the Society for Improving the Breed [*FAT-CATTLE*.] this Sketch of Tavistock Farm Yard, is dedicated.

74. [16 January 1802] The Duke of Bedford admires another triumph of selective breeding.

The Comforts of a Rumford Stove.

Vide Dr. Garnetts Lectures

75. [12 June 1800] Benjamin Thompson, Count Rumford, American-born inventor, philosopher, public benefactor and egotist, demonstrates the efficiency of his improved fireplace design.

"all Bond-Street trembled as he strode."

76. [8 May 1802] The Hon. James Duff, heir to the Earl of Fife, sets out on his
morning promenade.

Introduction of Citizen Volpone & his Suite, at Paris.—Vide, The Moniteur & Cobbetts Letters.—

77. [15 November 1802] Charles James Fox, "Citizen Volpone," is received by Bonaparte at the Tuileries on 3 September 1802, during the thirteen-month calm offered by the Peace of Amiens.

DILETTANTI-THEATRICALS ; — or — a Peep at the Green Room. — vide. Pic-Nic Orgies.

78. [18 February 1803] The Pic-nic Society, a fashionable but controversial amateur dramatic group, tunes up for a final fling.

The keenest Sportsman in Broomwell Camp. 1803.

Dedicated to Mrs. ———. d.r. of Henly without her myham.

by her hble Ser.t J.C. White.

— J.C. White del.

79. [Summer (?) 1803] A "hunting tableau" apparently dedicated to the proposition that one Major Tudor had been misbehaving while on volunteer maneuvers.

The CORSICAN-PEST; — or — BELZEBUB going to Supper.

80. [6 October 1803] Gillray speculates on Napoleon's anticipated descent to the infernal regions—an exercise in elementary voodoo which reflects a deep national concern over the possibility of French invasion.

BRITANNIA between DEATH and the DOCTORS. — "*Death may decide, when Doctor's disagree.*"

81. [20 May 1804] Political squabblings among her "physicians," Pitt, Addington and Fox, appear to leave the national patient vulnerable to Napoleon's sneak attack.

—— ci-devant Occupations —— or —— Madame Talian and the Empreſs Joſephine dancing Naked before Barraſs in the Winter of 1797.—— A Fact!

Barraſs (then in Power), being tired of Joſephine, promiſed Buonaparte a promotion, on condition, that he would take her off his hands:——Barraſs had, as usual, drank freely, & placed Buonaparte behind a Screen, while he amused himself with those two Ladies, who were then his humble-dependants.—Madame Talian is a beautiful Woman, tall & elegant; Joſephine is smaller & thin, with bad Teeth, something like Cloves.—it is needleſs to add, that Buonaparte accepted the Promotion & the Lady,—now, Empreſs of France! —3º

82. [20 February 1805] Literally "Former Pursuits." This facetious representation of the first meeting of the new Emperor and Empress of France was occasioned by their coronation on 2 December 1804. The young Bonaparte is supposedly weighing a proposition that he relieve the Director Barras of a superfluous mistress (Josephine) in exchange for a promotion.

The Plumb-pudding in danger;—or—State Epicures taking un Petit Souper.

—"the great Globe itself, and all which it inherit," is too small to satisfy such insatiable Appetites.

—vide Mr W—d-m's reminiscences, in y Oakland Magazine—

London.
Pub. Feby 26th 1805.
by H. Humphrey, esq.
St James's Street—

J. Gillray inv & fec.

83. [26 February 1805] "The world is sufficiently large for our two nations to live in it . . ."—peace overture from Napoleon to George III, 2 January 1805. In a classic essay on the arrogance of power, Pitt and Napoleon are shown carving out their respective spheres of influence.

POLITICAL-CANDOUR ; — i.e. Coalition-Resolutions" of June 14th 1805. — Pro bono Publico.

84. [21 June 1805] Charles James Fox defends his old rival, Pitt, against a charge of personal corruption. Gillray interprets the Whig leader's guarded tribute to the ailing, beleaguered Prime Minister as an attempt to charm his way into the administration. Pitt's approval, ambiguously expressed, is clarified by the inviting manner in which he taps a vacant spot on the "Treasury Bench."

ST. GEORGE and the DRAGON.

_____ a Design for an Equestrian Statue, from the Original in Windsor-Castle.

Published August 2ᵈ 1805 by H Humphrey 27 St James's Street.

85. [2 August 1805] King George III, as England's patron saint, prepares to deliver the coup de grâce as he frees Britannia from the clutches of Napoleon.

HARMONY before MATRIMONY.

86. [25 October 1805] "Pho! man, is not music the food of love? . . . she is so accomplished—so sweet a voice—so expert at her harpsichord—such a mistress of flat and sharp, squallante, rumblante, and quiverante! . . how she did chirrup . . . " (Sheridan, *The Rivals* [1775], Act II, Scene 1).

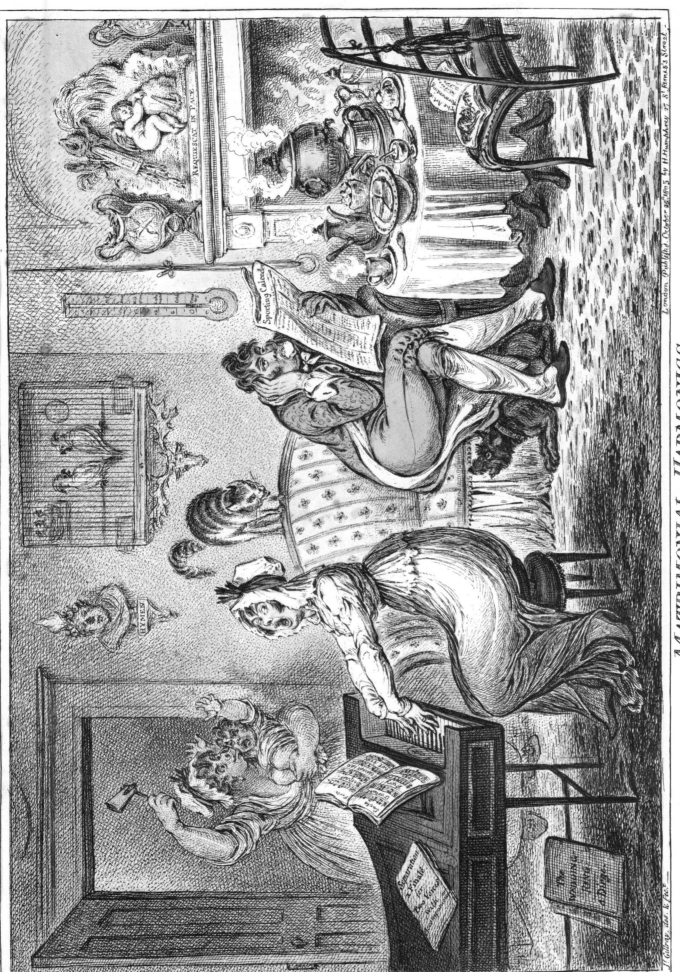

MATRIMONIAL-HARMONICS.

87. [25 October 1805] The inevitable dénouement of this cynical siren's song—marriage on the rocks. The lady's "Forte" recital, "Torture—Fury—Rage—Despair—I can-not can not bear," is evidently to be followed by the other composition lying on the piano: "Separation a Finale for Two Voices with Accompaniment." "The Wedding Ring—A Dirge" lies on the floor beneath.

Pub.d May 2, 1831, by John Fairburn.   Broadway, Ludgate Hill.

The POWERFUL ARM of PROVIDENCE.

An Allegorical Print, applicable to the Year 1831.

Dedicated to his most Gracious Majesty WILLIAM IV. His present Ministers & every Real Reformer in the United Kingdom.

88. [2 May 1831] The title, subtitle and dedication of this bizarre, apocalyptic vision were supplied in 1831 by an enthusiastic printseller named John Fairburn, who was waxing euphoric at the approach of the Great Reform Bill. The design, however, is the work of Gillray—unpublished in his lifetime—developed and executed between 1796 and 1807 for reasons which give free rein to speculation.

The FALL of ICARUS.

89. [20 April 1807] Richard Grenville, third Earl Temple, attempting a departure from office on wings of quill pens and sealing wax, is arrested in mid-flight by the stern sun of royal displeasure. Temple was alleged to have absconded with large quantities of government stationery.

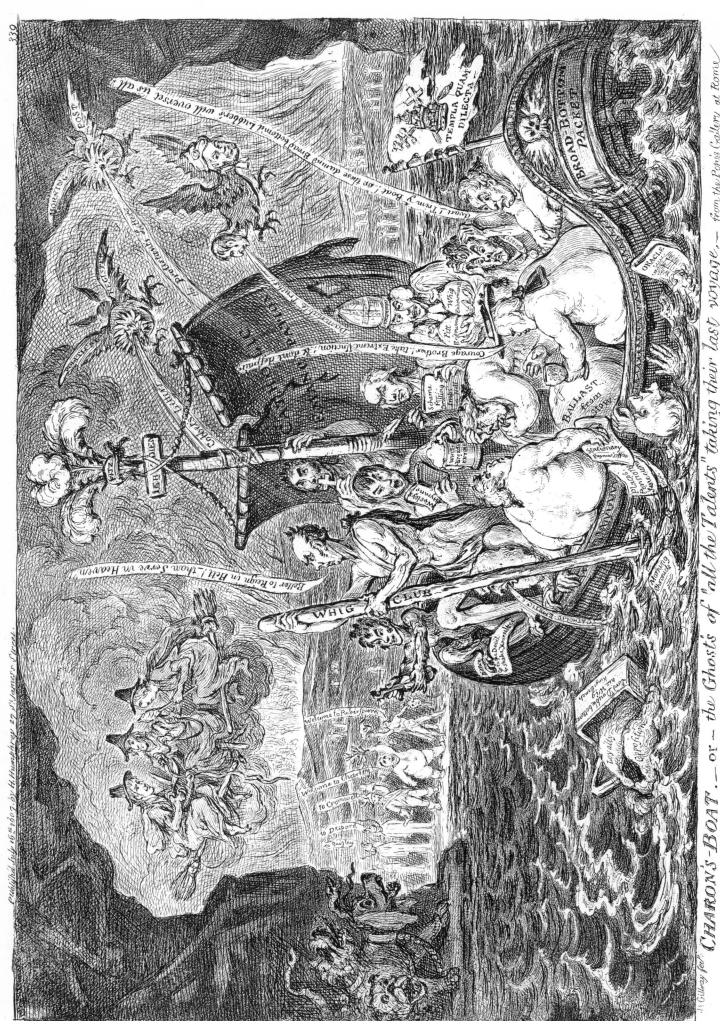

Pub. July 16th 2007. by H. Humphrey, 27 St. James's Street.

Js. Gillray fecit.

CHARON'S-BOAT.—or—the Ghosts of "all the Talents" taking their last voyage.—from the Pope's Gallery at Rome.

90. [16 July 1807] A final, belated farewell to the Grenville ministry, almost four months after their expulsion from office by George III on the issue of concessions to Roman Catholics. The role of Charon, mythical boatman of the river Styx, is filled by Charles Grey, Lord Howick, who introduced (5 March) the "fatal" bill which would have opened all military ranks to Catholics.

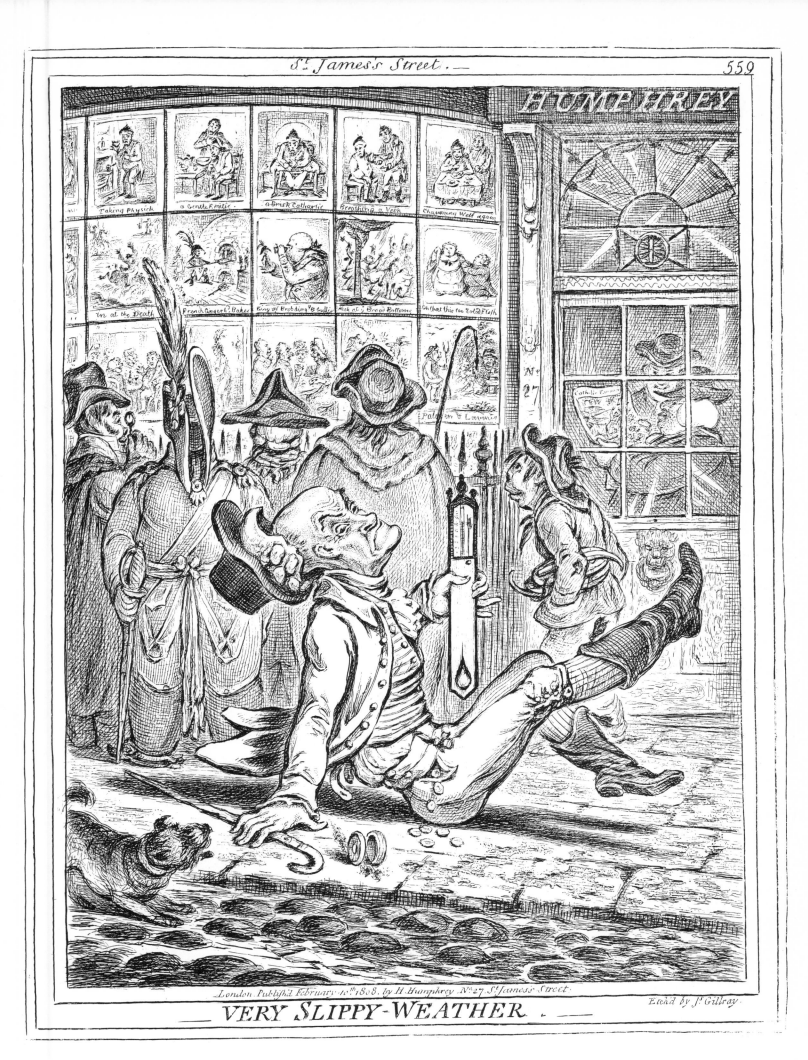

91. [10 February 1808] An assortment of loungers
check the window of Hannah Humphrey's printshop at 27 St. James's Street, Gillray's home, studio
and place of business after 1797. Etched after a
sketch by his amateur friend, the Rev. John Sneyd.

SPANISH-PATRIOTS attacking the FRENCH-BANDITTI.— Loyal Britons lending a lift.

92. [15 August 1808] Napoleon's troops were considered invincible until word arrived that some eighteen thousand of

them had surrendered to the Spanish general Castaños at
Baylén on 23 July.

Dreadful Descent of ♀ Roman Meteor. — The Turkish New-Moon, Rising in Blood. — The Spirit of Charles ♂ XII. — The Imperial Eagle emerging from a Cloud!

The Rhenish Confederation of Starved Rats, crawling out of the Mud. — Dutch-Frogs spitting out their spite. — American-Rattlesnake shaking his Tail. — Prussian Scare-Crow attempting to Fly!

THE VALLEY OF THE SHADOW OF DEATH.

Published Sept 24 1808 by H Humphrey at St James's Street London.

93. [24 September 1808] Napoleon, in the improbable guise of Christian from *Pilgrim's Progress*, is confronted by an aggregation of national adversaries: a grim vision of Imperial doom prompted by French difficulties in the Peninsula.

PANDORA opening her Box.

94. [22 February 1809] Mrs. Mary Anne Clarke, former mistress of the Duke of York, appears before the bar of the House of Commons to support charges that she had connived with the Duke, commander in chief of British forces, to sell army commissions at bargain prices. Mrs. Clarke was examined by the House on the first of February and on six subsequent days. The scandal absorbed the nation's attention for months and resulted, 20 March, in the resignation of the Duke.

Déposé a'la Bibliot. Nat. Rue Montmartre. N°.92.   *Les Invisibles. 1810.*   *et a'Londres, chez H. Humphrey, S'. James Street.*

95. [1810 (?)] A burlesque on the opporunities for self-concealment afforded by the extremes of "Empire" fashion; copied by Gillray from an anonymous French original.

— The Last Work of the late JAMES GILLRAY — Now first Published, May 15th. 1818. By G. HUMPHREY nephew and successor to the late Mrs. H. HUMPHREY — 27 St. James's Street —

London, January 9th 1811 —

J. Gillray Fect.

A BARBERS-SHOP in ASSIZE TIME. — from a Picture painted by H.W.Bunbury Esqr.

96. [Dated 9 January 1811; published 15 May 1818] Rustic candidates anticipating jury duty in a county assize, or court, are made presentable for their official service. The grand assizes were periodic biannual local sittings of the high court of justice, a long-standing tradition finally abolished in 1833. Gillray's last known engraving, this plate was executed during lucid intervals after his loss of reason in 1810, and published posthumously.

NOTES TO THE PLATES

N.B.: *Although for technical reasons the eight color plates (numbered I through VIII) are reproduced in one group (following page xxxii), in the present section the notes that describe them have been left in the proper chronological sequence. Thus, note I will be found after note 34; notes II and III after note 28; note IV after note 77; notes V and VI after note 81; note VII after note 87; and note VIII after note 91.*

[1]

THE CHURCH MILITANT. 5 September 1779

The Church of England is criticized for its energetic support of the unpopular war with the American colonies.

This satire is also a reflection on the Church's zeal for the prosecution of newly opened hostilities with Spain. The principal figure has been identified as William Markham, Archbishop of York (1719–1807). In what appears to be his first professional use of aquatint, the 23-year-old caricaturist added a light background tone. This, however, is virtually imperceptible in the present reproduction. The inscribed chants indicate a partiality for such spiritual concepts as indolence, self-indulgence, vengeance and the roast beef of British patriotism. The last, inadvertently engraved forward on the altar boys' hymnal, appears in reverse.

[2]

ARGUS. 15 May 1780

While Britannia grieves and the British lion slumbers in chains, the dozing King is surrounded by schemers.

In Greek mythology Argus was a giant with a hundred eyes, an alert and watchful guardian. George III, on the contrary, is portrayed as a somnolent dupe helpless in the hands of his Scottish advisers. The ragged Englishman allows: "I have let them quietly strip me of every Thing." The rebellious Irishman: "I'le take care of Myself & Family." A colonist behind the throne: "We in America have no Crown to Fight for or Loose." To the rear a squat Dutchman feeds on honey from the British hive. At Britannia's feet is a map of her realm from which America has been torn.

[3]

ST. GEORGE & THE DRAGON. 13 June 1782

Charles James Fox rushes to "reward" Admiral George Rodney for his services against the French.

On 12 April 1782 Admiral Rodney (1719–92) scored a decisive naval victory over the French in the West Indies, thereby creating a major embarrassment for the new Rockingham ministry, which had already issued a politically inspired order for his recall. The returning hero was honored with a barony and a modest pension. "Hold my dear Rodney," says Foreign Secretary Fox, "you have done enough. I will now make a Lord of you & you shall have the Happiness of never being heard of again." The monster's wings are covered with tiny French fleur-de-lis; it disgorges a band of frogs. See Plate 85.

[4]

A NEW ADMINISTRATION, OR—THE STATE QUACKS ADMINISTRING. 1 April 1783

After years of contentious rivalry, Lord North and Charles James Fox joined forces in February 1783 to "serve Britannia" in a notorious, short-lived coalition.

Following the resignation of the Earl of Shelburne, on February 24, George III delayed some five weeks before yielding to the inevitable and summoning the Duke of Portland to form a government dominated by the "unholy alliance" of Fox and North. North prepares to administer an enema. Britannia's cracked shield bears the combined crosses of St. George and St. Andrew—as on the national flag.

[5]

THE LORD OF THE VINEYARD. 3 April 1783

The new government formed on 2 April under the nominal leadership of the Duke of Portland was marked by a struggle for ascendancy between Fox and North. From the outset, Fox appeared to dominate.

North had already been characterized as a badger in a Gillray cartoon of 22 March 1782, which showed "The Fox stinking the Badger" out of his official "Nest."

[6]

WESTMINSTER SCHOOL. 4 February 1785

Schoolmaster Fox teaches the 25-year-old Prime Minister Pitt a thing or two about government.

The Fox-North coalition was replaced on 19 December 1783 by an administration headed by William Pitt the younger. When Gillray's caricature appeared, Pitt was losing ground in House debate on the propriety of the "scrutiny" or investigation he had authorized to restrain Fox from taking his seat for Westminster after the election of May 1784. Pitt was under strong pressure to introduce parliamentary reform, and subject to criticism on such lesser matters as the proposed reduction of tea duties and the imposition of a tax on windows instead.

Fox is cast in the role of Dr. Richard Busby (1606–95), legendary disciplinarian and celebrated master of Westminster School from 1638 to his death. He says: "That's all Twaddle! so here's for your India Task [tax]! there! there! there! & there's for blocking up the old Womens Windows & making them drink Tea in the dark! [etc.]" The next candidates for Fox's attention are supported, left to right, by Burke, Sheridan (with *School for Scandal* in his pocket) and Lord North. Although Pitt was indeed at a temporary disadvantage, Gillray's satire completely misrepresents Fox's position as one of strength.

[7]

A NEW WAY TO PAY THE NATIONAL-DEBT. 21 April 1786

King George and Queen Charlotte enjoy the bounty of their grateful land; a vision of royal avarice inspired by the King's disinclination to pay off the debts of his prodigal eldest son.

Pitt offers additional funds; Lord Sydney, the Home Secretary (right foreground), joins the military serenade. At the far right, the wealthy Duc d'Orléans offers the ragged Prince of Wales a note for £200,000 (see Plate 10). Handbills on the wall proclaim "Oeconomy an Old Song," "British Property a Farce" and "Charity a Romance." Another announces the execution of "Fifty-four Malefactors" for "robbing of a Hen-Roost." The facetious dedication is to Jacques Necker (1732–1804), Louis XVI's progressive minister of finance.

Gillray's ironic credit lines reinforce the "loyal" spirit of the title. Heliogabalus was the adopted name of the Roman Emperor Varius Avitus Bassanius (c. 205–222), profligate and extravagant (from Elagabalus, a Syrian sun god). The tyrannical minister Sejanus was a favorite of the Emperor Tiberius (42 B.C.–A.D. 37); the name was earlier applied by caricaturists to Walpole and Bute.

[8]

THE POLITICAL-BANDITTI ASSAILING THE SAVIOUR OF INDIA. First published 11 May 1786

Warren Hastings, Governor-General of British India (1773–85), is menaced by Opposition leaders Burke, North and Fox, who seek his impeachment on grounds of cruelty and corruption.

Hastings (1732–1818) was finally brought to trial in 1788 for his alleged misconduct of Indian affairs. The sensational trial finally petered out in acquittal seven years later. Gillray's initial responses were sympathetic to Hastings. Two years later, after his attitude (and his printshop) had changed (see Plates 13B, 14), this early expression of support was reissued by the original publisher.

[9]

THE BOARD OF CONTROUL. OR THE BLESSINGS OF A SCOTCH DICTATOR. 20 March 1787

Under the direction of Pitt's crony Henry Dundas, government management of East India Company affairs is seen to have a Scottish bias.

Dundas (1742–1811) receives a classically ragged and verminous band of obsequious "North Britons." Their leader bears an application: "We your Countrymen & Kinsmen make humble application to be appointed Governors or Directors in your India Department. . . ." Prime Minister Pitt and Home Secretary Sydney occupy themselves with a child's game, push-pin. The pictures on the wall recall the part played by charges of potential patronage abuse in the defeat of Fox's India bill (the direct cause of his government's downfall in December 1783). Gillray's ironic monogram "JS" salutes caricaturist James Sayers, a subsidized Pittite whose work against Fox was widely credited with a part in his defeat. Gillray, himself a "second-generation Scot," "seriously" and "humbly" dedicates the plate to proprietors of East India stock as from "their most obedient humble Servant, John English." Etching with aquatint.

[10]

MONSTROUS CRAWS, AT A NEW COALITION FEAST. 29 May 1787

Gillray commemorates a reconciliation of sorts between the Prince of Wales and his royal parents. On May 21 the King supported Pitt in a move to authorize discharge of the Prince's debts out of public funds.

According to a print published on May 14, a popular London sensation of the moment was the exhibition of three "wild-born human beings" with remarkable craws (or thyroid conditions?). Sitting at the open gates of the Treasury, the royal trio gorge on "John Bull's Blood." The Prince wears a fool's cap with his three-feathered emblem; his "craw" is comparatively empty. The King is clad as an old woman; his frugality and presumed taste for things Scottish are suggested by a plaid shawl. Four years after the Fox-North union, "coalition" was a word with powerful negative overtones. Etching with aquatint.

[11]

A MARCH TO THE BANK. 22 August 1787

The regular transit each evening and morning of a detachment of guards to and from the Bank of England was widely regarded as a nuisance to pedestrians.

During the Gordon Riots in June 1780, concern for the safety of the Bank of England led to the institution of a nightly guard detachment. At first the soldiers marched two abreast along the Strand, Fleet Street and Cheapside, jostling passers-by. By 1787 the guard consisted of one officer, two sergeants, two corporals, 29 men and a drummer-piper. After a series of complaints, *The London Chronicle* reported (July 19) that the Lord Mayor had been "desired to request the guard to march in single file." Some fifteen months later the same paper reported that the soldiers were still marching in their old formation, according to evidence given in an action for assault. Two years later a Lord Mayor of London met the column at Ludgate Hill, "but on making his remonstrance, was shoved off the footway by the Commanding Officer without any further ceremony" (*Reading Mercury*, 6 September 1790).

[12]

THE MORNING AFTER MARRIAGE—OR—A SCENE ON THE CONTINENT. 5 April 1788

A "nostalgic" and totally fanciful reconstruction of the notorious secret marriage of the Prince of Wales and Mrs. Maria Anne Fitzherbert, which actually took place at the bride's lodgings in Park Lane on 15 December 1785.

The first, and certainly the most chaste, of a series of

Gillray sorties into royal bedchambers. This plate is a sequel to a 1786 "illustration," reissued the week before, in which Gillray shows the Prince and his lady taking their vows before Edmund Burke in a Continental cathedral. In the earlier satire, Fox gives the bride away (most inaccurately, as Fox had opposed the union vehemently and it had taken place behind his back). Burke's Jesuitical garb was a jibe at his advocacy of political concessions for Roman Catholics.

The religious factor was fundamental. The Prince at 23 could not have entered into a valid marriage without the King's consent, nor was he anxious to. A valid marriage to the Catholic Mrs. Fitzherbert (who was 29 and twice widowed) would have blocked his succession to the throne under the Act of Settlement.

Mrs. Fitzherbert's sense of respectability thus sustained by the mock ceremony, the Prince continued to compound his extravagances and pay off his blackmailers. A great show of penitence and poverty in 1786 failed to move George III to bail him out. Thus it became necessary to turn to Parliament, and to his long-suffering ally, Fox. Fox's assurances to the Commons (30 April 1787) that he knew on "immediate authority" that the whispered wedding "not only never could have happened legally but never did happen in any way whatsoever" helped produce the funds which the Prince desperately needed. Naturally, Mrs. Fitzherbert was provoked with the luckless Fox, and to keep peace, young George broke with him, adopted Sheridan as his new "manager" in Parliament, and returned to his former life style.

The scene here is a French hotel. His Royal Highness luxuriates in a manner clearly reminiscent of the bride's attitude in the second tableau of Hogarth's popular *Marriage à la Mode* (1745). Mrs. Fitzherbert's pose is not unlike that of the most conspicuous strumpet in the third plate of *A Rake's Progress* (1735). Gillray's conception was dismissed by Joseph Grego in 1873: "The grace of the picture must be the apology for a certain Hogarth-like suggestiveness, which may be considered of questionable decorum" (*The Works of James Gillray, the Caricaturist*, London, p. 96). The Prince's garter, dangling askew, carries the royal motto, "Honi Soit Qui Mal Y . . . [Pense]" (Evil to him who evil thinks); the lady's, curling across her shoe, is inscribed with another erroneous tribute to Fox. "Plenipo" in the signature is short for plenipotentiary. Etching with stipple.

[13A]

THE PRINCESS'S BOW ALIAS THE BOW BEGUM. 1 May 1788

Rival caricaturist James Sayers rises to the defense of Hastings, ridiculing the emotional testimony of the Begum of Oude (concerning her economic exploitation by Hastings), the deference of Fox, Burke and Sheridan and the conspiratorial influence of Philip Francis (beneath the bench). See Plate 8.

[13B]

THE BOW TO THE THRONE,—alias—THE BEGGING
BOW. 6 May 1788

In Gillray's close parody, complete with "JS" monogram, Sayers' loyal jibe is twisted into a vicious indictment of the manner in which Hastings was thought to be enlisting the aid of Lord Chancellor Thurlow, Pitt, Queen Charlotte and the King (lower left). Oriental potentate Hastings is enthroned on a close-seat (or toilet) decorated with an inverted crown. The picture on the wall in Sayers' print shows the mountain of charges yielding up a mouse of a case. Gillray differs.

[14]

MARKET-DAY. 2 May 1788

In a pungent comment on the supposed venality of public men, Gillray shows leading members of the House of Lords placidly awaiting the pleasure of the highest bidder in the cattle pens at Smithfield.

This satire appeared in the context of the Opposition crusade against Warren Hastings, who departs past the pawnshop at left, atop the symbolic white horse of Hanover. The King is a calf, trussed and slung across Hasting's saddle. Lord Chancellor Thurlow stands at the center, leaning casually on his mace, purse in hand; he is obviously the big spender of the day. The Earl of Derby rises from a group of hesitant Opposition peers to propose an adjournment. "Thurlow's cattle" have upset a watchman's box and Fox (with lantern), Burke and Sheridan (with noisemaker) tumble to the ground. At the rear, on the balcony of a royal tavern promising "Good Entertainment for Man & Beast," Dundas and Pitt relax, content with their pipes and tobacco. Gillray appears to have had himself in mind when he drew the angry stockman (left center).

[15]

STATE-JUGGLERS. 16 May 1788

Pitt (producing decorations and honors), Hastings (vomiting gold) and Thurlow (exploding bombast) are represented as mountebank entertainers, practicing their impostures on an audience of grasping politicians.

The performance takes place beneath the sign of the Crown, atop which the King and Queen are represented as Punch and Judy. Queen Charlotte admires a snuffbox —allegedly a bribe from Hastings. Hastings' principal tormentors, Fox, Burke and Sheridan, are shown at the lower right. Fox is attempting to enjoy a piece of the action. A chimney sweep and a fishwife are conspicuous in the foreground. Gillray attributes the verse to Charles Churchill (1731–64); once again he employs James Sayers' monogram (see Plates 9, 13B). In actuality Pitt had long since disassociated himself from Hastings' defense.

[16]

FUTRELL VS. JACKSON. 10 June 1788

"Gentleman" John Jackson (1768–1845), future champion of England, celebrates his ring debut by trouncing the favored Thomas Fewtrell on 9 June 1788.

The interest in pugilism displayed by the Prince of Wales in the 1780s played a key role in the popularization of the sport. Capitalizing on the absence of any illustrated press, Gillray turned sports reporter on several occasions between 1788 and 1790, rushing "into print" after major contests with this sort of tableau. It is hard to say whether "Futrell vs. Jackson" is a piece of first-hand reporting. Gillray refers to the site, Swithin's Bottom, as "Smith in the Bottom," indicating that he may well have been present and heard it spoken that way. The place name is one piece of intelligence that a deputized assistant probably would have gotten right.

John Jackson was an unknown of nineteen, Fewtrell a veteran of twenty victories. It was reported that Jackson's "most sanguine friends had entertained doubts of his success," but the unfortunate Fewtrell was knocked down repeatedly and ultimately judged incompetent to face his junior "either in point of *science* or *bottom*" (endurance). The prevailing rules sanctioned Jackson's tactics as illustrated by Gillray—they also permitted the strategy by which he won the championship on 15 April 1795 —a combination of a vicious uppercut with an immobilizing grip on his opponent's hair.

At the time of his retirement in 1803, Jackson was described as having "practically realized the character of a gentleman. . . ." He became a close friend and sparring partner of Lord Byron. Together they decorated a large folding screen with prints and clippings tracing the manly art from 1785 to 1812. This montage, incorporating the Fewtrell print and the news accounts cited above, was given by Byron to his publisher, John Murray, and is preserved (on the same premises) by Murray's heirs.

Gillray shows the Prince seated center right beneath his crony, Colonel Hanger (see Plate 46) and Lord Derby. William Ward, Thomas Johnson and Richard Humphrey[s] were prominent boxers.

[17]

THE BUBBLES OF OPPOSITION. 19 July 1788

Charles James Fox attempts to float a new "opposition bubble," Lord John Townshend, his candidate for Parliament in a special Westminster election.

Devoid of the customary publisher's identification, this print appears to be one of a series commissioned from Gillray by a Pitt lieutenant on behalf of Townshend's opponent, Admiral Hood. Seven such plates critical of Townshend and Fox appeared between 19 and 31 July. A subsequent secret account submitted to the Treasury included £20 for a "Mr. Gilwray." However, Hood was defeated by Townshend on 28 July, and a subsequent bitter cartoon on the subject may indicate that Gillray remained unsatisfied. Fox mixes his "Devonshire Sope," indicative of the support of the Duke and Duchess of Devonshire, in a "Coalition Washing Tub" in which the faces of the infirm Lord North and the Duke of Portland (?) are visible. The largest bubble (center top) is that of the Prince of Wales. Those immediately beneath are, left to right, Burke, (possibly) the Marquess of Tichfield [Portland's son], Norfolk, Sheridan and Colonel Hanger (see Plate 46). The faces at the top left appear to be Windham and Lord Carlisle; at the lower left, Lord Stormont. Etching with aquatint.

[18]

THE MONSTER GOING TO TAKE HIS AFTERNOONS LUNCHEON. 10 May 1790

Public attention was drawn to the exploits of an unknown knife fanatic, the "Cutting Monster," wanted for several attacks on young women in the West End of London.

The "monster" was identified on 13 June as one Renwick Williams. He was brought to trial first on 9 July, and finally convicted and sentenced to two years' imprisonment on 12 December for injuring a young woman in St. James's Street. In an earlier version of this print, the victim's posterior is shielded by a porridge pot.

[19]

THE BALANCE OF POWER. 21 April 1791

The (celibate) Prime Minister Pitt attempts to impose an equilibrium on hostile relations between Turkish Sultan Selim III and Catherine the Great of Russia.

Anxious to prevent a Russian advance to the Mediterranean on 28 March, Pitt proposed an increase in British naval forces to support the underdog Turks. Catherine annexed the Crimea in 1783, and Turkey and Russia had been at war since 1787. Fox attacked Pitt's "balance of power" policy in the Commons on 29 March; Sheridan did so on 15 April. Gillray strikes his own balance by taking a cue from Sheridan, while inserting the notoriously impecunious Opposition leader as an embittered clown, bottom right. Pitt's parliamentary majority sagged during the heated debate and on 15 April he moderated an earlier ultimatum, allowing Catherine to retain her key Black Sea base at Orchakov. Pitt later described this crisis as the greatest mortification of his career. Russia and Turkey finally made peace four months later. Sheridan's reference to "the immortal Chatham" concerns the Prime Minister's father, William Pitt, first Earl of Chatham (1708–78, premier 1756–61 and 1766–68). The designation "posture master" was applied to acrobats, contortionists and teachers of calisthenics.

[20]

THE RIGHTS OF MAN; OR TOMMY PAINE, THE LITTLE AMERICAN TAYLOR, TAKING THE MEASURE OF THE CROWN, FOR A NEW PAIR OF REVOLUTION-BREECHES. 23 May 1791

The first part of Paine's *Rights of Man* was published 13 March 1791, dedicated to George Washington, in response to Edmund Burke's *Reflections on the Revolution in France* of the preceding November.

Thomas Paine (1737–1809), originally a maker of corsets at his father's shop in the Norfolk village of Thetford, established his credentials as a revolutionary propagandist with the influential American pamphlet *Common Sense* (10 January 1776). He returned to Europe in 1787 to promote his design for an iron bridge, but returned to politics after the fall of the Bastille. Threatened with imprisonment in England after the publication of *The Rights of Man, Part Two*, Paine fled to France in September 1792, where he was immediately elected a member of the Convention for Calais. Gillray's ironic dedication refers to *Common Sense*, and to the "Jacobine Clubs," making this in strict point of fact the earliest anti-Jacobin satire published in England. The name Jacobin was applied after 1789 to the Parisian club which met in the Convent of St. Jacques. After 1793 it was widely adopted in England as a broad term applicable to revolutionaries in general and to their principles. In Gillray's lengthy dialogue balloon, "Cabbage" is slang for pilfer, and "Flints" were London tailors who agitated for higher wages, as opposed to "Dungs," who accepted the statutory rates.

[21]

THE HOPES OF THE PARTY, PRIOR TO JULY 14TH. 19 July 1791

Charles James Fox presides over the public execution of George III, assisted by Opposition allies Horne Tooke, Sheridan and Sir Cecil Wray. Behind Sheridan, Joseph Priestley—controversial theologian and scientist—offers words of comfort.

Gillray locates his regicide in the Strand, before the Crown and Anchor Tavern, a popular radical meeting place. At the rear, an allegorical figure of Liberty floats above Temple Bar, the Wren gateway which stood at the head of Fleet Street from 1670 until 1878. She is flanked by the skulls of executed criminals; the statues indicated below are of Charles I (executed 1649) and Charles II. The spirit of Oliver Cromwell is also evoked by Fox's allusion to "the Man who chop'd the Calf's-head off a Hundred & Forty Years ago."

George III does not appear to grasp the gravity of his situation. After his derangement during the winter of 1788–89 and the consequent regency crisis, the state of the monarch's sanity was subject to continuing speculation. The Queen and Pitt, still under bitter criticism as alleged usurpers of the royal prerogative during the

King's illness (see Plate 22), are shown dangling from the lamp brackets at the upper right.

This plate probably was already in progress as a sort of salute to the second anniversary of the fall of the Bastille when "loyalist" riots in Birmingham obliged Gillray to shift his fantasy into the past tense. The Birmingham disturbances were occasioned by announced plans for a "Constitutional Society" Bastille Day dinner. The mob focussed its attention on Joseph Priestley (1733–1804), who was fully as unpopular for his activities as a dissenting minister as for his pro-French sympathies. Priestley's Birmingham house was sacked and his library and scientific apparatus were destroyed. Sir Cecil Wray (1735–1805), defeated by Fox in the celebrated Westminster election of 1784, had thrown his support to the Opposition. Gillray jibes at Wray for his 1784 plan to abolish Chelsea Hospital and put the revenue saved into "small beer" benefits for dispossessed former residents. (The caricaturist was born and raised in Chelsea, son of a hospital pensioner.)

[22]

WIERD-SISTERS; MINISTERS OF DARKNESS; MINIONS OF THE MOON. 23 December 1791

Continuing concern for the King's sanity is expressed in a haunting visual metaphor of lunacy. Anxious ministers Dundas, Pitt and Thurlow study the ascendant crescent profile of Queen Charlotte and the slumbering shadow of her royal husband.

From early November 1788 until mid-February 1789 George III had been deprived of his reason by a baffling disorder which has only recently been diagnosed as the rare hereditary metabolic disease porphyria. After three months of bitter medical-political wrangling, a regency bill was nearing enactment, the certain consequence of which would have been the elevation of the Prince of Wales and the substitution of a government headed by Fox and his friends for that of Pitt's. At the last possible moment the King experienced a complete recovery and the constitutional crisis evaporated. However, rumors persisted to the effect that Pitt's holding action had been aided by a "special relationship" with the Queen.

The appearance of Gillray's satire three years later probably owes more to the caricaturist's regard for the work of the Swiss painter Henry Fuseli (1741–1825) than to any widespread popular belief in the King's continued incapacity. Gillray's composition closely parodies Fuseli's well-known 1783 illustration of the witches' scene from *Macbeth* (Act I, Scene 3), and is "respectfully dedicated" to the older artist. There must have been some degree of association between them at this time. Gillray executed a "serious" engraving of a Fuseli drawing for the 1792 English edition of Lavater's *Essays on Physiognomy*, a project supervised by Fuseli himself. Including his "Wierd-Sisters," Gillray based four caricatures on works by Fuseli between October 1791 and June 1792. The last of these was modeled upon a painting completed by Fuseli twelve days earlier but not exhibited for seven years. Etching with aquatint.

[23]

A SPHERE, PROJECTING AGAINST A PLANE. 3 January 1792

A tangential encounter between Prime Minister Pitt and Mrs. Albinia Hobart, substantial lady of fashion.

Mrs. Hobart (1738–1816, Countess of Buckinghamshire after 1793) was a supporter of Fox celebrated for her private gaming table, her elaborate parties and her participation in amateur theatricals. Mrs. Hobart's grace as a dancer despite her amplitude encouraged mischievous speculation that she might be hollow.

[24]

FASHIONABLE CONTRASTS;—OR—THE DUCHESS'S LITTLE SHOE YEILDING TO THE MAGNITUDE OF THE DUKE'S FOOT. 24 January 1792

"A foreigner would suppose that several of our flimsy prints [newspapers] were conducted by shoe-makers . . . so much have they said about the Duchess of York's slipper" (*Morning Post*, 7 January 1792).

Frederica Charlotte Ulrica Catherine, the new Duchess of York, was small and not particularly attractive. She had been married in Berlin on 29 September 1791 to Frederick Augustus, Duke of York and Albany (1763–1827), the King's immensely popular second son. The Duke and Duchess returned to London on 19 November and a second wedding ceremony on 23 November at Buckingham House increased public excitement. Thereafter, the London papers fell over one another in their eagerness to comment appreciatively on the newcomer's grace and amiability (and majestic dowry). Particular attention was paid to her smallness of foot and elegance of dress. The diamond-encrusted shoes which she selected for the Queen's birthday celebration on 18 January were fussed over at great length. A tracing of the famous slipper was engraved (actual size: five and one half inches!) and sold. Accounts of the event the following day devoted approximately three times as much space to the Duchess' costume as to the Queen's. Gillray's "social note" appeared on 24 January.

[25]

ANTI-SACCHARRITES,—OR—JOHN BULL AND HIS FAMILY LEAVING OFF THE USE OF SUGAR. 27 March 1792

Gillray visualizes teatime at St. James's Palace. A proposed sugar boycott (to encourage the abolition of slavery in the West Indies) receives support at the highest level.

The King was noted for his frugal manner and the

extreme simplicity of his personal tastes. Queen Charlotte was thought to carry the family penchant for economy to the brink of avarice. Gillray suggests that their majesties might have an ulterior motive for recommending the virtues of unsweetened tea. The six princesses ranged in age from 26 to nine (Charlotte, 1766–1828; Augusta, 1768–1840; Elizabeth, 1770–1840; Mary, 1776–1857; Sophia, 1777–1848; and Amelia, 1783–1810). According to one of Gillray's earliest historians this print, circulated at the royal breakfast table, was the subject of much merriment. The same composition was pinned over the mantel of Rowlandson's friend Mathew Michell, where it caught the attention of the satiric poet "Peter Pindar" (John Wolcot, 1738–1819): "Yet he were a liar who would say 'Behold their *sweet* faces, for, by all that is holy! their pouting lips 'set one's teeth on edge!' "

A movement for the abolition of the slave trade commenced in Paris (1788) and was picked up by the British after the Crown assumed control of San Domingo in 1791. Seven days after Gillray's print was published, a motion providing for gradual abolition by January 1796 carried in the Commons, only to face postponement and rejection by the Lords.

[26]

A SPENCER & A THREAD-PAPER. 17 May 1792

The "lateral component" of this fashion plate is George, second Earl Spencer (1758–1834), who had wagered successfully that he could create a new style by chopping the skirts from his overcoat. According to one legend, the project was inspired by a riding accident which unceremoniously de-tailed his lordship's coat. A thread-paper was a pleated card used to divide skeins of thread; the phrase was popularly applied to slender individuals.

The initial reference to Lord Spencer's creation in the *Oxford English Dictionary* is for the year 1796. A member of Parliament before his elevation to the peerage, he served as First Lord of the Admiralty (1794–1801) and Home Secretary (1806–07). His attenuated companion remains unidentified. Etching with aquatint.

[27]

LE COCHON ET SES DEUX PETITS—OR—RICH PICKINGS FOR A NOBLE APPETITE. May 1792

Charles Howard, 11th Duke of Norfolk, Earl Marshal of England, appears in the company of a pair of courtesans (introduced after the fashion of sideshow curiosities).

The title means "the pig and its two little ones." The Duke of Norfolk, celebrated Whig, egalitarian and eccentric drunkard, was conspicuous for the extent and variety of his amours. The epithet "Royal Sovereign" appears to designate the larger lady, perhaps on account of her sway over the "Royal" Duke, so nicknamed for the frequency

with which he was "royally" intoxicated. Norfolk's prowess at the banquet table was legendary (a "six-bottle man"), as was his taste for random encounters with members of the opposite sex. According to the 1851 guide to Bohn's Gillray, the Duke "used to wear a grey coat, turned up with a black velvet collar, black small clothes [breeches], and black silk stockings, and would ask them, 'If they could take up with a country curate.' " A "stone" being fourteen pounds, the "lighter" of the two ladies would weigh in around four hundred; her other love has been identified as one Tom Wild, highwayman.

[28]

A CONNOISSEUR EXAMINING A COOPER. 18 June 1792

In a time of increasing revolutionary tension, George III takes a close look at the regicide "Protector," Oliver Cromwell, nemesis of King Charles I.

Events on the Continent were casting an increasing shadow across the Channel. King Gustaf III of Sweden, shot at the opera in Stockholm on 16 March, died on 29 March. At Paris the extremists were consolidating their power. In May a British government proclamation urged magistrates to exercise greater zeal in the control of riotous meetings and seditious publications.

George III blinks at a portrait of Cromwell by the miniaturist Samuel Cooper (1609–72), who painted the Protector (1599–1658) several times after 1650. Cooper's original life sketch, showing his subject "warts and all," is believed to be the one in the possession of the Dukes of Buccleuch. Gillray's version follows closely, with a shade more malevolence.

The King's illness of 1788–89 has affected his vision, and a considerable weight loss emphasized the characteristic protrusiveness of the royal eyeball. In another reference to George's notorious frugality, Gillray shows his ornate gold candlestick equipped with an auxiliary "save-all" designed to conserve tallow and wick to the last (symbolic?) end. The caricaturist facetiously signs this work (in Latin) as "drawn and executed from life."

[II.]   (color plate)

A VOLUPTUARY UNDER THE HORRORS OF DIGESTION. 2 July 1792

"The Good Life" as exemplified by the Prince of Wales's establishment at Carlton House.

The publication of this satire, and the one preceding, signaled a resolution on Gillray's part, at 26, to abandon his ambitions as a "serious" engraver, and commit all of his energies to caricature.

The Prince of Wales acquired Carlton House in 1783, engaging the architect Henry Holland to supervise extensive alterations. "Improvements" were in progress for much of the Prince's tenancy, but the residence was ready for a state levee on 8 February 1790. Gillray shows the Prince in his apartments overlooking Pall Mall, a summer breeze blowing in past Holland's unfinished Ionic colonnade. These pillars were salvaged for the portico of the National Gallery after Carlton House was pulled down in 1827.

At the time of Gillray's satire, the Prince was estranged from his parents by his politics, his choice of friends and his life style. He would be frustrated in efforts to follow his younger brothers into the military. Self-centered, self-indulgent, vain, his princely aptitude for enjoyment had boosted the royal physique to an estimated seventeen stone (238 pounds). The caricaturist surrounds his subject with the trappings of excess: a corkscrew on the watchfob, decanters of port and brandy on the table, empty wine bottles beneath. The elegance of the setting contrasts with a brimming chamberpot and a festoon of unpaid bills (the poulterer's, butcher's, baker's and, below, the doctor's). A convenient "clinic" on the shelf to the rear includes a box of "Leakes Pills" and "Velnos Vegetable Syrup" (domestic and French venereal disease nostrums), "Drops for a Stinking Breath" and some manner of preparation "For the Piles."

Above, the Prince's crown, three-feather emblem and motto "Ich Dien" (I serve) are bracketed with wine-bottle and wine-glass candle sconces and a new armorial device: empty plate with knife (dexter) and fork (sinister). The abstemious sage at top center is identified as "L: Cornaro [Age] 199." Luigi Cornaro of Padua (1467–1566) was the author of *Discorsi della Vita Sobria*, a treatise on longevity.

The account books on the floor by the dice and dice box allude to "Debts of Honor unpaid," the "Newmarket List" and a "Faro Partnership Account" with "Self, Archer, Hobart & Co." The second reference is to a alleged impropriety in the handling of the Prince's horse Escape at Newmarket the preceding November. The third, implying a financial interest in the notorious gambling parties of Lady Archer and Mrs. Hobart, is apparently a fantasy of Gillray's.

Reminiscing in 1854, William Makepeace Thackeray (born 1811) recalled "in one of those ancient Gillray portfolios, a print which used to cause a sort of terror in us youthful spectators":

... in which the Prince of Wales ... was represented as sitting alone in a magnificent hall after a voluptuous meal, and using a great steel fork in the guise of a toothpick. Fancy the first young gentleman living employing such a weapon in such a way! The most elegant Prince of Europe engaged with a two-pronged iron fork—the heir of Britannia with a *bident!* The man of genius who drew that picture saw little of the society which he satirized and amused. Gillray watched public characters as they walked by the shop in St. James's Street, or passed through the lobby of the House of Commons. His studio was a garret, or little better; his place of amusement, a tavern-parlour where his club held its nightly sittings over their pipes and sanded floor. You could not have society represented by men to whom it was not familiar....

It is a particularly significant measure of the gulf between Gillray and his Victorian successors that Thackeray—caricaturist and acute social historian—should have missed the point so completely. Although he was certainly a social and philosophical outsider, Gillray's failure to depict "the correct fork" hardly proves his ignorance of the *beau monde*. On the contrary, it is a virtuoso demonstration of an artist's continuing fascination with the interplay of grace and crudity which was so characteristic of his age. How effectively this device rivets our attention on the languid, bloated beauty of Gillray's fallen angel!

[III.] (color plate)

TEMPERANCE ENJOYING A FRUGAL MEAL. 28 July 1792

Contrasted with the Prince's life is the somewhat more severe regimen observed by his royal parents at Windsor.

The other half of the royal generation gap shows George III and Queen Charlotte in an orgy of self-denial and restraint. Gillray's painstaking sequel elaborates on themes of parsimony and avarice in a variety of ways. The King wears the "Windsor uniform," a blue coat with red lining and trim which he had introduced some twelve years earlier. He operates on a soft-boiled egg. His German-born Queen wolfs salad (or sauerkraut?), once again with a two-pronged "bident." Their tableware is gold, down to the massive, ornate flagon of "Aqua Regis" on the floor. They sit before or inside the bolted doorway of a strong room which displays a "Table of Interest" at "5 pr Cent."

His Majesty's patched breeches and shirtfront are protected by the table linen. His chair's upholstery is guarded from wear, as are the carpet and even the bell-pull. The fireplace with its frigid gnome and floral display of snow-drops, holly and mistletoe suggests a Spartan, chilly Christmas, contrasting with the sticky summertime of the companion piece. The mantelpiece candleholder (Munificence with empty cornucopias) bears holiday decorations; the candles are apparently being used one at a time in the interest of economy. Over empty scales, a painting of "The fall of Manna" shows a group of Jewish figures in the stock garb of contemporary usurers, gathering in the bounty. Over the King's head, an empty frame ("The Triumph of Benevolence") supports a miniature of the monarch as "The Man of Ross" (philanthropist John Kyrle, 1637–1724, memorialized by Pope: "The Man of Ross divides the weekly bread:/He feeds yon alms-house, neat, but void of state,/Where age and want sit smiling at the gate ..."). The top margin obscures two inapplicable visions, one of sharing—"Parting of the Loaves & Fishes"—and the other presumably of the heir apparent—"Epicurus IIII." The books at the lower right deal with the "Life of Old Elwe[s]," referring to a popular contemporary account of the career of a miser by Edward Topham (1751–1820), "Dr. Cheyne on the benifits of a Spare Diet" (George Cheyne, 1671–1743, was an advocate of vegetarianism) and an "Essay on the dearness of Provisions," harking back to a pamphlet debate of 1786.

[29]

THE ZENITH OF FRENCH GLORY;—THE PINNACLE OF LIBERTY. 12 February 1793

The execution of Louis XVI in Paris on 21 January was followed on 1 February by a declaration of war against England.

The early stages of the French Revolution met with wide approval across the Channel. Some four years before the Bastille was taken in July 1789, the poet William Cowper (if anything a Tory) railed against its "horrid Towr's," its dungeons and "cages of despair": "There's not an English heart that would not leap/To hear that ye were fall'n. . . ."

Through 1792, leaping hearts were increasingly subdued by reports of the consolidation of power in the hands of radical Jacobins. Already menaced by Austria and Prussia, the revolutionaries purged opposition at home with the massacres of 2–6 September. Royalty was abolished on 21 September and the Republic established. On 19 November French generals were urged to "grant fraternity and assistance to all people who wish to recover their liberty." The King, "Citizen Capet," was sentenced on 17 January and executed on 21 January. The news reached London three days later.

Gillray's "reconstruction" of the event shows the Place de la Révolution, formerly Place Louis XV (now Place de la Concorde), with a church dome (possibly l'Assomption) in flames at the rear. The atheistic character of the new regime is further demonstrated by the crucifix inscription ("Bon Soir Monsieur"), the treatment of the bishop and the two monks in the foreground, and the cap of "Libertas" which surmounts the bishop's crozier attached to the lamp bracket. At the next corner, a judge swings between the twin emblems of his office. The sansculotte fiddler is a bizarre mixture of crudity and finesse, from his bloody daggers to his patched bagwig and his fastidious little finger. The words "Ca Ira" beneath his tricolor cockade refer to a popular revolutionary street song of 1792 (roughly translated as "That will go" or "We're off and away").

Gillray's ironic underline, "Religion, Justice, Loyalty, & all the Bugbears of Unenlighten'd Minds, Farewell!," was joined on a second state by the title "A View in Perspective." This is one of the very first of many attempts at a realistic representation of the guillotine.

On 24 January the pro-Whig *Morning Chronicle* noted that: "The murder of the late French King, an act of such complicated injustice, cowardice, cruelty and impolicy, as is scarcely to be paralleled . . . will serve to make a war with France popular. . . ."

[30]

DUMOURIER DINING IN STATE AT ST. JAMES'S, ON THE 15TH OF MAY, 1793. 30 March 1793

Sketchy reports concerning a French invasion of Holland, led by General Dumouriez, contributed to speculation about his subsequent objectives. Priestley, Fox and Sheridan welcome their sansculotte visitor to London with a feast of ecclesiastical pudding, roast Pitt and stewed crown, liberally garnished with frogs.

A short-term prophecy, perhaps inspired by Burke's speech to the Commons on 22 March supporting Pitt's "Traitorous Correspondence Bill." Burke conceded that the measure gave the ministers "unusual powers" for dealing with subversive behavior, and that these might be misused. Even so, he felt this was "infinitely preferable to the situation we must be in if Dumourier and his barbarians are to come among us," to usurp the Government, to murder the King, to destroy the Constitution, and to introduce their "Visite Domiciliaire," their "Tribunal Révolutionnaire" and their "Douce Fraternité."

Charles-François Dumouriez (1739–1823), a career soldier and adventurer who joined the Jacobins in 1789, served briefly as Foreign Minister under the Girondists in the spring of 1792. Given command of the "Army of the Center" in August, he took the offensive against Prussia and Austria. Tales of an impending invasion into the Netherlands were circulating by early December. Newspaper reports in February 1793 suggested that Dumouriez had volunteered to visit England to talk peace. By this time, however, he had commenced a drive into Dutch Flanders which culminated in the fall of Breda (26 February) and of Gertruydenberg (1 March), stimulating mobilization of a British expeditionary force under the Duke of York. The French advance was halted by the Austrians at Neerwinden on 18 March, a fact not generally known in London until 26 March, when it probably caught Gillray in mid-etching. Already in deep trouble with the French government, Dumouriez concluded a secret treaty with the Austrians (25 March) for the evacuation of the Netherlands (completed 31 March) and defected to Austria (4 April). Ironically enough, Dumouriez did spend three days in London in mid-June, and settled in England in 1804, living on a government pension until his death. In actuality, he was short and stocky.

Gillray's satire rests on the prevailing atmosphere of rumor and uncertainty caused by tight government control of war news. His French guest is enthroned in something resembling the coronation chair (surmounted by the revolutionary *bonnet rouge*). He prepares to dine off a plate bearing the arms of George III. A Communion cup and two spoons decorated with the hand device of a baronet indicate his designs on the Church and the "establishment." His hosts are wearing the *bonnet rouge* with their aprons and oversleeves. The decanter of "Vin de Paris" on the table contains a red fluid in colored impressions.

Gillray's ambivalent cynicism is underscored by his signature ("Js. Gy. desn. et fect. pro bono publico") and by his dedication "To the worthy Members," etc.

The phrase "Pro Bono Publico" appeared in letters three feet high over Ashley's Punch House on Ludgate Hill, a circumstance which doubtless added to its contemporary significance. The "Crown and Anchor Society" was a fanatic band of superpatriots organized by one John Reeves in November 1792. Formally christened The Association for Preserving Liberty and Property against Levellers and Republicans, the group subsidized prints, issued pamphlets and encouraged the public to root out "French sympathizers" and other subversives. The caricaturist didn't much care for them.

[31]

JOHN BULL'S PROGRESS. 3 June 1793

Patriotic John, aroused from idyllic complacency by duty's call, returns to his destitute family as a gaunt, one-eyed cripple. A "moral history" after the fashion, but not the spirit, of Hogarth's celebrated "progresses" of sixty years before.

Under the emergencies of war and dearth, Gillray's John Bull took shape as a simple, "salt-of-the-earth" yeoman. He was practical, often canny and yet infinitely exploitable, a truly satirical figure—leagues apart from his magisterial Victorian successor.

The caricaturist's sympathy for enlisted men was surely intensified by the fact that his father had lost an arm at Fontenoy in 1745, and by the recollection of his boyhood spent in the shadow of the royal military hospital at Chelsea, where his father had been a patient and pensioner from 1746 to 1754. There is reason to believe that in 1775, when Gillray was nineteen, he may have executed a satire commiserating with the hard lot of the foot soldier in the American Revolution ("Six-Pence A Day," published by his first employer, William Humphrey, 26 October).

In 1793, notwithstanding a positive military situation (until late summer), much official tub-thumping and the offer of bounties to new recruits, enlistments were disappointing and desertions were high. In May, Gillray illustrated the "Fatigues of the Campaign in Flanders" as a drunken wenching party for the officers and a gargantuan KP detail for the men.

"John Bull's Progress" was his first attempt at a narrative sequence (or comic strip) as opposed to separate vignettes or paired contrasts. The homage to Hogarth's great moral cycles (A Harlot's Progress, 1732, and A Rake's Progress, 1735) reflects a general rise in Hogarthian interest following the sale of his widow's estate in April 1790. Alderman Boydell republished some 110 of the artist's Original Works in 1790, and commissioned John Ireland's two-volume 1791 commentary, Hogarth Illustrated, which was reissued in 1793. Caricaturists

John Nixon and Richard Newton produced "progresses" in 1792 and (February) 1793.

Gillray's sardonic inversion of the Hogarthian formula shows hardship and tragedy as a reward for virtue rather than for vice. In the third panel, John Bull's wife and children approach the gate of the government "Treasury," depicted as a pawnshop ("Money Lent by Authority"). The posted handbills announce: "Wanted a Number of Recruits to serve abroad" and "List of Bankrupts—John Bull. . . ." At John's "glorious Return" the family is evidently subsisting on a diet of bare bones and onions. John Bull wears the fur cap with brass plate which was regulation gear for grenadier companies, fusiliers and most regimental drummers.

[32]

FLANNEL-ARMOUR; — FEMALE PATRIOTISM, — OR — MODERN HEROES ACCOUTRED FOR THE WARS. 18 November 1793

With allied forces in disarray, and winter coming on, the proprietor of the Sun announced, on 1 November, that he was collecting flannel waistcoats for "our gallant Soldiers fighting in Flanders." The campaign was quickly taken up by other newspapers. By 6 November wagon-loads of underwear were pouring into London.

On 6 November, the True Briton thanked "the hundreds" who had already contributed flannel garments for the front. The campaign continued to gather steam, despite ridicule from the Opposition press and a plea from the Secretary of War (14 November) to the effect that there was a greater need for shoes. A storage depot was established in Soho Square and, according to the Oracle (15 November), there was hardly a village without a local collecting agency. On 13 November, Lloyd's Evening Post counseled the ladies of the realm that "further benevolence may be most advantageously applied in the furnishing of flannel caps, yarn stockings, socks, trowzers, and strong shoes." The following day, the same paper could report that female orphans of an asylum "patronized by her Majesty" and of another "under the patronage of his Grace the Duke of Leeds" were "busy making flannel caps for soldiers to be worn under their hats" (see A Newspaper History of England, 1792–1793, by Lucyle Werkmeister, Lincoln, Neb., 1967, pp. 415 and 423). Gillray's caricature on the 18th was supposed, by his early commentators, to have put a considerable chill on the whole project.

He shows a hypothetical fitting room or barracks. The troops are receiving conical (fool's?) caps; one beyond the fat lady at left center even appears to sport a tiny bell. Two prints on the wall, peeling and torn, insinuate a turning-away from Hannibal and Charles XII, commanders noted for their disregard of harsh weather. Gillray's interest in military costume conceivably was heightened by a month's visit to the front (commencing 30

August 1793) to collect material for Philip de Louther-bourg's battle tableau *The Grand Attack on Valenciennes.*

[33]

PRESENTATION OF THE MAHOMETAN CREDENTIALS—OR—THE FINAL RESOURCE OF FRENCH ATHEISTS. 26 December 1793

The Turkish plenipotentiary, a sort of playboy of the eastern world, advances on George III with an ambiguous proposal labeled "Powers for a new Connexion between the Port, England & France." His retinue of "French atheists" includes Sheridan, Fox and Priestley. A tricolor flag, "Vive la Republique," supports the notion of a Parisian plot.

The Porte was a designation for the government of the Ottoman Empire. This phallic fantasy has no discernible basis in political reality, and simply affords the caricaturist another chance to suggest the "subversive tendencies" of the Opposition leaders. A Turkish envoy had arrived in London late the previous year, giving rise to considerable humorous comment.

The King reacts in defensive consternation. Queen Charlotte and three of the older princesses show interest. Prime Minister Pitt, a simian mascot chained to a crown and bell, cowers at the royal knee. Home Secretary Dundas, in Highland dress, stands guard behind. Sheridan and Fox wear *bonnets rouges* decorated with crescent insignia. The following year Gillray catered to a continuing interest in things Turkish with thirteen meticulous costume plates, some of which he signed "Bierworth," probably his estimation of their value and importance.

[34]

FRENCH-TELEGRAPH MAKING SIGNALS IN THE DARK. 26 January 1795

Charles James Fox's continued opposition to the war is seen as a treasonous assertion of British weakness.

At the close of 1794, France's situation on the Continent was as strong as it had been during the greatest days of Louis XIV. Belgium and Spain were in hand, the Netherlands and Tuscany were falling and the Prussians had been pushed back to the Rhine. A French army crossed the Waal on 14 January en route to Amsterdam and the Dutch Stadtholder, William V, set sail for England on 18 January.

At home Fox, in a hopeless minority after the defection of Whig moderates under the Duke of Portland, repeatedly attacked the basis and conduct of "Mr. Pitt's war" as unjustified interference in the affairs of another country. The Opposition moved for peace in the Commons on 30 December and again on 6, 26, and 27 January. Gillray seems to imply that the enemy would interpret this stance as a mark of dissension and vulnerability. Fox is represented as a telegraph or semaphore tower on

the Channel coast. One arm signals to the invading fleet with a conspirator's dark lantern; the other points out London (dominated by the dome of St. Paul's), asleep and unprotected.

A *tachygraphe*, a mechanical semaphore system, was first proposed to the French National Convention in 1792 by its inventor, Claude Chappe. In operation between Paris and Lille by August 1794, the device consisted of a sixteen-foot horizontal beam with movable arms at each end, mounted on a tower and operated by cords and pulleys. It was reportedly capable of conveying a sentence, tower to tower, 100 miles in five minutes. An English variant was in use between London and Portsmouth by 1796. Etching with aquatint.

[I.]   (color plate)

PATRIOTIC REGENERATION,—VIZ.—PARLIAMENT REFORM'D, A LA FRANÇOISE. 2 March 1795

An imaginary, reconstituted "republican" House of Commons tries Prime Minister Pitt for his crimes against the "new order."

A satire on the variety of motions for parliamentary reform and on the Pitt government's reluctance to entertain any of them. Understandably less enthusiastic over constitutional modification than he had been before the fall of the Bastille, Pitt is said to have remarked, "It's not reform they want but revolution!"

Gillray has turned the reins of power over to Fox and his Whig colleagues, whom he imbues with the radical zeal of the activist corresponding societies. The former Opposition benches of the old Commons are filled with a motley crew of sansculotte proletarian delegates to the new legislature. A tricolor device supplants the royal arms over Fox's head. The great mace, symbol of the authority of the House, lies forgotten beneath the table. At the left, Fox sits in judgment above accusing counsel Erskine, whose trailing bill is headed "Guillotine." Erskine's "Defense of [Thomas] Hardy" (see his pocket) resulted five months earlier in the acquittal of the founder of the London Corresponding Society on a charge of high treason. His reference works are "Rosseau" [sic], "Voltaire," "Dr. Priestley," "Dr. Price" and [Thomas Paine's] "Rights of Man." Beside him, the impecunious Sheridan is keeping close track of confiscated valuables.

Clockwise from the lower right-hand corner, Norfolk, Derby and Grafton warm themselves with the "Holy Bible" and "Magna Charta"; Lansdowne tips the scales of justice in favor of "Libertas" (a hollow weight?) and "Citizen" Stanhope presents the charges against his brother-in-law, Pitt, who is brought before the bar by Lauderdale, the public executioner.

Assignats (sacks at lower left) were the dubious banknotes issued by the revolutionary French against the security of state lands. The load of coronets, mitres, orders and other establishment bric-a-brac (center) is destined for "Duke's Place," a notorious City enclave of dealers in stolen goods. Etching with aquatint. The autograph identifications on the impression of the print reproduced here are in Gillray's hand.

[35]

LIGHT EXPELLING DARKNESS—EVAPORATION OF STYGIAN EXHALATIONS. 30 April 1795

William Pitt, a serene Phoebus Apollo, guides the British sun through the perilous night of Whiggish obstruction, "French principles" and revolution.

The schizophrenic mixture of formal classicism and romantic expressionism is one of Gillray's most elaborate political allegories. Since it came at the nadir of Pitt's popularity, it is hard to imagine that the caricaturist wanted his mock sublimity taken in absolute seriousness.

The conception reflects the intensity of feeling stirred by Stanhope's motion against interference in French internal affairs (6 January), continuing calls for peace and Opposition proposals (24 and 30 March) for an inquiry on the state of the nation (a consequence of dearth, high food prices and civil unrest).

The tripartite British sun, with the Hebrew word for wisdom at its center, appears to radiate the royal arms. An Olympian, uncharacteristically muscular Pitt, crowned with laurel, holds extremely loose rein on the galloping pair. One of his feet rests on a prostrate shield, "Exit Python Republicanus"; behind the other is a large folio embellished with a lyre and the words "Magna Charta." Two cherubs bring up the rear. One holds the Bible, the other a scroll labeled "Brunswick Succession," showing a family tree of George III, bearing George IV and his potential issue, "And future Kings, and Monarchs yet unborn." (The Prince of Wales agreed to wed his cousin, Princess Caroline of Brunswick, in return for the payment of his debts. The marriage had been solemnized on 8 April.) The rampaging lion wears a fringed cloth with a picture of Britannia brandishing a birch scourge; he glares at the vanishing forms of Sheridan, Fox and Stanhope. The white horse of royalty (symbol of Hanover) carries the arms of Britain on his croup; his eye flashes lightning at the shades of Derby (top), Grafton, Lauderdale and Norfolk (who are losing their *bonnets-rouges*-cum-fool's caps). A month later, Gillray returned to the same imagery—but with Pitt as an horrific figure of Death, astride the "pale horse" of Hanover.

Overhead, the hooded figure of Justice scatters roses of approbation. Her scales are in balance, presumably poised between "Honorable Peace, or Everlasting War." On her staff the British flag waves triumphant over the tattered and tightly gripped tricolor pennant of the "Republicq." Devastated French warships and fleeing sansculotte dwarfs fill the sky behind. Serpents exiting upstage right accent the perniciousness of a "2d Edition" "Irruption of the Goths and Vandals" and a vaporous scroll of "Patriotic Propositions": "Peace, Peace on any Terms; Fraternization, Unconditional Submission; No

Law, no King, No God." (The bracketing of snakes and revolution, a spinoff of Benjamin Franklin's 1754 "Join, or Die" design, was first introduced by Gillray in an earlier wartime satire, "The American Rattle Snake" of 12 April 1782. See also Plate 93.)

Gillray had associated a hideous figure of the Greek Fury Alecto with the Whig Club on 4 July 1791 ("Alecto and her Train at the Gate of Pandaemonium"). Like the specter at the bottom left, it served as a spirit of revolution. The Whig Club was a group of diehard Foxites who met annually on their leader's birthday and on the anniversary of his return for Westminster in 1780.

The misty plots on the celestial roadway concern: "Jacobin Prophecies for breeding Sedition in England," "Scheme for raising the Catholicks in Ireland" and "A Plan for inflaming the Dissenters [Protestants] in Scotland." The furtive owl and bats (bottom, center and right)—eighteenth-century symbols of reaction and obscurantism—are Lansdowne, Michael Angelo Taylor and Erskine.

For a sequel, see Plate VIII.

[36]

A DECENT STORY. 4 November 1795

Port and good company.

Etched by Gillray from a rough sketch (in the author's possession) by the Rev. John Sneyd (1763–1835), Rector of Elford, Staffordshire. See detail in Mrs. Humphrey's window, Plate 91.

[37]

COPENHAGEN HOUSE. 16 November 1795

"Eyewitness account" of a mass meeting held on 26 October on the outskirts of London. Principal harangues were delivered by radical speakers John Thelwall (1764–1834, right), John Gale Jones (1769–1838, left) and William Hodgson (1745–1851, distant center).

Copenhagen House (and Fields), a popular Islington resort, just north of the central City, was the scene of a meeting called by the London Corresponding Society on 26 October to demand universal suffrage, annual parliaments and an end to the war. A second rally took place on 12 November to protest a seditious meeting bill (moved by Pitt on 10 November) and a "treasonable practices" bill (moved by Grenville on 6 November). These, in turn, had been reactions to the 26 October meeting and to a mob attack on the King's carriage, 29 October. Gillray updated his plate with a reference to the later meeting on the roulette table at the center: "Equality & no Sedition Bill."

His subtitle, " 'I tell you, Citizens, we mean to new-dress the Constitution and turn it, and set a new Nap upon it.' Shakespeare," harks back to talk of revolution in *Henry VI*, Part Two, Act IV, Scene 2. Shakespeare has an insurgent say: "I tell thee, Jack Cade the clothier means to dress the commonwealth, and turn it, and set a new nap upon it." Jack Cade was a leader of the Kentish Rebellion of May–July 1450 (entered London 1 July; withdrew 6 July; killed resisting arrest 12 July). By 1795 the textile term "nap" also carried the slang connotations "to cheat" or "to contract a venereal disease" (Hooper and Wigstead, *A Classical Dictionary of the Vulgar Tongue*, London, third edition, 1796, no pagination; first edition edited by Francis Grose, 1785).

At the lower left corner, a scroll of "Remonstrance" (supported by a barrel of "Real Democratic Gin by Thelwal & Co") carries the signatures of Jack Cade, Wat Tyler and Jack Straw. The last two were leaders of an uprising of Kentish and Essex peasants in June 1381. Tyler confronted the fourteen-year-old Richard II with demands for social equality and the abolition of serfdom. An old inn named Jack Straw's Castle was already a Hampstead Heath landmark in Gillray's time.

The three new signatories to the scroll are chimney sweeps. Their caps bear brass plates with the name of their employer, Thelwall, as required by the Chimney-Sweepers' Act of 1788. Speaker Jones is dressed as a butcher. His companion carries a "Rights of Citizens" proclamation. Thelwall's ragged umbrella is held by a dissenting minister. Another supporter displays the "Resolutions of the London Corresponding Society." He may be the meeting chairman, John Binns (1772–1860), but Binns was a plumber before he turned to journalism—not a barber, as the comb suggests. The proletarian audience includes Priestley (with folded arms, behind the gaming lady) and perhaps Fox (the stout party to her left, beneath Thelwall's fist).

Gillray's handling of the receding crowd masses may well derive from the elaborate multifigure tour-de-force watercolors which his friend Rowlandson produced during the mid-eighties. Gillray's regard for the seventeenth-century French master Callot is also in evidence.

[38]

Two-Penny Whist. 11 January 1796

Gillray's publisher, "Mistress" Hannah Humphrey, and her shop assistant, Betty, have some neighbors in for a friendly game.

Gillray had been working steadily for Hannah Humphrey since 1791, and apparently living under her roof since 1793. (His first satires in the late seventies were etched for her older brother William.) In 1796 they still resided at 37 New Bond Street, moving the following year to 27 St. James's Street.

"Mrs." Humphrey is at the center. The man opposite her is traditionally identified as a German named Tholdal and may well be Gillray's friend (and optician of sorts), A. F. Thoelden, whose letter of 19 August 1807 is preserved with the Gillray papers in the British Museum

(Add. MSS. 27,337, f. 108). He is "stricken" by Betty's disclosure of the ace of spades, with which she is taking her seventh consecutive trick. Her contented partner is a picture dealer and restorer named Mortimer. Quite apart from its interest as the only known likeness of Mrs. Humphrey, this has always been one of Gillray's most popular prints. The painter James Northcote (1746–1831) remarked to Hazlitt in 1826: "[Gillray] was a great man in his way. Why does not Mr. Lamb write an essay on the *Two-Penny Whist?*" (William Hazlitt, *Conversations of James Northcote, Esq., R.A.*, London, 1830, pp. 301–02).

[39]

The Fashionable Mamma,—or—The Convenience of Modern Dress. 15 February 1796

The free-flowing, classical "new look" introduced by Lady Charlotte Campbell in 1793 is associated with an offhand approach to *beau-monde* motherhood.

A baronet's carriage awaits without, footman at the ready, as the lady of the house does her duty. She dispenses with the wet nurse in accordance with current "natural" theory and vogue, derived from the doctrines of Rousseau. The "pocket-hole" slits, a characteristic of the clinging new style, are put to an ingenious new use. (According to Lady Charlotte Campbell's original inspiration, breasts were to be lightly covered or left bare.) The turban and the towering aigrettes carry the eye back to a picture of simpler times.

Thomas McLean's 1830 description of the print states that it was directed "as a public admonition" to a specific, but unspecified, viscountess.

[40]

Lady Godina's Rout;—or Peeping-Tom spying out Pope Joan. 12 March 1796

Lady Georgiana Gordon, clad in the very latest transparency, puts a roving eye to the test.

The *Classical Dictionary of the Vulgar Tongue* (1796 edition) defines "rout" as "a modern card meeting at a private house; also an order from the Secretary at War, directing the march and quartering of soldiers."

The second connotation is almost as applicable as the first to the situation of Lady Georgiana, the intensely marriageable daughter of Jane, Duchess of Gordon (1749–1812, in all probability the stout lady at the lower left). The Duchess' campaign to find suitable husbands for her ill-dowered daughters was conducted with military zeal. Three were eventually matched with dukes, one had to settle for a marquis. "Godina" is evidently an elision of Gordon and Godiva, the philanthropic equestrienne of eleventh-century Coventry; "Peeping Tom" was her solitary voyeur. Lady Georgiana's seven-year pursuit of the fifth Duke of Bedford (see Plate 74) ended in engagement shortly before his death in 1802. She subsequently married his younger brother and heir.

Pope Joan is a card game for three or more, involving a deck minus the eight of diamonds and a compartmentalized tray for stakes and counters.

The elderly man at the principal table was identified as "Dr. Sneyd" by Wright and Evans in 1851. Gillray's friend John Sneyd (see note to Plate 91) was only 33 at the time.

[41]

FASHIONABLE-JOCKEYSHIP. 1 June 1796

The Prince of Wales, resplendent in his uniform as an officer of the "English Light Horse," employs the good offices of Lord Jersey to pay a social call on Lady Jersey.

The Prince of Wales appointed George Bussey, fourth Earl of Jersey (1735–1805), as his Master of the Horse in 1795. On the verge of a farcical marriage to Caroline of Brunswick in April 1795, the Prince was still in love with Mrs. Fitzherbert but also deeply involved with Lady Jersey (1753–1821), who had married the Earl in 1770 —when the Prince was eight.

Before the arrival in England of the new Princess of Wales, Lady Jersey was conveniently designated as one of her "Ladies of the Bedchamber" (!) and sent to meet the boat. It was rumored that she had slipped a sexual depressant into the Princess's wedding-night supper and contributed to her discomfiture in a variety of other ingenious ways. This bizarre triangle continued, after a fashion, until the birth of an heir to the throne on 9 January 1796, nine months and one day after the wedding. The Prince regarded his obligations as discharged and immediately discontinued relations with his wife.

Through the spring this separation, and Lady Jersey's role in it, became steadily more appetizing as topics for gossip. On 30 May the London Chronicle observed that "every one pities and execrates the different parties." The slighted Princess received public ovations at the opera on 28 and 31 May. Ironically, the Prince's interest in Lady Jersey began to wane at about the same time that he broke off with his wife. Lady Jersey remained in the "service" of the Princess until 25 June, and continued her efforts to captivate the Prince for years thereafter.

The Prince, in full dress (helmet, gloves and spurs), holds rein on Lord Jersey's queue and forms the sign of the cuckold over his head. The Princess's coronet, with its triple plume, rests on a close-seat (privy) with an earl's coronet and the monógram J. The canopy of Lady Jersey's four-poster is decorated with a coronet and antler emblem. Gillray inscribes the work as "ad. vivam del. et fect." (drawn and etched from life).

Joseph Grego excused the inclusion of a detail showing the central pair in his 1873 Gillray "as illustrative of the eccentricities of military costume." On 3 May, another Gillray print had saluted the royal "Light Horseman" with lines from Henry IV, Part One, describing another heir to the throne: "I saw him with his Beaver on . . . Rise from the ground like feather'd Mercury . . . And witch the world with noble Horsemanship" (Act IV, Scene 1).

[42]

THE CANEING IN CONDIUT STREET: 1 October 1796

A bellicose Lord Camelford menaces his former commander, the explorer George Vancouver, during a chance encounter in Mayfair.

Thomas Pitt (1775–1804), a cousin of the Prime Minister, joined Vancouver's Pacific expedition in April 1791 as a midshipman. In consequence of his insubordination at sea, Captain Vancouver ordered him flogged and placed in irons. Pitt left the ship Discovery in Indian waters and eventually returned to England aboard the Resistance with the rank of lieutenant. During his absence, his father had died. Accordingly the 21-year-old officer arrived back in London in September 1796 as the second Baron Camelford of Boconnoc.

Vancouver had returned in October 1795 and was preparing his journals for publication. He gave this project as his reason for declining the new Lord Camelford's immediate demand for satisfaction. Shortly thereafter the two accidentally met in Conduit Street (spelling transposed by Gillray), close by the caricaturist's shop at 37 New Bond Street. Camelford was prevented from striking his former superior by onlookers. Vancouver died in 1798 at the age of forty. Camelford lost his life six years later in a duel at the age of 29.

Gillray appears to sympathize with Camelford, perhaps owing to rising criticism against the harshness of naval discipline. (The mutiny on the Bounty occurred 28 April 1789.) Two very young sailor boys watch gleefully as Vancouver's brother (John?) grapples with the enraged peer. From the letter in the brother's pocket, Gillray seems to have identified him with a Charles Vancouver who wrote on agriculture between 1794 and 1813: "Chas Rearcovers' Letter to be publish'd after the Parties are bound to keep ye Peace."

The proximity of the "South Sea Fur Warehouse," and the Captain's fur mantle marked "This Present from the King of Owyhee [Hawaii] to George III forgot to be deliver'd," hint at commercial improprieties. Trailing from Vancouver's pocket is a "List of those disgraced during the Voyage—put under Arrest all the Ships Crew —Put into Irons, every Gentleman on Board—Broke every Man of Honor & Spirit—Promoted Spies. . . ." His foot rests on a booklet: "Every Officer is the Guardian of his own Honor.—Lord Grenvill's Letter." He has evidently dropped the pile of shackles "For the Navy" which lie behind him. His speech refers to a rumor that he had been en route to the Lord Chancellor to ask for protection from Camelford at the time of the incident.

[43]

SUPPLEMENTARY MILITIA, TURNING OUT FOR
TWENTY DAYS AMUSEMENT. 25 November 1796

One mixed company of patriots responds to Prime Minister Pitt's proposal of 18 October for a supplementary militia of sixty thousand men.

There was direct reference to the possibility of a French "descent on these kingdoms" in the speech from the throne on 6 October, a menace which Opposition leaders derided as illusory. On 18 October the government presented a defense package that included a request for a sixty-thousand-man militia, six units of ten thousand, to be called up in rotation for twenty-day training periods. Fox denounced the plan as "a measure for impressing the subjects of this country into the land service." (An abortive French invasion of Ireland in late December tended to buttress popular concern.)

Gillray's stalwart tradesmen march in close order, bayonets fixed, and their uniform coats and crossed bandoliers clashing with decidedly nonregulation footgear and miscellaneous accessories. They are led by a sturdy butcher carrying a banner on which St. George is about to dispatch the dragon.

The front rank is composed, left to right, of a rickety cobbler; a gouty bricklayer; a gaunt, tattered painter; a tailor with shears and tape-measure; and a hairdresser with pretensions to fashion. The double-amputee drummer may be a self-portrait. (He wears a grenadier's cap. The trailing sleeve or flap of the drummer's livery should end in a tuft or tassel, rather than fool's bells.) The artist has traditionally been identified as the portrait painter John Hoppner, R.A. (1758–1810), who was neither ugly nor impoverished.

[44]

HET COMMITTÈ VAN NOODLYDENDE. Summer 1796

"Charity begins at home": The "Committee of Public Assistance" in the new Batavian Republic gets down to business. A propaganda print commissioned for distribution in the Netherlands.

While Parliament was in recess (30 June to 16 September) Gillray occupied himself with finishing and etching twenty satires attacking the French puppet republic established in Holland the previous year. The series, *Hollandia Regenerata*, was based on drawings by David Hess, a 26-year-old Swiss officer and native of Zurich, who served with the Dutch from about 1788 to 1796. (His regard for Gillray is suggested by the fact that many of his later caricatures were signed "Gillray, junior.")

The project was either instigated, or promoted in London, by Sir Francis Baring (1740–1810), a wealthy merchant, and by Commander William Hope (1766–1831), later vice-admiral (see Hill, *Mr. Gillray The Caricaturist*, London, 1965, pp. 73–80). According to a pamphlet written two years later by Sir John Dalrymple,

who convinced Gillray to try a similar notion for English consumption:

> During the present Revolutions of Holland a Series of Engravings was Published . . . forming a Kind of History, whereby men were taught their Duty in public Life by their Fears and their Dangers. Twelve thousand Copies were circulated in that Country at a trifling Expense. The Antidote however came too late for the Poison.

Hollandia Regenerata was evidently printed in London (in both red and black ink) and bound in book form with facing pages of commentary in Dutch, French and English. The series develops allegations of greed, exploitation and incompetence on the part of the Batavian leaders and their French Svengalis. The title of Plate 11, reproduced here, translates literally as "The Committee for the Distressed." An accompanying explanation concludes with the Biblical passage James ii, 15, 16: "If a brother or sister be naked and be destitute of daily food; and one of you say unto them; Depart in peace, be ye warmed, and be ye filled; notwithstanding ye give them not those things, which are needful to the body; what doth it profit?"

[45]

EENIGE DER REPRESENTANTEN VAN HET VOLK VAN
HOLLAND. Summer 1796

A birch rod or scourge labeled "Some of the Representatives of the People of Holland." Another subsidized gesture at the overthrow of the Batavian Republic, strikingly modern in conception.

Plate 18 from *Hollandia Regenerata*. The commentary, in Dutch and English: "Ezekiel vii. 11. Violence is risen up into a rod of wickedness." On 26 December 1796 the *Morning Post* pointed happily to the existence of these caricatures as "a mark of the approach of Freedom" in the Batavian Republic, presumably in ignorance of their local origin.

[46]

STAGGERING-BOBS, A TALE FOR SCOTCHMEN. 1 December 1796

Colonel George Hanger (man-about-town, eccentric and sometimes crony of the Prince of Wales) defends the prowess of his low-slung pony.

George Hanger (1751–1824, fourth Baron Coleraine after 1814) was one of Gillray's regular favorites (see Plate 16). Seven days earlier Mrs. Humphrey published his "Georgey a' Cock-horse," which showed Hanger parading down lower Grosvenor Street on his celebrated Scotch pony. This earlier print appears to have caused some ugly talk about Hanger's noble steed, presumably by George Hay, 16th Earl of Erroll, at Steven's Coffee House in St. James's Street (see Gillray's dedication). Erroll (1767–98), a Pittite, was a newly designated representative (Scottish) peer in the House of Lords.

Colonel Hanger is shown in profile, almost exactly as in the earlier view, with round hat, neckcloth, shirt frill and his fashionable "supple-jack" bludgeon, riding atop his exhausted pony's fabled potential cargo of calves. "Staggering Bob, with his yellow pumps" was contemporary Scots vernacular for a newly dropped calf with his yellow hoofs, ready to be killed for veal.

Baron Karl Friedrich von Münchausen (1720–97) was a garrulous, hyperbolic soldier of fortune. His adventures were first popularized in a pamphlet by Rudolf Erich Raspe, published at Göttingen (where Hanger had been to university) in 1785. Hanger's "own" rambling discourse is a reasonable parody of the style displayed in his (1801) *Life, Adventures and Opinions*. Richard Tattersall (1724–95) was a noted horse auctioneer whose establishment at Hyde Park Corner attracted the enthusiastic patronage of the Prince of Wales and his circle.

On 1 July 1797, the *Morning Post* referred to one or the other of Gillray's efforts as "the celebrated equestrian figure of George Hanger and his 'Pony.'"

[47]

END OF THE IRISH INVASION;—OR—THE DESTRUCTION OF THE FRENCH ARMADA. 20 January 1797

A disastrous day for the Opposition in the House of Commons (30 December 1796) coincides with a gale at Bantry Bay (27 December) that confounded a major French naval assault on southwest Ireland.

A French force of 15,000 regular troops under the command of General Lazare Hoche (see Plate 55) sailed from Brest on 15 December in a flotilla of transports escorted by twenty frigates and seventeen ships of the line. Hoche and his Irish advisers expected that a landing in the southwest of Ireland would touch off a popular uprising against the British. This plan was frustrated by a timely concurrence of wretched weather, poor discipline and inept seamanship. The "French Armada" came a cropper in much the same fashion as its Spanish prototype some 208 years before.

News of the dispersal of Hoche's fleet reached London on 31 December, one day after government winds in the House of Commons had blown the Opposition into a similarly desperate strait. Dundas strongly attacked Fox's pacific stand on the war. An address moved by Pitt offering "zealous support for measures likely to bring the war to a safe and honourable issue" found the embattled Foxites in a minority of 37 to 212.

Gillray shows the four winds, Pitt, Dundas, Grenville and Windham. The first two are blowing devastation on the ship "Le Revolutionare," which sports Fox as the carved figurehead. Another French warship, "L'Egalité," with tattered tricolor ensign, "Vive Egalite," is going down with all hands. In the foreground, the "Revolutionary Jolly Boat" (or dinghy) is swamped by a blast from Windham, the Secretary at War, confounding Sheridan,

Edward "Liberty" Hall (secretary of the Whig Club), Erskine, M. A. Taylor and Thelwall, who is losing a scroll of his "lectures" (see Plate 37). A sixth individual, boots in the air, has apparently lost a deck of cards. Etching with aquatint, reissued 1 June 1799 at a time of widespread French military setbacks.

[48]

"THE FEAST OF REASON, & THE FLOW OF SOUL."— I:E:—THE WITS OF THE AGE, SETTING THE TABLE IN A ROAR. 4 February 1797

The air is heavy with *bon mots, jeux d'esprit* and ribtickling rejoinders as Opposition wags enjoy a wild night at their tavern club.

John Courtenay, right (1741–1816, essayist, poet, orator, M.P. and abusive joker), chairman of a smoking club, gets off a "straight line" to Colonel Hanger (see Plate 46). Georgey's response convulses Fox ("O charming! charming!"), Sheridan ("Excellent!—damme Georgey, Excellent") and Michael Angelo Taylor ("Bravo! the best Thing I ever heard, said, damme").

Hanger has spilled his wine and broken his glass, conceivably in the full flush of a toast. Sheridan clutches his "Brandy," Taylor his "Mum" (a popular German beer brewed of barley malt and wheat, originally imported from Brunswick), and Courtenay is drinking "Champaign." The pipe-smoking simian in the Liberty cap over his head is sarcastically associated with Juvenal (Decimus Junius Juvenalis, A.D. 60?–140?), ferocious Roman moral satirist. The first part of Gillray's title is taken from Pope's *Imitation of Horace*, Book II, Satire 1 (c. 1733): "There, my retreat the best companions grace,/ Chiefs out of war, and statesmen out of place./ There St. John mingles with my friendly bowl/ The feast of reason and the flow of soul." The second part is based on Hamlet's allocution to Yorick's skull (Act V, Scene 1): "Where be your gibes now? your gambols? your songs? your flashes of merriment, that were wont to set the table on a roar?"

[49]

THE TABLE'S TURN'D. 4 March 1797

Left: Billy Pitt in the claws of Devil Fox as 1400 French terrorists land in South Wales. Right: Billy confounds his old devil with news of the defeat of the Spanish fleet at Cape St. Vincent.

Some 1400 French convicts and desperados, dubbed the *Légion Noire*, anchored at Ilfracombe in the Bristol Channel on 23 February. Their leader, one Colonel Tate (late of the U.S. Army), had orders to sack and burn Bristol, which he abandoned on learning of the approach of a large volunteer force. Crossing the Channel, Tate landed his brigade on the Pembrokeshire coast, where they were intimidated by village women (in scarlet cloaks) and subdued by local volunteers and by the

Pembrokeshire militia, which took them into custody. First word of the landing reached London two days later, precipitating a run on the Bank (see Plate 50). News of Tate's surrender arrived on Sunday, 26 February. The Opposition seized on the incident as an indication of weak coastal defense and general lack of preparedness.

Although Fox long had maintained that there was no invasion threat, he agreed with Pitt (31 October 1796) on the need to resist such an attack: ". . . be vigilant against the French; be vigilant also against the minister of this country. . . ." Gillray's hairy devil glories in Pitt's embarrassment: "Ha! Traitor!—there's the French landed in Wales! what d'ye think of that, Traitor?"

This brief exultation was terminated by the information (3 March) that Sir John Jervis (1735–1823) had defeated the Spanish fleet at Cape St. Vincent (off the southwest point of Portugal) on 14 February. This key triumph thwarted a French plan to join the Dutch and Spanish fleets with their own in an all-out assault on England.

In the second panel, Pitt waves a copy of the (London) *Gazette*, an official state journal published Tuesdays and Saturdays. It proclaims the "Defeat of the Spanish Fleet; by Sir John Jarvis." In his diary for 4 March, Lord Glenbervie observed that the "glorious news . . . occasioned a great flatness on the Opposition side of the debate last night on Mr. Whitbread's motion for an enquiry into the conduct of Administration relating to the defense of Ireland. . . ." "Ha! Mr. Devil!" says Pitt, "We've Beat the Spanish Fleet what d'ye think of that, Mr. Devil?"

Gillray's satire probably was originally conceived as a study of Opposition attitudes before and after news of the surrender of Colonel Tate reached London (special editions of the *Gazette* had come out on 25, 26 and 27 February). The news of Jervis' victory on Friday, 3 March, provided a perfect opportunity for a last-minute update.

[50]
MIDAS, TRANSMUTING ALL INTO PAPER. 9 March 1797

A financial panic triggered by Tate's landing in Wales forced the Bank of England to suspend gold payments on February 26.

> Of Augustus and Rome
> The poets still warble,
> How he found it of brick
> And left it of marble.
>
> So of Pitt and of England
> Men may say without vapour,
> That he found it of gold
> And left it of paper.
> —contemporary epigram

A satire on Pitt's political ascendancy, Opposition weakness and the French menace. A colossal Pitt, wearing a crown of the new one-pound notes, straddles the rotunda of the "Bank of England" (apparently a privy). His throat, the mouth of a sack of gold coins, is secured by a padlock, "Power of securing Public Credit." The "Key of Public Property" dangles from the little finger of his left hand.

Three joyous cabinet cherubs, Grenville, Windham and Dundas, affirm the "Prosperous state of British Finances. & the new plan for diminishing the National Debt—with Hints on the increase of Commerce." (On 28 February, Pitt said that the sudden drain on gold was unrelated to "any circumstance which could infer either the deficiency of the Bank or the unprosperous situation of the country. The rate of foreign exchanges were never more flourishing. . . .")

Inside the bank, the situation is greeted with apparent alarm. A stereotyped Jewish usurer departs with "Scrip"; two onlookers clutch their "Dividends."

In the distance, a fleet approaches from Brest and the sky is filled with an irradiated horde of dagger-waving sansculottes.

Gillray's accompanying "History of Midas" draws freely on the *Metamorphoses* of Ovid (43 B.C.–A.D. 18), who codified a series of legends concerning a king of Phrygia some 700 years earlier. Midas was supposed to have received one wish from the god Dionysus in return for favors conferred on the wine-demon Silenus. Granted the "golden touch," he later was released from it on condition that he bathe in the river Pactolus. In another tale, Midas was given donkey's ears by Apollo. These the king hid beneath a turban, concealed from everyone but his barber. Unable to contain his secret, the barber whispered it into a hole—which soon sprouted a crop of tattletale reeds. Gillray's version of the legend may be read beneath the picture. His reference to Midas' dedication to Bacchus is a direct hit at Pitt's known fondness for claret and port. Gillray's "Sedges" are (clockwise from the left) Grey, Sheridan, Fox, Erskine and Taylor. All wearing the *bonnet rouge*; all whisper, "Midas has Ears."

[51]
LE BAISER A LA WIRTEMBOURG. 15 April 1797

Prince Frederick of Württemberg greets his bride-to-be, Princess Charlotte, eldest daughter of the King. Published to mark the arrival in London of the "Great Bellygerent" for his marriage on 17 May.

Gillray's subtitle reference to the hardness of the times reflects a certain lack of enthusiasm for the Princess' dowry of £80,000. The matronly Princess Charlotte (born 1766) was perhaps the least marriageable of George III's bevy of daughters.

The Prince, bedripped and bedangled with ribbons, stars and orders, meets his fiancée more than halfway. Joseph Farington, the painter, noted in his diary that "[his] fat gives him an appearance like deformity . . . his manners are agreeable," adding on the authority of Lady Inchiquin that "each of them was agreeably disappointed at finding the other of better appearance than they expected" (*Diary*, James Grieg, ed., Lond, 1922–28, vol. 1, p. 207). He became Duke of Württemberg in 1797 and King in 1806 (see Plate VII), and died in 1816. His wife survived him, living until 1828.

[52]

LA PROMENADE EN FAMILLE.—A SKETCH FROM LIFE. 23 April 1797

The Duke of Clarence (1765–1837, later King William IV) takes a Sunday stroll with his great and good friend Dorothea Jordan and their three children.

The Duke of Clarence was the nautically inclined third son of George III (enlisted as able seaman at fifteen; stationed at New York 1782; promoted to captain 1785; rear admiral 1790). He formed an attachment with the noted actress and comedienne Mrs. Jordan which lasted from 1791 until 1811. By the time that the Duke felt obliged to withdraw in search of a potential queen and legitimate heirs, this liaison had produced ten children, eventually ennobled as Fitzclarences.

Dorothea Jordan (1762–1816) first acted in Dublin (1777) and made her London debut at Drury Lane in October 1785. She was supposed to have been the author of *The Spoiled Child*, a farce in which she appeared (1790) and to which the book in her hand refers: "Act IIId. enter Little Pickle" ("pickle" was accepted jargon for an "arch, waggish fellow" (*A Classical Dictionary of the Vulgar Tongue*, London, 1796). Mrs. Jordan's farewell performance at Covent Garden occurred in 1814. She died, and was buried, at St. Cloud near Paris.

Gillray's signpost "From Richmond To Bushy" alludes to Mrs. Jordan's home, Petersham House, at Richmond, and to Bushy Park, a royal preserve near Hampton Court of which the Duke of Clarence held the sinecure "rangership." The overland distance, about eight miles, would help to explain the royal fatigue.

The combination go-cart and phaeton is decorated with a crown and chamberpot design ("jordan" was a popular euphemism for chamberpot). From the Duke's pockets project a toy battleship, a belled whistle, a toy windmill and a doll. Drawn by Gillray "from life."

[53]

A CORNER, NEAR THE BANK;—OR—AN EXAMPLE FOR FATHERS. 26 September 1797

A pair of "trawlers" catch the fancy of an adventurous soul.

Unfortunately, modern scholarship has yet to improve on Thomas McLean's 1830 explanation: "This subject was designed to 'show up' the decrepid old P——, a notorious debauchée, too well known in the city for his depravity. He was a clerk at the Bank of England, and made himself infamous by his constantly associating with the frail ones of Elbow-lane. The resemblance of this hoary sinner was too striking, not to be recognized by all the frequenter's of Lloyd's, the Bank, and the Exchange."

Gillray's elegant tarts are decked out in an overblown style of the previous decade. Their anonymous admirer carries a volume of "Modest Prints."

[54]

THE FRIEND OF HUMANITY AND THE KNIFE-GRINDER. 4 December 1797

Gillray illustrates a poem from the new Pittite satirical weekly, *The Anti-Jacobin*. The verses ridicule "bleeding-heart liberals" in the abstract; the caricaturist zeroes in on George Tierney, parsimonious Whig M.P. for the Borough of Southwark, leading Opposition spokesman after the "secession" of Fox in May.

The Anti-Jacobin commenced publication on 20 November 1797, providing a brilliant circle of junior (and occasionally senior) ministers with a vehicle to combat the "lies, misrepresentations and mistakes" of the Opposition press.

The paper operated from "secret" editorial quarters on the second floor of a vacant house in Piccadilly next door to its printer. The moving force was George Canning (see p. xxii), aided by his Eton classmate John Hookham Frere, classicist and diplomat, and William Gifford, satirist, scholar and editor. They promised in their first number to share some of the "effusions of the *Jacobin* muse which happen to fall in our way," accompanied by "humble" imitations "in further illustration" of their principles.

The 23-year-old Robert Southey was the first "Bard of Freedom" upon whose "wood-notes wild" the editors of *The Anti-Jacobin* opened fire. They selected Southey's poem "The Widow" (Cold was the night wind; drifting fast the snows fell;/ Wide were the downs, and shelterless and naked;/ When a poor wand'rer struggled on her journey,/ Weary and way-sore . . .") as typical of a movement for "aggravating discontent in the inferior orders," and proceeded to improve upon it in their second issue (27 November) with the (famous) lines transcribed beneath Gillray's plate, published seven days later. ("A human being, in the lowest state of penury and distress, is a treasure to the reasoner of this cast," they observed.)

At this point Canning was successfully concluding a campaign of some two years' duration to secure Gillray's cooperation, and this unsigned etching is obviously one of the first fruits of the partnership. Frere wrote to Gillray's friend Rev. John Sneyd on 14 November asking for assistance in visualizing "A Jacobinical philanthropist first trying to excite discontent in an old ragged drunken knife grinder," presumably for Gillray's edification. "I need not remind you," Frere continued, "who so well understand the analogy between physiognomy and alliteration that the words 'needy knife grinder' indicate a thin long red nose, but I beg you to observe how carefully we have provided for the scenery and the background, the Checquers [tavern] and the parish stocks with the coach at a distance and a pampered menial behind." Apparently Sneyd's sketch did not reach the caricaturist in time and Frere was unhappy with the final result. The published satire eliminates the stocks, forsakes the "parish" for the city and adds a gratuitous swipe at Tierney. "Gillray has certainly bedevilled it and destroyed all the simplicity of the idea," Frere complained to Sneyd.

Tierney is not caricatured. The tavern sign hangs from a beam inscribed "Best Brown Stout." The lintel bears the words "Dealer in Brandy Rum & Gin." Gillray's "bedevilment" has a certain cogency. Tierney had just been returned as M.P. for Southwark after he successfully challenged his opponent with notorious breaches of the (commonly ignored) Treating Act, forbidding the dispensation of free beer.

[55]
THE APOTHEOSIS OF HOCHE. 11 [January] 1798

The late Lazare Hoche, fire-breathing French general and Anglophobe, rises from his blood-stained country into an extraordinary sansculotte heaven. Probably the most elaborate political "cartoon" ever published.

Lazare Hoche (1767–97) was an early aspirant for the role of post-revolutionary strongman which Bonaparte eventually claimed in November 1799. As early as 1793, when Hoche became a general at 27, he talked of leading an invasion of Britain. After pacifying a royalist peasant uprising in the Vendée (1795; see the lower right corner) and defeating an émigré army at Quiberon the same year, he appears to have thought of little else. He commanded the abortive assault on Ireland in December 1796 (see Plate 47) and helped plan the activities of the *Légion Noire* (Plate 49) in February 1797. Hoche was still trying to coordinate French and Dutch forces for another cross-Channel project when he died suddenly (apparently of natural causes) on 19 September at Wetzlar, his headquarters on the Rhine. The 31-year-old hero was accorded a state funeral in the grandest Parisian manner.

Gillray's vision of deification may well have been an effort to redeem himself with his associates at *The Anti-Jacobin* after their unhappiness with "The Friend of Humanity." In mid-December J. H. Frere informed John Sneyd that the caricaturist had not been seen for days. "I have taken your idea of the Jacobin Decalogue for an Apotheosis of Hoche—which I suggested to Gillray."

The result, some three weeks later, shows Hoche plucking a guillotine-lyre as he rides a rainbow into a grisly baroque Paradise dominated by a triangular symbol of Equality, irradiated with a sunburst of bayonets and daggers. Just below is Sneyd's decalogue of inverted commandments.

Hoche is welcomed by a mixed congregation of Jacobin cherubs, furies, severed winged heads, headless figures waving palm(?) fronds, monsters and revolutionaries who were themselves casualties of the Revolution. This last group (above Hoche at ten o'clock) includes Jean-Marie Roland (1734–93), a moderate Jacobin who committed suicide; Jean-Paul Marat (1743–93), assassinated in his bath; and a gathering of Girondist "martyrs" proscribed by the Convention on 31 May 1793. These are: Pétion (mayor of Paris 1791; suicide 1794); Barbaroux (lawyer, guillotined 1794); Louvet de Couvrai (scroll: "Recit de mes Perils"; novelist, politician, 1760–97, guillotined); and the Marquis de Condorcet (1743–94, mathematician and philosopher, presumed suicide in prison). More than one-sixth of the 361 deputies who condemned Louis XVI died violent deaths before 1799.

Gillray's plate was accompanied by a leaflet, presumably the work of Frere, purporting to be a description of Hoche's elevation, translated from a French newspaper. It is a blueprint for the satire: "The Soul of the Hero arose from the Dust, and reclining on the Tri-Coloured Bow of Heaven, tuned his soft Lyre . . . while millions of amputated heads charm his virtuous ears with the songs of Liberty!" (There is a copy of this extremely rare leaflet in the House of Lords Library, London.)

[56]
THE TREE OF LIBERTY,—WITH, THE DEVIL TEMPTING JOHN BULL. 23 May 1798

Pockets bulging with the (golden) pippins of constitutional monarchy, John Bull declines the rotten fruit of "Reform" dangled before him by Charles James Fox.

With the arrest and examination of leaders of various English radical groups, violent overthrow of the government continued to be a prime topic of speculation. At a meeting of the Whig Club on 1 May, Fox proposed toasts to "The sovereignty of the people of Great Britain" and "The sufferers in the cause of freedom in Ireland." Calling on "Friends of Liberty" to resist foreign domination, he said that "in happier times . . . it will be equally their duty to use every effort—I mean every justified and legal effort—to shake off the yoke of our English tyrants" (*Morning Post*, 2 May—a suggestion which particularly angered Gillray's "associates" on *The Anti-Jacobin*, drawing fire on 7 May). On 9 May the King struck Fox's name from the list of privy councillors.

On 4 January 1798, Fox had asked for "a radical reform" and "a complete and fundamental change of administration." Gillray's Opposition tree is based on "Envy," "Ambition" and "Disappointment"; its principal branches are the "Rights of Man" and "Profligacy." The former, capped with a "Libertè" bonnet, bears the fruit of "Democracy," "Plunder," "Revolution," "Murder," "Treason," "Slavery," "Conspiracy," "Corresponding Society" and "Whig Club." The latter branch supports "Atheism," "Blasphemy," "Impiety," "Deism" and "Age of Reason" (Paine's deistic book). To the rear, the British

Oak, its roots the "Commons," "King" and "Lords," its trunk of "Justice" dividing into "Laws" and "Religion," bears a crown and the golden pippins of "Freedom," "Happiness" and "Security."

The planting of a "tree of liberty," garlanded and betokened, was an established ceremony for French troops taking new territory, inspired by the "maypoles" erected by dissidents in colonial America as early as 1766. One of Gillray's first impressions on landing at Ostend in 1793 was of a pole on the quay "with the imperial [Austrian] arms on the top—on the spot where the Tree of Liberty had stood" (MS in author's possession).

John Bull turns down the "N'apple," since his "Pokes" (sacks or [?] pockets) are full of "Pippins" (slang for things admired) "from off t'other Tree." "Besides," he adds, "I hate Medlars, they're so domn'd rotten, that I'se afraid they'll gee me the Guts-ach for all their vine looks!" In addition to the pun on "meddler," the medlar serves the caricaturist's purpose well. It is a hedge tree of European origin bearing an astringent fruit which is not considered edible until on the point of decay: "vulgarly called an open a-se; of which it is more truly than delicately said, that it is never ripe till it is rotten as a t--d" (*A Classical Dictionary of the Vulgar Tongue*, London, 1796).

[57]

UNITED IRISHMEN IN TRAINING. 13 June 1798
UNITED IRISHMEN UPON DUTY. 12 June 1798

Deprived of leadership and denied French support, radical peasant factions of the "United Irishmen" commenced a month-long rampage on 23 May.

Societies of "United Irishmen" were formed in 1791 at various places to press for emancipation from Britain and for parliamentary reform. By 1795 the movement had been driven underground and, strengthened by working-class and peasant elements, was turning militant.

On 12 March 1798, their national "Directory" of leaders was arrested at Dublin, and five weeks later an undisciplined agrarian revolt ignited in several spots, notably County Wexford and East Ulster. After four weeks of fanatic anti-Protestant terrorism and pillage, loyal government troops prevailed. The city of Wexford, last point of major resistance, was reoccupied on 21 June.

Gillray's "trainees" practice their uncertain infantry skills on the effigy of a British soldier. They stand before the "Tree of Liberty" alehouse (see Plate 56), licensed for dispensation of "True French Spirits." Gillray's men "upon Duty" sack and burn the cottage of a sturdy peasant. The sword of the principal ruffian is labeled "Liberty." He wears a tricolor cockade and branch of green on his hat in colored impressions. The road leading to a military camp (flying the tricolor flag of "Equality") is crowded with expropriated livestock, primarily sheep. Beyond, underneath a waning moon, a town goes up in flames. Etchings with aquatint.

[58]

JOHN BULL TAKING A LUNCHEON:—OR—BRITISH COOKS, CRAMMING OLD GRUMBLE-GIZZARD WITH BONNE-CHÉRE. 24 October 1798

Horatio Nelson and his fellow admirals serve up a victory feast of French "Frigasees," guaranteed to tickle the national taste buds.

On 1 August 1798, Admiral Nelson's triumphant victory over the French fleet at Aboukir Bay, near Alexandria, stranded Bonaparte in Egypt. News of this event reached England on 26 September, upsetting the expectations and predictions of the Opposition. (Sheridan and Fox—"Oh, Curse his Guts, he'll take a chop at Us, next" —are shown through the window in full flight.)

Gillray uses the opportunity to salute both Navy and nation on a run of good fortune. John Bull, solidly entrenched beside a brimming jug of "True British Stout," tucks in with gusto, despite his disclaimer. He is working on a platter of demasted French warships, "Soup and Bouilli"—boiled beef, generally considered baby food. Nelson, minus the arm he lost at Tenerife (24 July 1797) and showing the head wound received on 1 August, carries a "List of French Ships—Taken Burnt & destroy[ed]."

He is flanked by Earl Howe (1726–99), Admiral of the Fleet, victor of the "Glorious First of June" (1794). At the far right, Admiral Duncan brings in "Dutch Cheese," alluding to the defeat on 11 October 1797 of a Franco-Dutch expedition to Ireland. Above and to the rear are additional entrees à la Gardiner, Bridport and Vincent. Sir Alan Gardiner served with Howe on the "First of June," a battle in which Gillray had a special interest (he spent some days at Portsmouth collecting material for P. J. de Loutherbourg's elaborate 1795 painting now in the National Maritime Museum, Greenwich). Admiral Sir Alexander Hood, later Viscount Bridport, was commander of the continental blockade (1797–1800) and, after 1796, Vice-Admiral of England. Admiral Sir John Jervis was created Earl of St. Vincent after the Battle of Cape St. Vincent in 14 February 1797 (see Plate 49). As a result of the same conflict, Nelson's expertise was widely praised for the first time. A paragraph in *The Times* of 13 March 1797, "Nelson's New Art of Cookery," may have given Gillray his lead.

John Bull's beribboned hat hangs over a print (?) of "Buonaparte in Egypt." A last course, "Desert à la Warren," is extended on a cake dish at top center. Two weeks before this satire was etched, on 11 and 12 October, Commodore Sir John Borlase Warren foiled yet another French invasion attempt on Ireland.

[59]

DOUBLÛRES OF CHARACTERS;—OR—STRIKING RESEMBLANCES IN PHISIOGNOMY. 1 November 1798

A short course in the art of caricature, "dedicated" to the celebrated Swiss physiognomist Johann Kaspar Lavater. Gillray's "Characters" are Fox, Sheridan, Norfolk, Tierney, Sir Francis Burdett, Derby and Bedford, all prominent Opposition leaders.

One of Gillray's rare periodical projects, this plate was published as a foldout in the *Anti-Jacobin Review and Magazine*, created to continue the work of Canning's original (see Plate 54), which had been terminated in July.

Lavater's influential treatise *Physiognomische Fragmente* (1775–78) argued that there was a direct and exact correlation between appearance, nature and moral character. This work was an immediate success; it was translated into French (1781–83) and into English (1789–98). Gillray etched a single illustration, after Fuseli, for the latter (1792). Lavater praises that in art which he finds morally uplifting. Raphael's purity was exemplary, Rembrandt's faces struck him as base and Hogarth's as singularly evil. He analyzed Fox in 1788 and saw nothing alarming.

Gillray plays on Fox as the Devil (see Plates 49, 56), Sheridan as avaricious (Plate I) and Norfolk as a drunk. Burdett (1770–1844), anti-war M.P. and advocate of reform, is compared with "Sixteen-string Jack," a highwayman. For the Duke of Bedford, see Plate 74; Newmarket was, and is, a celebrated mecca for racing enthusiasts on the Suffolk-Cambridgeshire border. Soft-ground etching.

[60]

STEALING OFF;—OR—PRUDENT SECESION. 6 November 1798

Charles James Fox quits the House of Commons in terror as his cringing colleagues eat their "disloyal" words. William Pitt, offstage, confronts them with an inventory of governmental triumphs and accomplishments in one hand, and "proof" of their treason in the other.

Fox still remained in the self-imposed exile from the House of Commons which began in May 1797. In his frozen leap, he is joined by fellow "secessionists" Charles Grey (an "Opposition Gray-Hound") and M. A. Taylor.

Gillray looks forward to the new sitting of Parliament on 20 November, when after a recess of some four and a half months the Opposition would have to face up to a number of new "embarrassments." He shows the embattled Whigs, "cornered" by "successes": "Destruction of Buonaparte," "Capture of the French Navy," "End of the Irish Rebellion," "Voluntary Associations," "Europe Arming" and "Britannia Ruling the Waves." The document in the unseen Premier's left hand, "O'Conner's list of Secret Traitors," refers to Author O'Connor (1763–1852), an Irish patriot acquitted of treason at Maidstone, Kent, in May 1798 after testimony in his behalf by Fox, Sheridan, Erskine, the Duke of Norfolk and the future sixth Duke of Bedford. O'Connor's subsequent admission of guilt, in testimony on 21 August before a committee

of the Irish House of Commons, was a devastating blow to Opposition credibility.

Pitt commands: "Read o'er This!—and after This! And then to Breakfast, with what appetite you may!!!" (a reference to *Henry VIII*, Act III, Scene 2). The candle stubs in the sconces suggest an all-night session. In the foreground of Gillray's "democratic Déjeuné," Tierney consumes an "Homage to the French Conv[ention]" and Sheridan munches "Loyalty of the Irish Nation." They are pressing in to fill the vacant space between them, marked by the hat of "C. Fox." Behind them, Sir George Shuckburgh eats "French lib[erty]," the egotistical Erskine eats "my own Loyalty," an unidentified member·eats "Peace or Ruin," Burdett eats "Egalité" (see Plate VI) and John Nicholls (1745–1802, M.P. for Tregony, Cornwall) eats a "Letter to W Pitt." The Speaker's chair is (apparently) occupied by Henry Addington, who held the post from 1789 to 1801. The great mace is in its proper place, unlike Plate I. Etching with aquatint.

[61]

FIGHTING FOR THE DUNGHILL:—OR—JACK TAR SETTL'ING BUONAPARTE. 20 November 1798

Another patriotic spin-off of Nelson's August victory in the Battle of the Nile: John Bull's seagoing alter ego sends the French menace reeling.

The British sailor wears the inscription "Britannia Rules the W[aves]" on his hat. His adversary, lacerated, nose bleeding, abdomen sporting a bruise labelled "Nelson," appears about to fall into oblivion. Bonaparte wears a huge cocked hat with tricolor cockade and sleeve ruffles which perpetuate the durable stereotype of the Frenchman as a ragged fop. Jack Tar's toe rests on Malta, which commenced a revolt against French occupation on 2 September, under the protection of a British blockade. Etching with aquatint.

[62]

SIEGE DE LA COLONNE DE POMPÉE.—SCIENCE IN THE PILLORY. 6 March 1799

Personal letters from disgruntled French officers in Bonaparte's Egyptian command had been intercepted by the British Navy and published in London. Gillray offered this vision of French "savants" in difficulties with the natives, assuring his audience that it had been etched "from the Original Intercepted Drawing."

When Bonaparte arrived in Egypt in July 1798, he was accompanied by a 170-man scientific commission which included engineers, mechanics, surveyors, cartographers, interpreters, mathematicians, artists, musicians and poets. The Institut d'Egypte was officially installed at Cairo on 23 August, with a library, workshop, botanical collection and printing plant. Field parties of archaeologists were sent out, one of which eventually located the Rosetta Stone.

George Canning wrote an anonymous introduction to the third series of intercepted letters, published in 1800, and as Under-secretary of State in the Foreign Office, was probably instrumental in getting them into print. It seems highly likely that Canning (or one of his friends; see Plate 54) assisted in the conception of this satire, which is based on several sheets of detailed "suggestions" in the British Museum (Add. MSS. 27,337, ff. 191–204).

According to R. S. Kirby's *Wonderful and Scientific Museum*, published in 1803, the column in question (erected in honor of Diocletian rather than Pompey) stood a quarter of a league beyond the south gate of Alexandria (vol. 1, p. 95). It was 114 feet tall and made of red granite. A base fifteen feet square supported a ninety-foot shaft surmounted by a Corinthian capital. The pillar was visible from the sea, and had long been an aid to navigation. That it could actually have accommodated the group shown by Gillray was demonstrated in 1781 by eight inebriated officers of the British navy who managed to hold a party on the top.

The column was reportedly measured by some of Bonaparte's *savants* while they were weak from thirst and hunger—a spectacle one of them later described as "un beau sujet de caricature" (François Charles-Roux, *Bonaparte, Gouverneur d'Egypte*, Paris, 1936, p. 131). According to the inscription, the incident "illustrated" took place on "5 Frimaire, 7th Year of the Republic" (27 November 1798).

Atop the column, the leader clutches a proclamation: "Vive Mohamet Qui protegoit les Sciences" (Long live Mohammed, defender of science). The colleague who clutches him has a "Plan for Burning Mecca" in his pocket. Various other plans, measuring instruments, tables and reference works rain down on the attackers. The Bedouin at the bottom left is felled by a "Project for Fraternization with the Bedouins." To his right a marksman brings down the balloon "Diligence d'Abissynie" (Abyssinian coach). Its former passengers drop pamphlets concerning "The Velocity of Falling Bodies" and "Aerial Navigation." The desperate soul about to lose his grip on the capital carries a "Plan for Making Man Immortal." The verses at the bottom right contrast the supposed burning of the ancient (Greek) library at Alexandria by one "Amru" (probably Amr Ibn Al-as, c. 580–644, Muslim conquerer of Alexandria, 642) with current practices. The "Hebert" mentioned in the verses was Jacques-René Hébert (1757–94), savage Jacobin editor and propagandist.

[63]

THE TWIN STARS, CASTOR & POLLUX. 7 May 1799

George Barclay and Charles Sturt, concurrent Members of Parliament for the town of Bridport, Dorset, are cast as the inseparable twin brothers of Greek mythology.

Messrs. Barclay and Sturt cannot be found to have distinguished themselves above and beyond their generosity of proportion and their shared constituency. (Bridport enjoyed double representation from the thirteenth century until 1868, and a single member until 1885, when county voting districts were redrawn.)

George Barclay (c. 1759–1819), son of a London merchant, was first returned for Bridport in March 1795, and subsequently in 1796, 1802 and 1806. He was a director of the Royal Exchange Assurance Company, and notwithstanding the tankard, appears to have had no connection with the family of brewers. His companion, Charles Sturt (1763–1812) of Crichel More, Dorset, sat for Bridport from 1784 until 1802. Judging from this composition's place in a six-plate *New Pantheon of Democratic Mythology*, both were aligned with the Opposition.

In Greek mythology, Castor and Pollux were sons of Leda and Zeus (masquerading as a swan during his courtship). They were renowned for their athletic prowess, and ultimately enshrined as heavenly constellations.

[64]

THE GOUT. 14 May 1799
A soft-ground etching.

[65]

THE STATE OF THE WAR—OR—THE MONKEY-RACE IN DANGER. 20 May 1799

Armies of the Second Coalition (Great Britain, Russia, Turkey and Austria) inflicted a series of defeats and reversals on French forces in Europe and the Mideast during the spring of 1799.

Simian French troops, wearing cockaded *bonnets rouges*, fall prey to the ferocity of a British lion, a crescent-headed Turkish monster, a Russian bear and the Austrian double-headed eagle. The Turk menaces an ape-like officer who drops a paper marked "Organisation of Egypt, & Triumph of Buonaparte" (see Plate 62). On the day this satire was published, Bonaparte finally abandoned the siege of Acre against Turks supported by the British, and withdrew toward Egypt (see Plate 67). For the time being, the French were falling back before the Austrians in Germany and before the Austrians and Russians in Italy.

[66]

ALLIED-POWERS, UN-BOOT-ING EGALITÈ. 1 September 1799

The powers of the Second Coalition gang up on France (personified by Bonaparte), depriving him of his ill-gotten Italian "boot" and booty.

A patriotic summary of continuing French difficulties at the hands of the Russians and the Austrians in Italy, the Turks in the Mideast, the British at sea and the surreptitious Dutch (thought to be on the verge of regaining their autonomy; see Plates 44 and 45).

While Britannia ruled the waves, after a fashion (1796–97), the French had been extending their grasp on the Continent. Young General Bonaparte's Italian conquests made him a national hero. However, the balance began to shift with his expedition to Egypt (commencing in May 1798), which provoked the alliance of Britain, Russia and Turkey. The generally meddlesome foreign policy of the French Directory increased the attractiveness of concerted action, and the Austrians finally resumed hostilities with France in March 1799, eighteen months after Bonaparte had forced them out of the First Coalition. Russians and Austrians, under the Russian General Suvorov, defeated the French at Cassano on 27 April, took Turin on 26 May and completed the French defeat in Italy with the Battle of Trebbia, 17–19 June.

Gillray's Austrian is a fierce hussar. His Turk prepares to add Bonaparte's nose to his collection of appendages with a sword labeled "St Jean d Acre" (see Plate 67). John Bull, or rather Jack Tar (see Plate 61), wears ribbons saluting Admirals Nelson, Duncan and Bridport (see Plate 58). He holds the Frenchman immobile for the Turk (see Plate 67), his right foot firmly planted on the "Dutch Cheese" which a fat Dutchman (resembling the exiled Stadtholder, William V) is preparing to claim. The paper, "Secret Expedition," beneath the latter's knee, refers to an abortive English attempt to liberate Holland with the aid of Russians and loyal Orangists. The mission embarked on 13 August from Ramsgate and Deal, and captured the Dutch fleet on 30 August. (This news reached London two days after the print was published.) In the background, tiny Dutch (?) figures cavort around a burning "liberty tree."

The ascendancy of the Second Coalition was to be short-lived. Pitt's campaign in the Netherlands was abandoned as an utter failure by mid-October. Meanwhile, Bonaparte had been acquainted with the critical state of French domestic affairs (ironically through newspapers supplied to his officers by Sidney Smith), and as this satire appeared, was rushing back from Egypt to fill the vacuum on the home front.

[67]

Sir Sidney Smith. 10 November 1799

British hero of the siege of Acre: a "straight" ceremonial portrait which points up Gillray's singular incapacity for flattery.

As this extraordinary likeness implies, Sir William Sidney Smith (1764–1840) was mercurial, arrogant and vain. At the time of publication he was the toast of the town, *in absentia*, for his successful support of the embattled Turkish fortress town of St. Jean d'Acre on the Syrian coast (present-day Israel) just north of Haifa.

Bonaparte, still isolated in Egypt after Nelson's victory of August 1798 (Plate 58), laid siege to Acre on 21

March 1799. Smith, nominally envoy plenipotentiary to Constantinople, led a British squadron which effectively provisioned the embattled pasha of Acre. He also intercepted French artillery arriving by sea, adding these to the defensive batteries of the tiny peninsular bastion. After 61 days, Bonaparte withdrew on 20 May; some 2200 of 13,000 French troops had been killed, another 2300 were severely wounded or ill. It was his first defeat, and the only one he would suffer before the battle of Aspern in May 1809.

Smith had enlisted in the navy at eleven in 1775. He was a captain at seventeen, knighted at 27 and a rear admiral at 41 (in 1805). Always something of a firebrand and adventurer, Smith was chasing French privateers when he was captured off Normandy in April 1796 and held prisoner in Paris for two years. Sir Sidney escaped from the Temple on 24 April 1798, as Bonaparte's Egyptian task force gathered at Toulon.

Napoleon managed to make his retreat from Acre look like a triumphal procession. This illusion was capped by his decisive victory on 26 July over the Turkish army (again supported by Sir Sidney), which had chased him back into Egypt. French officers visiting Smith's flagship to arrange an exchange of prisoners returned to their commander with European newspapers which brought him up to date on domestic military, political and financial crises. Bonaparte reached France on 9 October and wrested power from the Council of Five Hundred by martial coup the day this plate was published. Etching with aquatint, colored by hand.

[68]

French-Taylor, fitting John Bull with a "Jean de Bry." 18 November 1799

The latest Parisian monstrosity is tried and found wanting: a satire on sartorial and political "freedom" under the Directory.

A spoof on the grotesque, extravagant and purposely sloppy fashions for men which blossomed in Paris after the fall of the puritanical Jacobins, and on the spectrum of official costumes prescribed for government functionaries (these had been designed for them in 1795 by the painter David).

Gillray's John Bull, even more oafish and salt-of-the-earth than usual, falls prey to the spirit of revolution in the stock guise of a ragged French fop (in earlier days he was more apt to be a gentleman's gentleman or a dancing-master). John is crammed into a bizarre overstuffed jacket named in honor of the revolutionary politician and diplomat Jean-Antoine de Bry (1760–1834), who had narrowly escaped assassination at the Congress of Rastatt (Austria) on the 28th of April preceding. Gillray's notion of this style coincides roughly with the garment worn by De Bry for his portrait by David (reproduced in *Art News Annual*, 1945–46, p. xl).

The Englishman stands on a volume of "Nouveaux Costumes"; he is decked out in bizarre tasseled jackboots and a curled Brutus wig. On the wall, a framed set of "Des Habillement François" show simian figures in David's exotic neoclassical outfits: "Membre du Directo[ire]," "Conseil des Anciens," "Ministre," "Conseil des 5 Cents" (Council of Five Hundred), "Juge ——" and "Administrat[ion Municipale]." These hang over a list of rules "pour les Modes" which terminates, ironically, "Vive la Libertè." Gillray previously travestied these garments one by one in a series of *French Habits* worn by the English Opposition (April–May 1798).

The tailor explains the joys of liberation from the "tight Aristocrat Sleeve," urging "von leetel National Cockade" to achieve the Paris "look." John is unconvinced.

[69]

DEMOCRACY;—OR—A SKETCH OF THE LIFE OF BUONAPARTE. 12 May 1800

In February 1800, Bonaparte's takeover as First Consul was confirmed by plebiscite and he moved into the royal palace, Les Tuileries, as virtual monarch. Gillray travesties his rise as a "mushroom" of the French Revolution.

This savage "history" is one of the earliest prototypes of the modern Sunday adventure comic. Executed with a sparkle and finesse reminiscent of Callot, the sequence marks the rise of a preoccupation with finely wrought "book" illustrations that may well have inspired the illfated 1801 edition of the *Poetry of The Anti-Jacobin* (see p. xxii). Two weeks later Gillray signed a memorandum with a publisher calling for the execution of some forty designs over the following six months.

In May 1801, Gillray expressed reservations about a commission to illustrate a new biography of the French leader. "I fear there will be very little room for humour in the life of such a cut throat," he wrote.

The caricaturist's initial treatment of the subject traces Bonaparte's progress from his childhood in Corsica: "Democratic Innocence." Napoleon was born at Ajaccio on 15 August 1768, second of eight children of Carlo and Letizia Buonaparte to survive infancy. His father, of noble birth but comparatively humble circumstances, was then a chief lieutenant of the Coriscan nationalist Paoli. Napoleon had four brothers, three of whom would become kings, and three sisters, including a future queen and a grand duchess.

"Democratic Humility." At nine, young Bonaparte was taken to France and placed in the Collège of Autun, under a military scholarship solicited from the Crown by his father. After three months he was transferred to a military school at Brienne. In October 1784 he commenced a year's study at the Ecole Militaire in Paris, from which he emerged at sixteen as a second lieutenant

of artillery. Gillray shows the commandant with plans of fortifications and a volume, "Principe Militaire," sitting beneath a plaque "by the benevolence of the King." The most prominent student carries a book, "Sur l'Exercise Manuel." A portrait of Louis XVI is decapitated by the upper margin.

"Democratic Gratitude" refers to Bonaparte's "whiffof-grapeshot" defense of the National Convention against a (partially) Royalist uprising on the 13th of Vendémiaire (5 October 1795). The banner is inscribed "Vive lè Egalité."

"Democratic Religion." In the East, Napoleon had encouraged his Moslem "hosts" to believe that he and his men were contemplating an imminent conversion to Islam. His proclamation to the Arabic people on landing in Egypt was published in the *London Chronicle* (27 September 1798): "The French are true Mussulmen. Not long since they marched to Rome, and overthrew the Throne of the Pope, who excited the Christians against the Professors of Islamism." One Turk (extreme left) reads a book, "Alcoran" (the Koran). Bonaparte is smoking a hookah.

"Democratic Courage." General Bonaparte deserts his ragged, sleeping troops at the approach of a Turkish army. For his departure from Egypt (18 August 1799) see note to Plate 67.

"Democratic Honor." Under the banner of "Libertè," Bonaparte tramples the "Constitution de l'Ann. 3" (1795): a view of the coup d'état of the 19th of Brumaire (10 November 1799). The Council of Five Hundred, wearing David's formal costume (see Plate 68), is put to flight. "Arrests" and "Orders" litter the floor. The presidential canopy is labelled "Vive la Convention Une & Indivisible." In actuality, the president was Napoleon's brother, Lucien, who supported the coup.

"Democratic Glory" shows the new First Consul, supported by the military, wearing the costume and hat of a member of the Directory. His scepter is tipped by a microscopic figure of Fame, his throne by a sunburst and an eagle clutching a terrestrial globe. These emblems of ascendancy, conquest and domination are given an Eastern twist by the palm-tree motif, the incense burner and the abject character of the "Homage du Senat Conservatif" at the lower right. A group in the garments of the Council of Five Hundred presents an "Adresse du Corps Legislatif." A figure to the left of the Consul extends an "Address de Tribunate." The ex-abbé Emmanuel Sieyès is introduced as a conspiratorial influence behind the throne; in actuality he had been demoted from Director to Senator.

The visionary dénouement, "Democratic Consolations," promises an "Apotheosis" for Bonaparte similar to that provided Lazare Hoche two years before (Plate 55). A woman's hand extends a cup of poison; the head of his truckle-bed is a guillotine.

Etching, colored by hand. Each panel of the original measures 4⅛ by 4¼ inches.

[70]

DIDO, IN DESPAIR! 6 February 1801

Emma, Lady Hamilton, turns from a slumbering spouse to lament the departure of her "Aeneas"—Lord Nelson.

Dido, founder and Queen of Carthage, was coupled by Vergil with the mythical Trojan hero Aeneas. According to the poet, she committed suicide after her peripatetic lover obeyed a command from Jupiter, ordering him on to Italy and duty.

In 1793 Horatio Nelson made the acquaintance of Sir William Hamilton (1730–1803), British minister at Naples, and his celebrated wife Emma, then in her late twenties. Lady Hamilton helped to secure provisions for Nelson's fleet on his Mediterranean pursuit of Bonaparte in 1798 (see Plate 58), and their friendship ripened after his return from the Battle of the Nile.

After Hamilton's recall, the trio returned to London together overland with fanfare and popular adulation. Arriving in November 1800, Nelson formally separated from his wife, and the public received continuing indications of his high regard for Lady Hamilton. On 1 January 1801 he was promoted to vice admiral and on 17 January he hoisted his flag as second in command of the Channel fleet. On or about 30 January, Emma Hamilton gave birth to his daughter, Horatia. (Nelson sailed for the Baltic on 12 March and led a daring attack on Copenhagen, 2 April.)

Gillray's heroine postures theatrically. An open album on the divan, "Studies of Academic Attitudes taken from the Life," refers to a series of twelve drawings by F. Rehberg published in 1794, showing Lady Hamilton's famous "attitudes" or public tableau-vivant evocations of paintings and statues. A garter, "The Hero of the Nile," lies between her slippers. The *objets d'art* at the lower right include a booklet, "Antiquities of Herculaneum, Naples Caprea &c," medallions, coins and statuettes of Pri[apus, Greek god of fertility (?)], Messalina (unfaithful third wife of the Roman emperor Claudius), Venus and a satyr. On the dressing table: a flask of maraschino, a comb, a pincushion, a "Composing Draught" and a container of "Rouge à la Naples."

After the Peace of Amiens (March 1802), Nelson and the Hamiltons settled down in the former's house at Merton, Surrey, for a brief, blissful *ménage à trois*.

[71]

A COGNOCENTI CONTEMPLATING YE BEAUTIES OF YE ANTIQUE. 11 February 1801

Connoisseur Sir William Hamilton rivets his gaze on a damaged bust of Lais, celebrated mistress of an ancient philosopher. His other "treasures" are equally pertinent to the highly public affair between his wife and Lord Nelson.

The caricaturist expands on the possibilities of the bric-a-brac introduced into Dido's bedchamber the previous week (preceding plate). Sir William Hamilton served as British envoy to the Court of Naples from 1764 until 1800. He was a noted antiquarian and collector; many of his acquisitions in time found their way to the British Museum. Hamilton was also a student of the action of volcanos, on which subject he produced several treatises between 1772 and 1783.

At the upper left a meretricious figure of Cleopatra, gin bottle in hand, reaches toward a Mark Antony resembling Nelson. They are bracketed by the horns of Apis, sacred bull god of ancient Egypt. At the top center a volcano erupts, and at the right Hamilton, framed under cuckold's antlers, is shown as the Emperor Claudius (41–54 A.D.; see preceding note). A frigid figure of Midas, with the ears of an ass (see Plate 50), is below.

Beneath Apis, a headless figure displays a bunch of grapes, the three Graces dance on a cracked chamberpot and Cupid weeps over a bent arrow. The central figure of Lady Hamilton as Lais alludes to the Corinthian mistress of the philosopher Aristippus of Cyrene (B.C. 435(?)–356), a lady of legendary beauty. Among the items on the floor there is a damaged pitcher with marine embellishment and a jester's scepter.

Hamilton died on 6 April 1803.

[72]

LILLIPUTIAN-SUBSTITUTES, EQUIPING FOR PUBLIC SERVICE. 28 May 1801

After seventeen years as First Lord of the Treasury, William Pitt stepped down on 7 March as the result of a disagreement with the King regarding political concessions for Roman Catholics. A new Tory administration formed by Pitt's close friend Henry Addington is welcomed by Gillray in the spirit of Jonathan Swift.

On 5 May, Charles James Fox told the Whig Club that a situation might arise "in which the King may not only rule us by his Jack-boot, but we may be governed by his Jack-boot's Jackboot." The new Prime Minister, balancing on the "Treasury Bench," decked out in Pitt's Windsor coat and enormous boot, reflects on the splendid fit of his new uniform.

At the left, Lord Eldon is enveloped in the trailing wig of Loughborough, his predecessor as Lord Chancellor. He exults: "O such a Day as This, so renown'd so victorious, Such a Day as This, was never seen!" In front of Addington, Hawkesbury, the new Foreign Secretary, wallows in the outsized breeches of Lord Grenville. To the right, Lord Hobart sports the tent-like kilt of Dundas, whom he succeeded as Secretary of State for War and the Colonies. His references to crocodiles and the Baltic concern Nelson's victories at Aboukir Bay and Copenhagen. His weapon, a "little Andrew Ferrara," takes its name from one Andrea Ferrar, a noted Highland cutler famous for his broadswords.

At the right, Sylvester Douglas, Lord Glenbervie, the new Joint Paymaster-General, tries on "Mr. C[an]n[in]g's Old Slippers." The background figures are, from the extreme left, Lord St. Vincent, who succeeded Lord Spencer at the Admiralty; Edward Law (created Baron Ellenborough in 1802), the new Attorney-General; and Charles Yorke, who followed Windham as Secretary of State for War. The two new Treasury secretaries (wearing inkwells) are John Hiley Addington, the Prime Minister's brother, and Nicholas Vansittart, later a Chancellor of the Exchequer.

Gillray's patron, Canning, resigned with Pitt and there is little question that the caricaturist's pension (see p. xxii) was promptly halted by the Addingtonians. Canning had been extremely loath to give up his place, and to turn over to Glenbervie the house that went with it. This plate, signed by Gillray as having been drawn and etched (but not invented) by him, almost surely is of Canning's, or Canningite, inspiration. It marks the starting shot of a lively barrage of verse and epigram in which Canning and his friends charged the Addington government with incompetence, insignificance and nepotism. The following comment on a proposal for blockhouses in the Thames estuary is a fair example:

> If blocks can the nation deliver,
> Two places are safe from the French;
> The first is the mouth of the river,
> The second the Treasury Bench.

[73]
ANACREONTICK'S IN FULL SONG. 1 December 1801

As the hour approaches four in the morning, a tavern club raises its collective voice in the "Anacreontic Anthem," a melody applied some thirteen years later to Francis Scott Key's "Star Spangled Banner."

Anacreon was a Greek lyric poet of the sixth century B.C. with a legendary fondness for wine and themes of love. His distinctive meter and philosophy were perpetuated by later Greek writers in a body of *Anacreontea*, of which some eighty poems or fragments were translated by Thomas Moore and published in 1800 as *Odes of Anacreon*. A group of free and festive spirits formed the Anacreontick Society in 1766, customarily opening their meetings with the "Anacreontick Song" (from which Gillray derived the lines at the top of the composition). The society flourished for some four decades, joined by a variety of other music and drinking clubs for patrons of almost any class and taste. In the nineteenth century this tradition gradually evolved through the tavern "music saloon" to the elaborate "music halls" of the high Victorian era.

A stanza of the "Anacreontick Song" published in 1801 (see the song sheet at extreme left) concludes with an exhortation from "Anacreon in Heav'n" (to the tune of "the rockets' red glare"):

> Voice, fiddle and flute, no longer be mute,
> I'll lend you my name and inspire you to boot.
> And besides I'll instruct you like me to entwine,
> The myrtle of Venus with Bacchus's vine.

(Myrtle, an aromatic evergreen shrub, was traditionally an emblem of love; "Bacchus's vine" is, of course, the grape.)

A songbook, the *Anacreontic Collection* (no date), contains this description of the Society: "His Royal Highness, the Prince of Wales and the Duke of Orleans are members . . . the other contributory members are chiefly bon-vivant noblemen, military officers of rank, gentlemen of the learned professions, rich and respectable citizens, and other men of distinction in life." Gillray's gathering includes a mixture of bucolic "squires" and city bucks, with a slumbering Unitarian minister and an officer added for good measure.

The portrait is of the "patron saint," quill in one hand, verses in the other. Beneath the clock a tiny figure of Time, clutching a wine bottle, straddles a barrel in the manner of artists' representations of Bacchus. The incidental debris includes the makings of a fruit punch, wine bottles, glasses, clay pipes and a snuffbox. Etching with aquatint.

[74]
FAT-CATTLE. 16 January 1802

The Duke of Bedford admires another triumph of selective breeding.

Francis Russell, the fifth Duke of Bedford (1765–1802), first president of the Smithfield Club, was noted for his accomplishments as a breeder of sheep and cattle. A member of the Prince of Wales's circle as a young man, the Duke devoted a large part of his later life to agricultural experimentation. He died (unmarried) some six weeks after the publication of this plate, and was succeeded by his brother.

The ironic reference to Burke recalls the stateman's scathing attack on the Duke in his "Letter to a Noble Lord" of February 1796. This blast came as an answer to Bedford's criticism of Burke's pension in the House of Lords (1 December 1795).

The *Illustrative Description* of Gillray's work published in 1830 observed that there was no beauty without utility. "What beauty can be discovered in an oil-cake-fed oblong ox, or a cubical ram, is only to be known by the scientific; and as for the utility of gorging a sow on barley-meal until she becomes prematurely barren, and is choaked of fat, it is a question to be answered only by the elite of the Agricultural Society."

(The caul is an intestinal fold. Tallow, a hard whitish fat, was sought for candles, leather dressings, soaps and lubricants.)

[75]
THE COMFORTS OF A RUMFORD STOVE. 12 June 1800

Benjamin Thompson, Count Rumford, American-born inventor, philosopher, public benefactor and egotist, demonstrates the efficiency of his improved fireplace design.

Benjamin Thompson was born at Woburn, Massachusetts, on 26 March 1753. After an early career as schoolmaster and soldier, activities as a loyalist spy prompted his imprisonment and flight to England in 1776. In London, 1766–80, Thompson pursued science and politics, returning to the colonies in 1781 as lieutenant colonel of the King's American Dragoons, a unit of his own devising. After the Revolution, he entered the service of the Elector of Bavaria at Munich, by whom he was knighted (1784) and raised to the honor of Count in the Holy Roman Empire (1791). (Thompson selected the title Rumford after the original name of Concord, New Hampshire, where he had lived from 1772 to 1774.)

During the decade prior to his relocation in London (1795) Rumford wrote extensively on heat, radiation, fuel economy and the science of cookery. His "new contrivance for roasting meat" was quickly dubbed the "Rumford Roaster" and achieved wide acceptance on both sides of the Atlantic. (One of the Count's later contributions was a blueprint for the drip coffeepot.)

The first volume of Rumford's collected works, published late in 1796, included an essay on "Chimney Fireplaces with Proposals for Improving Them to Save Fuel, to Render Dwelling Houses More Comfortable and Salubrious, and Effectually to Prevent Chimneys from Smoking." His innovations hinged on a new understanding of the action of convection currents, and involved the introduction of the modern narrow throat, smoke shelf and damper. Rumford's new fireplace had been installed in a number of fashionable London homes by early 1796, and a letter of commendation from Sir John Sinclair, President of the Board of Agriculture, was included with the essay referred to above. The satirist Peter Pindar hailed the Count as "Knight of the dish-clout":

> Lo, every parlour, drawing room, I see,
> Boasts of thy stoves and talks of naught but thee.

In 1799 Rumford founded the Royal Institution, dedicated, said its prospectus, to the "general diffusion of a spirit of experimental investigation . . . among the higher ranks of society." Cynics noted that the Institution's proposed display of mechanical inventions appeared to revolve around the Count's own achievements, and that the initial series of lectures, delivered by Dr. Thomas Garnett (1766–1802), were preoccupied with matters of heat, cold, shelter and cookery. These lectures were in progress when Gillray's caricature appeared.

According to McLean's 1830 commentary, Rumford purchased a number of impressions of this plate at Mrs. Humphrey's, distributing them to friends with the inscription: "This is so much more like the Count—than he is himself, that when you look upon it, you cannot fail to think of your humble servant—the donor." Rumford moved to France in 1802 and died at Auteuil in 1814.

[76]

—"ALL BOND-STREET TREMBLED AS HE STRODE."—
8 May 1802

The Hon. James Duff, heir to the Earl of Fife, sets out on his morning promenade.

Colonel James Duff (1776–1857), 26 at the time this caricature appeared, is modishly decked out in a coat resembling the "Jean de Bry" of Plate 68.

Duff was educated at Edinburgh, and married in September 1779 to Mary Caroline Manners. In 1808 he enlisted his purse and person in the Spanish army and fought against the French in the Peninsular campaign, retiring with the rank of major general in 1810. Duff was wounded at the battle of Talavera (27–28 July 1809). The same year he succeeded to the family title as the fourth Earl of Fife in the Scottish peerage, and in 1827 entered the English peerage as the first Baron Fife. He was a great friend and confidant of George IV.

[77]

INTRODUCTION OF CITIZEN VOLPONE & HIS SUITE, AT PARIS. 15 November 1802

Charles James Fox, "Citizen Volpone," is received by Bonaparte at the Tuileries on 3 September 1802, during the thirteen-month calm offered by the Peace of Amiens.

The signing of the Peace of Amiens on 27 March led to a temporary respite in the long war with France. Perhaps the most celebrated of the stream of English tourists to take advantage of this opportunity was Charles James Fox. Still in his "retirement" from parliamentary affairs (see Plate 60), the Opposition leader was seeking source material for his history of James II and the Revolution of 1688. (Note the "Original Jacobin Manuscript" protruding from his pocket.)

Fox was received with great ceremony and adulation as befitted a long-time advocate of peace with the French. He was welcomed at Calais by the exiled Irish patriot-traitor Arthur O'Connor (see Plate 60) and journeyed to Paris, where he remained twelve days. Gillray's delegation is composed, left to right, of O'Connor (a paper, "Trial of O'Conner at Maid[stone]" is in his pocket); Mrs. Fox, Elizabeth Armistead, whose marriage to "The Man of the People" had been revealed on the eve of departure; Fox himself; Thomas Erskine; Lady Holland; Lord Holland (Fox's nephew); and, groveling, Robert Adair. Adair (1763–1855), a Whig M.P., was supposed to have intrigued against Pitt in Russia (1791) and to have written pro-French articles for the *Morning Chronicle*. His pockets contain "Revolutionary Odes, by Citizen Baw-ba-dara" (Bob Adair; alluding to an *Anti-Jacobin* joke of Canning's) and "Intelligence for the Morning Chronicle."

Bonaparte had moved one step closer to monarchical status the previous month when he was confirmed by plebiscite as First Consul for life. He is shown in the seat of the "Roi Soleil," guarded by a quartet of Mameluke warriors, presumably souvenirs of the Egyptian campaign. Fox's secretary, J. B. Trotter, reported on his employer's presentation to the French ruler: Fox "bestowed not one word of admiration, or applause" upon his host; in turn this "extraordinary and elevated character . . . addressed a few questions and answers relative to Mr. Fox's tour" and terminated the interview (see Trotter's *Memoirs of the Latter Years of . . . Fox*, 1811). According to Bonaparte's valet, the First Consul failed "à lui inspirer une haute idée de sa personne."

News accounts of the audience reached London later in the week, moving William Cobbett to heights of irony in an open letter to Fox: "Sir,—I have never till now thought of you as a person of any political consequence." Cobbett went on (*Annual Register*, 18 September 1802) to suggest that Fox's reserved behavior was calculated for maximum political effect at home.

The *Moniteur* (see Gillray's subtitle) was Napoleon's daily journal of official information, originally founded in 1789 by the revolutionaries Brissot, Condorcet and Clavière.

[IV.] (color plate)

A Phantasmagoria;—Scene—Conjuring-up an Armed Skeleton. 5 January 1803

Macbeth's witches—Prime Minister Addington, Hawkesbury and Fox—summon up a frightful vision of Britannia at peace, debilitated by concessions to the French.

A satire on the Addington government's military economies and its alleged appeasement of Bonaparte, cast in terms of a popular spook show which was playing nightly at the Lyceum Theatre in The Strand.

"Phantasmagoria" was a term coined (c. 1802) by M. De Philipsthal for his theatrical entertainment in which spectral figures projected on gauze screens were made to increase and decrease in size, advance and retreat, dissolve, vanish and pass into one another. De Philipsthal's advertisements promised to introduce:

> Phantoms or Apparitions of the Dead or Absent, in a way more compleately illusive than has ever been offered to the Eye in a public Theatre, as the Objects freely originate in the Air, and unfold themselves under various Forms and Sizes, such as Imagination alone has hitherto painted them, occasionally assuming the figure and most perfect Resemblance of the Heroes and other distinguished Characters of past and present Times (reproduced by Milbourne Christopher in *Panorama of Magic*, N.Y., 1962, pp. 32–33).

(An earlier public experiment in lantern magic by Gillray's painter friend de Loutherbourg—the "Eidophusikon"—had attracted much comment in 1781.)

By the end of 1802 major fissures were opening in the uncertain peace concluded at Amiens the previous March. Napoleon was blocking British commerce with Holland and Italy, and moving against Switzerland. Addington was coming under increasing fire for sweeping cutbacks in the regular army and in naval manpower, as a result of which he claimed a saving of 25 million pounds. Addington's Foreign Secretary, Lord Hawkesbury, was being criticized for his generosity at the conference table, as the commercial advantages promised as a consequence of peace failed to materialize. (De Philipsthal explained that his "Spectrology" professed "to expose the Practices of artful Impostors" and to "open the Eyes of those who still foster an absurd Belief in Ghosts or Disembodied Spirits.")

Gillray's "phantasmagoria" is based on the cauldron scene from *Macbeth* (Act IV, Scene 1) in which the three witches produce the apparition of an armed head to speak a warning. Addington gestures with mistletoe (?) and serpent (the incantation speaks of "fillet of a fenny snake" and "root of hemlock") as he ladles coin into a pot containing the tail and paw of the British lion. The sack of guineas at his side, "To make the Gruel Thick & Slab" (also from Shakespeare's chant) suggests a heavy, sticky concoction. Hawkesbury feeds the flames with documents representing the strategic conquests and advantages he is accused of discarding: "Dominion of the Sea," "Continental Alliances," "Switzerland" ·(whose independence had been presumed), "Honduras," "Egypt" (theoretically returned to Turkish rule), the "Cape" [of Good Hope] (relinquished to Holland), "Malta" (to be restored to the Knights of St. John) and the "West Indies." The last paper to go is labeled, microscopically, "Brit[ish] Isles." "Gibralter" and "Ireland" are being held in reserve.

William Wilberforce kneels in the foreground, singing a "Hymn of Peace." He had supported the peace and opposed all alliances with Continental powers in a speech on 24 November. To his right, the Gallic cock, in *bonnet rouge*, crows atop the lion's severed head. The third witch, Fox, is exultant. He had recently returned from Paris, and was openly delighted with the peace.

This is one of six Gillray political satires appearing between December 1802 and August 1803 which were published, inexplicably, by the caricaturist himself, rather than by his "landlady," Mrs. Humphrey.

[78]

Dilettanti-Theatricals;—or—A Peep at the Green Room. 18 February 1803

The Pic-nic Society, a fashionable but controversial amateur dramatic group, tunes up for a final fling.

The Pic-nic Society, organized early in 1802 by Lady Buckinghamshire and Lt. Col. Henry Francis Greville, was an elite amateur theatrical group dedicated to elaborate "pot-luck" suppers and the presentation of farces, burlettas, pantomimes and masquerades. The *Morning Herald* of 16 March 1802 reported that the society "met last night for the first time, in the Tottenham Street Rooms," where one act of a popular French play, translated for the occasion, was performed. The entertainment concluded with a supper, brought in from a tavern. (Subsequently, members provided the meal themselves, determining their obligations by drawing lots from "a capacious silken bag.") From the outset the project was regarded as unwelcome competition by professional actors and managers of the licensed theaters. Richard Brinsley Sheridan reportedly instigated a lively newspaper and pamphlet assault which charged the Pic-nics with licentious and immoral behavior. The atmosphere was charged from the beginning. A report of the debut stated that the ballerina Parisot disapproved and refused to participate. "It being apprehended that the public peace might be disturbed by this irregular assemblage, the Bow Street officers held themselves in readiness to act during the whole of the evening. . . ." The club soon transferred activities to the "highly proper" Argyle Rooms, near Oxford Circus (see John Ashton, *The Dawn of the XIXth Century in England*, London, 1886, pp. 354–55). Under continual criticism, including two earlier satires by Gillray, the Pic-nics expired shortly before their first anniversary, barely a week after the publication of "Dilettanti-Theatricals." On 28 February 1803 *The Times* reported that "The Pic-nic Society is at an end. Many of its members, at a late meeting, wished to continue the Theatrical amusements but no person would undertake the management of them."

Gillray situated his assemblage in the greenroom, the traditional offstage lounge for actors and actresses. In a commentary on the plate, the German periodical *London und Paris* (vol. 11, 1803, pp. 253–54) observed that "specialists of Hogarth caricatures will note that Gillray had two shades of his master and predecessor in mind," namely "Strolling Actresses Dressing in a Barn" and the "Midnight Modern Conversation." Also, the figure of Lady Salisbury, getting into costume for "the Part of Squire Groom," left center, appears to derive from the "posture woman" (a sort of strip-tease artist) in the third plate of Hogarth's *Rake's Progress*. The Marchioness of Salisbury (1750–1835) was a noted sportswoman; "Squire Groom" remains a mystery. Albinia, Countess of Buckinghamshire, the stout party at the central dressing table, is preparing for the part of Roxana, presumably the jealous first wife of the central character in Nathaniel Lee's 1677 play *The Rival Queens, or the Death of Alexander the Great*. Her bulk contrasts with the tiny figure of Lord Mount Edgcumbe (1764–1839) at the bottom left corner, who brushes up for the role of Alexander. He, in turn, is silhouetted against the towering form of Lord Cholmondeley (1747–1827), a dour, porcine Cupid wearing the (Latin) inscription "Love Conquers All." The orchestral group beyond him consists of Lords Carlisle, Spooner, Derby and Salisbury (the Lord Chamberlain, 1783–1804), respectively occupied by the bassoon, triangle, French horn and violin. Two singers, tradition-

ally identified as the "Misses Abraham," trill "Bravura Airs à la Billington" (Mrs. Elizabeth Billington, 1768–1818, celebrated and highly paid singer, was one of the Pic-nics' major detractors).

In the right foreground, the playwright and fop Lumley Skeffington cavorts with the deformed Lord Kirkcudbright. Behind Skeffington, the Prince of Wales dances with Mrs. Fitzherbert and another lady. Behind the ornamental screen, "Old Q" (the Marquis of Queensbury), Colonel Hanger (see Plate 46) and a third gentleman bestow their attentions on three ladies. The screen is decorated with club "deities": Handel, St. Cecilia (patroness of music and singing), Shakespeare, Melpomene (the muse of tragedy), David Garrick (the actor, 1717–79) and Thalia (the muse of comedy). Reynolds' admired 1775 portrait of Sheridan's first wife, Elizabeth Linley, as St. Cecilia, was parodied by Gillray in 1782. The saint's inclusion here may have been intended as a subliminal reference to the (hostile) Sheridan.

A flagon of usquebaugh (whiskey) and a glass stand, partially draped, beneath the dressing table.

[79]

THE KEENEST SPORTSMAN IN BROOMSWELL CAMP. Summer (?) 1803

A "hunting tableau" apparently dedicated to the proposition that one Major Tudor had been misbehaving while on volunteer maneuvers.

A rakish officer in regimentals quickens to the pursuit of the hare (?) indicated by the bucolic guide. He prepares to unleash an aristocratic whippet (which is contrasted with the countryman's mongrel).

Gillray evidently executed this plate as a special commission for his amateur client J. C. White. Presumably it was a private joke of extremely limited circulation, intended to discomfit the subject. White may have been the same patron "J. C." or "I. C." for whom Gillray etched a quartet of sporting subjects and one rustic comedy in 1800, and another hunt scene in 1807.

The copperplate must have remained with Gillray, as it appeared in the 1830 collection, with the explanatory innuendo that "Major T-d-r" was not the only keen sportsman at Broomswell Camp. The location of this jolly installation is unspecified and remains obscure, although the landscape could be Welsh. (Tenby is a fishing town on Carmarthen Bay, Pembrokeshire, in the south of Wales.)

With the nation confronted by the resumption of hostilities in May, and by a new invasion threat, the summer and autumn of 1803 were conspicuous for the activity of local volunteer units. A royal message on 8 March had ordered out the militia, eventually some 75,000 strong. By December an additional 340,000 volunteers had answered the call. These self-administered companies, exempt from other service, were far too numerous to be properly equipped and trained. Etching, colored by hand.

[80]

THE CORSICAN PEST;—OR—BELZEBUB GOING TO SUPPER. 6 October 1803

Gillray speculates on Napoleon's anticipated descent to the infernal regions—an exercise in elementary voodoo which reflects a deep national concern over the possibility of French invasion.

This pseudo-horrific vision was apparently conceived as an illustration to an eight-stanza poem (later attributed to the watercolorist Paul Sandby, 1725–1809), published below the title. The poet operates on the premise that Bonaparte and his legions mean to swim the Channel like "hungry Sharks, some night in the dark . . . to frighten our Children & Women":

When these Gallic Foisters, gape wide for our Oisters,
Old Neptune will rise up with Glee,
Souse and Pickle them quick, to be sent to Old Nick,
As a Treat from the God of the Sea,—Tol de rol.

Belzebub will rejoice, at a Supper so nice,
And make all his Devils feast hearty,
But the little-tit-bit, on a fork, he would spit
The Consular-Chief-Buonapartè!—Tol de rol.

The Devil wears a cockaded *bonnet-rouge*-cum-fool's cap. His dining table is a gory butcher's block, covered with a cloth ringed by a tricolor border. His cutlery, manufactured by "Taleyrand" (Talleyrand, 1754–1838, French foreign minister), lies between the "sacramental cup" of French "Atheism" and the "Infernal salt." Satan's "Favourite French Wines of the Consular Vintage" include the "Sang" (blood) of Switzerland, England and Holland. From offstage right, servants produce "Crocodile Soup" and "Mahomedan Gravy," references to Bonaparte's Egyptian experiences (see Plates 58, 62 and 69). The royal throne is a guillotine, beneath which the skulls of Robespierre and Marat can be seen. A group of simian corpses, the (invasion) "Armée D'Angletarre," dangles from a rack in the oven.

Bonaparte is seen as a "savory," a piquant anchovy to be taken on the toast awaiting below: a final complement to the Jacobin feast. The imp above him applies brimstone. Two others, at the left, bring frogs and salamanders to the roast. Another, with bellows, sits atop a bulging sack of "Fuel for Everlasting Flames," allegations of Napoleonic atrocities then receiving much public attention. These include: "Poisoning 580 wounded French soldiers," "Massacre of 3800 Turks at Jaffa," "Murdering 1500 Women at Toulon" and "Assassination of Captive Swiss." Already in the fire are charges of treachery, murder, blasphemy, breach of faith, cruelty, envy, perjury, ingratitude, devastation and avarice. Gillray's ironically inflated statistics and his hyperbolic torrent of dispraise appear to mock the floodtide of atrocity literature then inundating the country.

The song sheet at the lower right, "Invasion of Great Britain—a Catch" is "to be perform'd after Supper—with a full Chorus of his Highness's Band." This sarcasm was particularly timely. The First Consul was devoting the month of October to plans for his cross-Channel assault. On the sixth, as Gillray's print appeared, he inspected the shipyard of the Invalides and took an excursion on the Seine in one of his new gunboats.

A reduced copy of this print was published in the Weimar periodical *London und Paris* two months later, with a Gallic rooster decorously substituted for the French leader.

[81]

BRITANNIA BETWEEN DEATH AND THE DOCTOR'S. 20 May 1804

Political squabblings among her "physicians," Pitt, Addington and Fox, appear to leave the national patient vulnerable to Napoleon's sneak attack.

William Pitt's lack of enthusiasm for his successor, Addington, grew after the Peace of Amiens (see Plate 77). After a hesitation prompted by the return of the King's mental disorder (February–April 1804), Pitt joined Fox in spirited attack on the administration. With his majority cut to 37 after a defense vote on 25 April, Addington resigned on the 29th and Pitt was asked to form a new government.

Gillray's conception to the contrary, Pitt had been anxious to head a "broad-based" coalition ministry, including Fox as Foreign Secretary. George III was unalterably opposed to this last suggestion, and with the King's health and stability still causing grave concern, Pitt did not press it. On 18 May the monarch gave formal assent to a government composed of Addington's ministers and Pitt's intimates; Addington himself departed (he would return to office briefly the next year). A spirit of faction prevailed.

Gillray's quotation is adapted from the first line of Pope's "Epistle" to Lord Bathurst, from his *Moral Essays* of 1732: "Who shall decide when doctors disagree,/ And soundest casuists doubt, like you and me?" Pitt dominates the composition, brandishing an irradiated, crown-stoppered bottle of "Constitutional Restorative." A treatise on the "Art of Restoring Health" projects from his pocket. The prostrate Fox holds a *bonnet rouge* fools' cap in one hand and a vial of "Republican Balsam" in the other. A pair of dice, "Whig Pills," fall from the shaker at his side.

This satire turns on the derisive nickname of "the Doctor" which Canning conferred on Addington shortly after the latter became prime minister in 1801 (Addington's father had been a court physician). Gillray shows the outgoing premier at the left, dropping a "Composing Draft"; a clyster pipe is in his coat pocket. At the extreme right, Napoleon-Death (in a cocked hat with tricolor plumes) overturns Britannia's bedside table, scattering Addington's "Prescription" and nostrums. The patient wears a medallion portrait of the King on her bodice, a probable reference to George III's own precarious condition. This is one of the few prints to suggest (accurately) that invasion was still a real possibility in 1804. Etching (with almost imperceptible aquatint).

[V.] (color plate)
L'ASSEMBLÉE NATIONALE;—OR GRAND COOPERATIVE MEETING AT ST. ANN'S HILL. 18 June 1804

St. Anne's Hill, Fox's estate near Chertsey in Surrey, provides the locale for a Whig reception in the French manner which appears to follow or anticipate the establishment of a regency under the Prince of Wales.

Notwithstanding his stated desire for a comprehensive coalition government to face the national emergency, Pitt had returned to power one month earlier atop an exceedingly "narrow-bottomed" administration (see Plate 81). Gillray seized the opportunity to round up the factions which had been excluded for one bizarre gala in honor of Mr. and Mrs. Fox, the Prince of Wales (bisected by the right margin) and Mrs. Fitzherbert, ensconced on the sofa.

With the King's health once again very much at issue, there was considerable talk of a regency. The Prince met endlessly with his would-be ministers at regular "Cabinet" dinners in Carlton House, laying plans for a "cooperation" to be headed by Fox and Grenville. The word "coalition" would have evoked unfortunate echoes of the Fox-North partnership of 1783 (see Plates 4 and 5), and was avoided. Grenville and his family refused to serve with Pitt after the King's rejection of Fox as foreign secretary, and stood with the Foxites, the Prince's friends and lesser interests in a swollen, intrigue-ridden Opposition.

"L'Assemblée Nationale" purports to be a levée given by Fox for these several factions; the caricaturist's groupings have political and social significance. Under the intense gaze of Napoleon-Atlas (top center; see Plate 77), Fox and his wife greet the "three Grenvilles," Buckingham, Grenville and Temple. Behind the host, Moira, leader of the Prince's adherents, looks unhappily at the new arrivals. Behind Mrs. Fox is the Duchess of Devonshire with her brother, Lord Spencer (Plate 26), and her sister, Lady Bessborough. Like Grenville (and Windham), Spencer was a defector from the government party. The Prince is attended by Michael Angelo Taylor and a fawning dog, "Tommy Tattle," apparently Thomas Tyrwhitt, M.P., formerly his private secretary. The Prince faces his brother, the Duke of Clarence, who is flanked left and right by the heads of Col. John McMahon, his factotum, and the Duke of York. Clarence is accompanied by the actress Dorothea Jordan (see Plate 52), who studies her favorite role of Nell, an "innocent country girl," in Charles Coffey's 1731 play The Devil to Pay. Gillray's subtitle, "the Farce of Equality," is applied to her thirteen-year liaison with the Duke. Mrs. Fitzherbert (by then commencing her final descent from favor) receives a "Coalition Masquerade" ticket from Lord Carlisle. Behind her Erskine and Grey scan with

enthusiasm the "Arraignments for the new Broad-Bottom'd Administration." The former finds himself ("Citizen Ego") as a "Lord High" of some sort; the latter is listed as a "Greyhound."

The epithet "broad-bottomed" had been applied to a comprehensive ministry as early as 1744; in 1804 it was doubly apt as an allusion to the bulky posteriors of the Grenvilles.

At the lower left, the sixth Duke of Bedford sits with the Duke of Norfolk. The former, a cattleman like his brother (Plate 74), advances a "Scheme for Improving of the Old English Breed"—evidently by crossing it with the "French Ram." His hat contains a "Plan for Sheering the British Bull." Norfolk, a famous two-fisted tippler, has turned from the port bottles beneath his chair to a tankard and glass of "Whitbread's Entire," an allusion to Samuel Whitbread, Foxite M.P. for Bedford and son of the founder of the Whitbread brewery. Behind them, Robert Adair talks with M.P.s Tyrwhitt Jones and General George Walpole, over a copy of The Morning Chronicle containing "Verses upon the Death of ye Doctor" by "Bawb A Dara" (see Plate 77). To the right, Windham takes snuff from a conspiratorial Sheridan. The queue following the Grenvilles consists of Lord and Lady Derby, Lady Buckinghamshire, John Nicholls (see Plate 60), the Duchess of Gordon, Lord Cholmondeley and Lord and Lady Salisbury in the doorway. At the rear, Tierney (Plate 54) confers with the independent radicals Horne Tooke and Burdett.

The portrait of George III ("Pater Patriae") is in eclipse at the left; a painting over the Prince's friends at the right depicts tiny native "Worshipers of the Rising Sun." According to Bryan's Dictionary of Painters and Engravers (1849, p. 283), Fox is represented by Gillray as the First Consul of England, holding court after the execution of the old King and the proclamation of the Republic. The chances are excellent that this puckish interpretation had been handed down from Gillray himself. A second innuendo, both mischievous and prescient, is supplied by the quote from Henry IV, Part I, (Act I, Scene 2) in the Prince's coat pocket: "I know you all, & shall awhile [uphold/ The unyok'd humour of your idleness . . .].". In this speech, Shakespeare has the future Henry V reveal his intention to desert the licentious companions of his youth as soon as it serves his basic interests.

"L'Assemblée Nationale" is one of Gillray's rarest etchings, probably because of the offense which these nuances gave to the Prince and his friends. George Stanley, writing the 1849 Bryan's article cited above, added that "a large sum of money" was accepted for its suppression and that the Heir Apparent then ordered the copperplate destroyed. Some such transaction undoubtedly occurred. Stanley understood that the metal was preserved by deceitful associates of the Prince and that it would appear in the collection then being published by H. G. Bohn. It did not. Etching, colored by hand.

[VI.]   (color plate)

MIDDLESEX-ELECTION, 1804. 7 August 1804

In a boisterous Hogarthian setting, various Opposition leaders (wearing proletarian dress) celebrate and assist the anticipated return of Sir Francis Burdett as Member of Parliament for Middlesex.

Sir Francis Burdett, M.P. and radical reformer, proceeds in triumph to the hustings at Brentford (some eight miles west of Charing Cross). A hotly contested parliamentary by-election (23 July–6 August) between the Independent Burdett and an unpopular ministerial candidate, G. B. Mainwaring, was gleefully seized by the Opposition as an opportunity to embarrass the Pitt government.

After 1768, when John Wilkes fought a celebrated volatile (and ultimately unsuccessful) contest against Court and ministerial influence for the approval of the same constituency, Middlesex elections possessed a special egalitarian significance. Burdett first stood for the district in 1802, defeating the incumbent William Mainwaring in a struggle marked on both sides by bribery, coercion, deception and ruffianism. This election commenced on the eve of the thirteenth anniversary of the fall of the Bastille. Burdett announced his intention to campaign principally on the maladministration of Cold Bath Fields Prison in central London, with which his opponent had become identified as a magistrate and friend of the prison governor, Aris.

Although Burdett outpolled Mainwaring by almost three hundred votes, his claim to the victory was challenged amidst allegations of fraud and corruption. On 9 July 1804 a select committee of the House of Commons held that neither candidate was entitled to the seat and a special election was ordered by the House. What followed was a rerun of the 1802 donnybrook, with Burdett, supported by the Radicals and Whigs, facing G. B. Mainwaring, son of the former incumbent. After a lively neck-and-neck competition—the results of which Pitt received daily by special messenger—Mainwaring had a majority of five, 2828 to 2823, at the close of polling on 6 August. A review of disputed votes subsequently increased Burdett's total by six, but these were disallowed and Mainwaring was returned as the duly elected member. Petitions, counter-petitions and investigations kept the controversy alive for another eighteen months. Burdett's expenses in the two races were estimated to have been as high as £100,000. In 1807 he was elected member for Westminster, and retained the seat for thirty years.

Gillray patterned his composition after the final plate of Hogarth's 1747 series *Industry and Idleness*, which shows the industrious apprentice received in state as the Lord Mayor of London. Gillray's vision is evidently based on a recollection of Burdett's tumultuous cavalcade to Brentford from his home in Piccadilly on the first day of the poll in 1802 (see M. W. Patterson, *Sir Francis Burdett and His Times (1770–1844)*, London, 1931, pp.

132–72). Twenty butchers led the procession, keeping time with marrowbone and cleaver. Banners streamed, flags bore the inscription "Burdett and no Bastille," and the candidate's chariot was attended by "gentlemen outriders." At Kew Bridge, an enthusiastic populace removed the horses from the carriage and drew it to the hustings en masse.

Gillray's open barouche is pulled by (left to right) William Cobbett (?; face obscured); Col. William Bosville (1745–1813, radical, eccentric and bon vivant); Charles Grey (the tallest); and six peers: Carlisle, as a tailor; Spencer; Bedford, a farmboy; Northumberland, a shoemaker (?) in leather apron; Derby, a postboy; and Lansdowne. Fox, a chimney sweep, and the Duke of Norfolk, a butcher, bringing up the rear.

Burdett's coachman is the Radical doyen, John Horne Tooke, his mentor and principal ally of Wilkes in the 1768 election. Tooke's pockets emit a stream of manuscripts: "Speeches for Sir Francis on ye Hustings," "Hints," an "Address to the Mob," "Bills for all the Pissing Pots," "Sir Francis's Patriotic Speech on the Defence of the Country," etc. etc. The carriage panels are decorated with a dove of peace exhibiting the banner of "Egalitè" (Burdett visited France in 1802), a firebrand "Torch of Liberty" and a mug (with the profile of "Buonaparte")—"Plenty" at "Three Pence a Pot." One rear wheel crushes a dog, Sir William Curtis, ("A Cur-'tis"), a contractor who had backed another Court candidate. Burdett's "gentlemen outriders" are Sheridan, Tierney and Erskine. Sheridan hoists a banner depicting Pitt as "Governor [Aris] in All His Glory," flogging a half-nude Britannia. (In 1798 and 1800, Burdett had called for parliamentary inquiry into the alleged abuse of prisoners at Cold Bath Fields. On the latter occasion he referred to atrocities committed upon a girl detained to give evidence against a rapist. Burdett repeatedly charged the prison's governor, Aris, with corruption, sadism and discrimination against political offenders.) Tierney carries a giant key, surmounted by the streamer "No Bastille"; Erskine's flag supports this "Good-Old Cause" beneath a *bonnet rouge*.

The trio of butchers in concert at the lower right are Tyrwhitt Jones, General Walpole and Adair (see Plate V). At the opposite corner, the Prince of Wales's interests are represented by the military drummer, Lord Moira, accompanied on the horn by a hawker for the *Morning Chronicle*. A "Ministerial" rat hangs from the gibbet over his head, beneath a standard demanding "Independence & Free Elections." Adjacent handbills call for the "Triomphe de la Liberté," "The Rats A là Lenterne" and "Wanted a number of Recruits for the Coalition Dinner" (see Plate V).

The thin figure gesticulating on the center platform of the hustings is probably intended for candidate Mainwaring. The mob's antipathy to him is suggested by the accumulation of thrown debris on the roof and by the flying gobs of mud aimed at the flag, crown, mitre and woolsack which identify "The Constitution" public house (which corresponds to the King's Head Tavern in Hogarth's 1747 prototype). "Good Entertainment" is promised over the doorway, before which a full-scale riot appears to be in progress. Placards above the entrance announce "Mainwaring—King & Country" and "No Despard." (Col. Edward Marcus Despard, 1751–1803, previously championed by Burdett while imprisoned at Cold Bath Fields, had been convicted of a plot to overthrow the government, and executed on 21 February 1803.) Just below, a bagwig on a staff identifies "The Old-W[h]ig Interest." The politicians and mob alike wear blue and orange Burdett ribbons in their hats.

Gillray's subtitle was utilized in *David Copperfield* (1849–50, Chapter XXX), where Dickens gives it a more nautical cast. A "long pull" was also used to describe a generous or excessive serving of drink, generally beer.

Evidently the administration appreciated Gillray's continuing loyalty. On 13 August 1804 the caricaturist acknowledged grateful receipt of a Treasury "present" of £50, delivered into his hands by George Canning (D. Hill, *Mr. Gillray The Caricaturist*, London, 1965, p. 111).

Etching with aquatint, colored by hand.

[82]

—CI-DEVANT OCCUPATIONS—OR—MADAME TALIAN AND THE EMPRESS JOSEPHINE DANCING NAKED BEFORE BARRASS IN THE WINTER OF 1797.—A FACT!— 20 February 1805

Literally "Former Pursuits." This facetious representation of the first meeting of the new Emperor and Empress of France was occasioned by their coronation on 2 December 1804. The young Bonaparte is supposedly weighing a proposition that he relieve the Director Barras of a superfluous mistress (Josephine) in exchange for a promotion.

When Josephine de Beauharnais first captivated General Buonaparte in 1795, she was under the "protection" of Paul-Jean-François-Nicolas, Comte de Barras (1755–1829), venal, licentious politician, former terrorist and member of the Directory (1796–99). As Gillray implies, Barras had tired of Josephine, a penniless 32-year-old widow with two children and expensive tastes. He wished to transfer his attentions to Madame Thérèse Tallien (1773–1835), ten years younger, who was radiantly beautiful, highly fashionable and the daughter of an influential Spanish banker.

Apparently, Barras and Madame Tallien played Cupid; somehow Napoleon and Josephine each received the false impression that the other was a person of considerable means. An existing relationship was legitimized in a civil ceremony on 9 March 1796 and the speed with which the bridegroom then departed to take command of French forces in Italy fostered a notion that the marriage had

been part of a devious bargain with Barras. In actuality the reassignment seems to have been prompted by a desire to remove the ambitious General Bonaparte from competition in domestic politics. Gillray links the supposed deal with the infamous mission to Egypt of 1798–99 (see the folding screen and Plates 58, 62 and 67) rather than the earlier Italian campaign, from which Bonaparte returned triumphant in December 1797. The caricaturist's emphatic assertion that his postdated canard is "A Fact!" underscores the characteristic sarcasm and ambivalence of the work. Gillray at once ridicules Napoleon's parvenu rise and the excesses of Francophobic propaganda prevalent in England between 1803 and 1807.

Barras is enthroned beneath an infant Bacchus in *bonnet rouge*. His table (decorated in a satyr-and-cloven-hoof motif) supports a paper, "Egypt Commission pour Buonapartè—Barrass," anchored by a bottle of burgundy. For the decanter of maraschino and the obscured portrait of Messalina above it, see Plate 70. The screen which hides Napoleon is embellished, just above him, with the prophetic suggestion of an imperial crown floating above a pile of red-bonneted skulls. These are probably the French soldiers poisoned at Jaffa in 1799 (see Plate 80). The vignette of Cupid astride a crocodile on the banks of the Nile reconciles the parallel themes of business and pleasure. Etching with aquatint.

[83]

THE PLUMB-PUDDING IN DANGER;—OR—STATE EPICURES TAKING UN PETIT SOUPER. 26 February 1805

"The world is sufficiently large for our two nations to live in it . . ."—peace overture from Napoleon to George III, 2 January 1805. In a classic essay on the arrogance of power, Pitt and Napoleon are shown carving out their respective spheres of influence.

Notwithstanding its apparent indispensability to later generations of cartoonists, the world did not become a staple prop of the craft until Gillray's day. In 1701, the Dutchman Romeyne de Hooghe had drawn Louis XIV as Apollo, creaking over the planet in a broken chariot. The first truly caricatural use of the globe as a central element is apparently George Townshend's 1756 view of the Duke of Cumberland atop a terrestrial ball as the "Gloria Mundi." Hogarth includes an allegorical detail of a flaming world in "The Times, Plate I" of 1762.

Twenty years later the young Gillray borrowed Townshend's sarcastic "Glory of the World" to portray Charles James Fox. In Gillray's "Giant Factotum" (1797) the globe is a plaything of Pitt's; and the caricaturist continued to employ the image in a number of contexts (see Plates 61 and 88), of which the "Plumb-pudding" was the most memorable. Often copied, reproduced and parodied, this is probably Gillray's best-known work.

On 2 January 1805, Napoleon addressed a letter to George III stressing his desire for peace and asking what

Britain, at its "highest point of prosperity," could hope to gain from war. Pitt viewed this initiative with skepticism, properly enough, as the Emperor had written the King of Spain the same day urging militancy against England. (Spain declared war on England on 12 December; a formal alliance with France was concluded on 5 January.) Napoleon was answered formally and evasively through diplomatic channels, and on 15 January, a new session of Parliament opened with a speech from the throne calling for measures "to prosecute the war with vigour." William Windham, former Secretary at War, spoke in opposition to the government's policy on 15 January and 21 February. However, a search of Cobbett's *Political Register*, which Windham supported, and to which he occasionally contributed, fails to produce Gillray's attributed "eccentricity." The reference to "the great Globe itself" comes from *The Tempest*, Act IV, Scene 1.

Gillray's gargantuan protagonists are both in uniform. (Two years earlier Pitt organized and commanded a volunteer militia corps for the defense of the Cinque Ports.) The Englishman's chair is decorated with a royal lion bearing the ancient Cross of St. George, traditional emblem of an admiral's flagship (although slightly etched diagonals, reinforced with blue stripes on colored impressions, come closer to an approximation of the "Union Jack"). His plate carries the royal arms and his implements are a knife and (Neptune's?) trident. Napoleon's plate is marked with a crown, his chair with an imperial eagle perched atop a revolutionary *bonnet rouge*. He serves himself with sword and fork.

Beneath Pitt's knife, the notation "West Indies" is a reminder of continuing, long-standing friction there between the two countries. It is unlikely that Gillray would have been aware of a French naval feint in progress at that moment, conceived to lure British ships from their Continental blockade and facilitate the long-planned cross-Channel invasion. A squadron escaped from Rochefort on 11 January, arrived in the West Indies on 20 February and proceeded to harass British possessions there for some six weeks.

[84]

POLITICAL-CANDOUR;—I.E.—COALITION-"RESOLUTIONS" OF JUNE 14TH 1805.—PRO BONO PUBLICO.—
21 June 1805

Charles James Fox defends his old rival, Pitt, against a charge of personal corruption. Gillray interprets the Whig leader's guarded tribute to the ailing, beleaguered Prime Minister as an attempt to charm his way into the administration. Pitt's approval, ambiguously expressed, is clarified by the inviting manner in which he taps a vacant spot on the "Treasury Bench."

Gillray's satire reflects the currency of (accurate) rumors that Pitt still desired to strengthen his feeble government by the inclusion of Fox and Grenville. This

proposition was frustrated by the King's opposition to Fox, as it had been the year before (see Plate 81).

In the spring of 1805, Pitt's political problems had been aggravated, and his spirits badly shaken, by the loss of his First Lord of the Admiralty. Henry Dundas (now Viscount Melville), the Prime Minister's long-time ally and comrade, was forced to leave office after a committee of inquiry raised serious questions of official misconduct concerning his behavior as treasurer of the navy during the 1790s. On 8 April the Whig radical Samuel Whitbread introduced a motion before Parliament urging condemnation of Melville as an evident preliminary to impeachment.

At four A.M. on 9 April the House divided evenly, 216 to 216, on the crucial first question put to it. The speaker, Abbott, "after looking as white as a sheet, and pausing for ten minutes" (Lord Fitzharris, quoted by Stanhope in *Life of William Pitt*, vol. iv, London, 1862, pp. 283–84), cast a tie-breaking vote for censure. Pitt wept. Later in the day Melville resigned.

Despite this withdrawal, Whitbread continued to press for formal impeachment, principally on the unfounded accusation that Melville had approved the private, speculative use of navy department funds by his subordinate Alexander Trotter. (Gross negligence would have been a fairer indictment.) The unfolding scrutiny into Melville's affairs produced a separate charge against Pitt himself, that his 1796 advance of £40,000 in surplus navy money to government agents Boyd and Benfield was the result of a corrupt private arrangement. (Actually the transaction proceeded from the need to make payment on a sensitive government loan during an inflation crisis.) Whitbread brought this subject up for debate on 14 June, where the payment was explained to the satisfaction of the House as "highly expedient" and "most beneficial" although "not strictly conformable to law" (Stanhope, *Pitt*, iv, p. 311). At the outset, the Prime Minister inquired if he should retire during the discussion of a matter personally affecting himself. He was assured by the House that such a gesture was unnecessary. Fox then rose to make the remarks which inspired Gillray's tableau.

According to the record in *Hansard's Debates* (vol. 5, pp. 413–14):

Mr. Fox assured the Right Honourable Gentleman that he should have felt as sincere sorrow as any member in that House if it had appeared from the result of the inquiry, that the Right Honourable Gentleman was guilty to the same degree as Lord Melville. However he might have differed . . . however he might have thought his general conduct deserving of blame; however he might think him blameable in this instance; yet he should have felt uneasy and unhappy had it turned out . . . that the Right Honourable Gentleman was personally corrupt. For himself, he could declare that he never entertained such an opinion of him, and he was happy that the results of the inquiry did not justify the adoption of even a sentiment of suspicion on that ground. Although he had frequently condemned the public conduct of the Right Honourable Gentleman; although he had on many occasions uttered sentiments respecting him, which he should have felt it treason against his country and his conscience to suppress, still he never expressed a suspicion that the Right Honourable Gentleman was capable of personal corruption, nor did he ever entertain such a suspicion. However he might charge him with that species that appertained to general neglect of duty, his mind entirely acquitted him of that kind of sordid corruption alluded to by [Whitbread].

The speaker's chair is occupied by Charles Abbott (1757–1829), perhaps diminished in Gillray's eyes by his vote against Melville. Before him, a scroll of "Resolutions respecting the Chancellor of the Exchequer" (Pitt) rests on the great mace. This paper refers to the £40000," the "Bank of England," Messrs. "Boyd & Benfield" (Walter Boyd, 1754–1837, and Paul Benfield, d. 1810, financiers, loan contractors and members of Parliament, declared bankrupt in 1799) and (Alexander) "Trotter." The last word is apparently "participation." Fox conceals "Arraignments for a new Coalition"; his hat contains plans for a "Political Union, to save the Country from Buonaparte and the Doctor" (Addington, now Viscount Sidmouth; see Plate 81). Beside him, an overturned mug of brewer Whitbread's "Entire" spills its froth on the floor.

Fox's sentiments are supported by a number of speeches by his colleagues, from the left: Lord Henry Petty, Tierney, Erskine, Wilberforce, Windham and Grey. Petty marvels: "an Immaculate Statesman!—just like my own Papa" (his father, the Marquis of Lansdowne—an ex-Prime Minister with a reputation for duplicity—had died on 7 May). Tierney, who fought a duel with Pitt in 1798, says sourly, "O! how I shall enjoy to sit down with him, upon the Bench of Honesty." Erskine: "—he scorns a dirty Cause, I vow to G-d!" Wilberforce, whose speech against Melville on 9 April had been decisive: "O he's an Angel of Light!—a Cherubim of Glory!" Windham holds "Notes & Speeches for the [William Cobbett's] *Political Register*" (see Plate 83) and muses: "—why, He deserves a Statue of Gold more than Porcupine [Cobbett] himself!" Grey shields two documents, "Enquiries into the Public [Offices?]" and "State of the [Nation?]" as he muses: "yes I find they'll be all prov'd Honest, so I'll destroy my Papers too!"

Sheridan's (silent) figure is partially obscured by Fox. Indebted to Melville for a previous kindness, he took no part in the attack on him.

This is the last Gillray caricature of Pitt published during the Prime Minister's lifetime. Etching, colored by hand.

[85]

ST. GEORGE AND THE DRAGON.—A DESIGN FOR AN EQUESTRIAN STATUE, FROM THE ORIGINAL IN WINDSOR-CASTLE. 2 August 1805

King George III, as England's patron saint, prepares to deliver the coup de grâce as he frees Britannia from the clutches of Napoleon.

This patriotic "bas-relief" was etched by Gillray from an original watercolor drawing by Captain Thomas Braddyll (1778–1862) preserved in the print room of the British Museum. Thomas Richmond Gale Braddyll of Conishead Priory, Lancashire, was a captain in the Coldstream Guards by 1803 and had advanced to the rank of colonel by 1810. Between June 1803 and August 1805 he supplied Gillray with the inspiration and design for four Napoleonic satires, including a pair of celebrated tableaux from Swift showing "The King of Brobdingnag [George III] and Gulliver [Napoleon]" (26 June 1803 and 10 February 1804).

The King wears the uniform of the Royal Horse Guards ("the Blues"), in which he had been painted five years earlier by Sir William Beechey (painting now at Buckingham Palace). The coat was blue, with scarlet facings and gold lace, complemented by buff breeches. As in the portrait, Gillray shows the order of the Garter; the wide red sash is spurious. The shabrack, or ornamental saddlecloth, is decorated with a crown-and-garter emblem. The fur-trimmed holster cap (on the pommel of an invisible saddle) seems to bear the same marking. (Unlike his sons, the King never held rank in the military. For years the Horse Guards preserved a coat said to have been the one in which he was painted by Beechey; see Miller and Dawnay, *Military Drawings and Paintings in the Collection of Her Majesty the Queen*, London, 1970, vol. 1, p. 92.)

George is poised to administer a second stroke; his first has cleft the Imperial crown and opened a huge gash in the Imperial skull. Britannia has dropped her spear and shield; the latter displays the Union Jack, adopted in 1801. Braddyll's buoyant image celebrates the alignment of the third coalition (England, Russia, Austria and Sweden) against the French. It also coincides with the last serious threat of a cross-Channel assault.

At the moment "St. George" appeared in Mrs. Humphrey's window, Napoleon was setting out for Boulogne, where some 90,000 men and 2000 vessels awaited his pleasure. Eleven days later, news of an Austrian declaration of war diverted the Emperor's attention to the east, forcing final abandonment of his cherished invasion of England. By the first of September, Boulogne had been evacuated and the French army was marching to meet the forces of the third coalition on the Danube. Etching with aquatint.

[86]

HARMONY BEFORE MATRIMONY. 25 October 1805

"Pho! man, is not music the food of love? . . . she is so accomplished—so sweet a voice—so expert at her harpischord—such a mistress of flat and sharp, squallante, rumblante, and quiverante! . . . how she did chirrup . . ." (Sheridan, *The Rivals* [1775], Act II, Scene 1).

Gillray celebrates the joys of courtship in the first tableau of an often reproduced pair. (His inscription, "Js. Gillray, des. & ft.," suggests that the original notions were supplied by one of his "silent partners.")

The tremendous popularity of amateur music in clubs, societies and homes offered a wide target to the caricaturists. Gillray dealt with the general topic on several occasions (see Plates 73 and 78), returning to the subject of domestic recitals again in 1809 and 1810, again after the inventions of others ("Farmer Giles & His Wife shewing off their daughter Betty," 1 January 1809, and "A Little Music," 20 May 1810). Here the harp is the symbol and instrument of romance and fascination, in contrast to the malevolent piano of the companion piece.

The central "message" of affectionate involvement is elaborated in a variety of ways: the narcissistic butterfly at the mirror, the intertwined roses, the chinoiserie serenade on the vase, the goldfish, the cherub's-head table bracket, the playful cats, the heart-shaped vessel (with sphinx embellishment), the burgeoning palm motif on the pilaster at the right and the pot of myrtle (?) supported by a grinning satyr.

The man holds a songbook, "Duets de l'Amour"; the thin volume of Ovid on the table between the couple alludes to the Roman poet (43 B.C.–A.D. ?17), celebrated for his love themes. In the medallion above, Cupid discards his traditional weapons for a blunderbuss, which he fires broadside at two billing doves. The decorative bas-relief to the left is dominated by the crossed torches of Hymen, Greek deity of marriage, that to the right by Cupid's bow and loaded quiver. Gillray's original watercolor drawing (author's collection; see illustration) displays a less cynical vignette of Cupid entrancing a second cherubic figure with a violin solo. The heart-shaped character of the sphinx vase has not yet been established and the young man's feet twist and undulate in a marvelously coy manner, abandoned in the etching.

Original watercolor drawing for Plate 86.

[87]

MATRIMONIAL-HARMONICS. 25 October 1805

The inevitable dénouement of this cynical siren's song —marriage on the rocks. The lady's "Forte" recital, "Torture—Fury—Rage—Despair—I cannot cannot bear," is evidently to be followed by the other composition lying on the piano: "Separation a Finale for Two Voices with Accompaniment." "The Wedding Ring—A Dirge" lies on the floor beneath.

Gillray's bitter sequence may have owed some of its inspiration to the four-plate "history" of *Modern Love* apparently painted by John Collet (c. 1725–80) in 1765 but not published until 1782, after his death. Collet followed an upper-class romance from "Courtship" through "Elopement" and "Honey-Moon" to "Discordant Matrimony." There might also be an unsympathetic echo of Francis Wheatley's *The Life of A Country Girl*, a saccharine salute to bucolic simplicity and married life, first exhibited at the Royal Academy in 1792. Anticipating the Gillray prints, a parallel distinction between *Courtship* and *Marriage* was drawn by William Williams (active c. 1758–c. 1797) in a pair of paintings dated 1797 (reproduced by Sacheverell Sitwell in *Narrative Pictures*, London, 1936, Plates 62 and 63).

The hour is suggested by the morning cap, the dressing gown and slippers, and by the breakfast table (at which the lady has seemingly forsaken her tea for "Hollands" (gin). The book at her place lies open to "The Art of Tormenting," illustrated by a copy of the cat-and-mouse vignette which Gillray had etched for W. Miller of Old Bond Street in 1803 (impressions in the Tilden Collection, New York Public Library, dated 1 January 1804, apparently a book illustration). An empty purse hangs from the back of the chair, hinting at a disagreement over economics.

The discord is heightened by the heir apparent and the noisemaker in the doorway, the quarrelsome cockatoos (who have a trio of unhappy offspring themselves) and the cat and dog. The latter's collar identifies him as Benedick, and by inference his feline adversary would be Beatrice (the disputatious lovers of *Much Ado About Nothing*).

The bust on the wall is of the marriage god Hymen, disfigured by disease, his garland aflame. Stag's antlers supporting the birdcage hint gratuitously at infidelity. The thermometer sits at "Freezing" (the alternatives being "Cold," "Luke Warm," "Milk Warm," "Warm," "Hot" and "Boil[ing]"). Over the fire, Cupid "rests in peace," his quiver upended, his torch fallen. The mantelpiece vase, with angry serpents for handles, is decorated with a crossed bow-and-torch design. The beleaguered husband, his teeth clamped on a roll (or lemon?) escapes into his "Sporting Calender" (*The Sporting Magazine; or Monthly Calendar of the Transactions of the Turf* was founded in London in 1793).

[VII.] (color plate)

TIDDY-DOLL, THE GREAT FRENCH-GINGERBREAD-BAKER, DRAWING OUT A NEW BATCH OF KINGS.—HIS MAN, HOPPING TALLEY, MIXING UP THE DOUGH. 23 January 1806

Napoleon at the apex of his power, seven weeks after the French triumphs at Austerlitz, confirms the new Imperial ascendancy over Bavaria, Württemberg and Baden by converting their electors into satellite monarchs. He is assisted by his foreign minister, the clubfooted Talleyrand. Tiddy-Dol Ford (d. 1752) was a colorful Mayfair pitchman memorialized by Hogarth in the eleventh plate of *Industry and Idleness* (1747).

The morale boost provided the English by Nelson's final victory (at Trafalgar, 21 October 1805) was balanced and temporarily eclipsed by the overwhelming defeat which Napoleon inflicted on the Austrians at Austerlitz (2 December). As a consequence of the Treaty of Pressburg (26 December), the electors of Bavaria, Württemberg and Baden were recognized as kings. (For the obese King Frederick II of Württemberg, see Plate 51.) The unexpected news of Austerlitz is generally credited with hastening the total collapse of Pitt's health. His mournful injunction to roll up the map of Europe ("it will not be wanted these ten years") occurred on or about 12 January and he died on 23 January, the day when Gillray's satire appeared.

Hogarth's original "Tiddy-Dol" wore a laced coat, white apron and feathered cocked hat, his gingerbread by his side in a two-handled wicker basket. Ford's nickname derived from a fondness for chanting the chorus of a popular ballad ("Ti-tid-dy, ti-ti, ti-tidy-dy . . . tid-dy, tid-dy dol") in hawking his wares; he was noted for lively patter, approximated on the side of the red-bonnet cornucopia, bottom left: "Hot Spiced Gingerbread! all hot—come who dips in my luckey Bag." Gillray's hamper is stuffed with "True Corsican Kinglings for Home Consumption & Exportation"; Napoleon was preparing to replace the crowned heads of Europe with a mixed circle of relatives and favorites. The cornucopia spews crowns, coronets, scepters, decorations and a cardinal's hat, presumably the one awarded Napoleon's uncle Joseph Fesch in February 1803.

In the foreground, a "Corsican Besom [broom] of Destruction" has swept mementos and symbols of Napoleon's conquests into the "Ash-Hole for broken Gingerbread." These include a broken ship (Venice), a crowned skull (Spain), the Italian boot, the papal tiara, Switzerland, the Netherlands, the Austrian eagle, Holland (a broad Dutch posterior), a cap of Liberty and the tricolor flag of the French Revolution. To the left, cannonballs provide the "New-French Oven" with "Fuel"; to the right, Sheridan, Fox, Burdett, Moira, Tierney and Derby are "Little Dough Viceroys, intended for the next new Batch!" These rest on a bureau in which the baker stores his "Kings & Queens," "Crowns & Sceptres" and "Suns & Moons."

At the rear, Talleyrand prepares Hungary, Poland and Turkey in the "Political Kneading Trough"; he is assisted by the Prussian eagle, which tears greedily at Hanover. Talleyrand's mitre and vestments allude to his ecclesiastical background, and to his tenure as bishop of Autun, 1789–91. Despite his own melancholic turn of mind, Gillray's professional response to the catastrophic turn of events on the Continent is characteristically upbeat. A preliminary sketch, with initial drafts of the inscriptions, is preserved in the Tilden Collection, New York Public Library. One of these, "Tiddy Doll the 1st," would have underscored the Emperor's own parvenu stigma. However, here as in other Napoleonic satires, Gillray preferred to show the enemy as a demonic little menace rather than as an ineffectual buffoon.

[88]

THE POWERFUL ARM OF PROVIDENCE. 2 May 1831

The title, subtitle and dedication of this bizarre, apocalyptic vision were supplied in 1831 by an enthusiastic printseller named John Fairburn, who was waxing euphoric at the approach of the Great Reform Bill. The design, however, is the work of Gillray—unpublished in his lifetime—developed and executed between 1796 and 1807 for purposes which give free rein to speculation.

For a variety of excellent reasons, this curious composition has never been associated with Gillray; it is perhaps the rarest, and certainly one of the most perplexing, of his "published" designs. The caricaturist seems to be encroaching on the prophetic fancies of William Blake, briefly a fellow student of his at the Royal Academy Schools in 1779.

The etching technique is Gillray's throughout; the extreme finesse of execution leads one to suspect that it was a work of the mid-nineties (compare, for example, the handling of the cloud masses and the draped figure with those in Plate 35). Perhaps Gillray's first thought was an allegory of revolution and regeneration as an extension of the creation of the universe, possibly with some relevance to the upheavals in France. It may have originated as an outside commission for a book illustration or frontispiece. Whatever the case, the finished work was preceded by at least three preliminary drawings: a sketch of an exploding world (Curzon Collection, Oxford), a similar view in which hands are suggested at the center of a vortex, and a working pencil study on transfer paper establishing the explosion, the arc and the enigmatic lady in their final relationship (both in the Tilden Collection, New York Public Library).

Gillray's representation of the creation of the universe is most un-Blakeian in its faithful attention to scientific detail. The planets are represented in proper order, Mercury, Venus and Mars identified by their traditional symbols, the Earth by its lone moon, Jupiter by its four principal moons, and Saturn by a suggested ring and nine (?) satellites. Uranus, discovered in 1781, is not included —unless it is the terra firma on which the lady dances,

and thus the departure point of the whole exercise. (The "new" planet was named "Georgium Sidus" in honor of the King, a distinction recognized in England until 1850.) The celestial spectacle also embraces the Milky Way, a couple of meteor showers and the apparent birth of a comet, its tail correctly aimed away from the sun.

None of the preliminary sketches have reference to the terrestrial globe at the center, which appears to have been inserted later in a tenuous attempt to convert an abandoned illustration into a comment on the movement to outlaw the African slave trade. The spotlight on the "dark continent" may have been intended to encourage or celebrate the passage of a bill to abolish "all manner of dealing and trading in the purchase, sale, barter or transfer of slaves." Such a measure finally received the royal assent on 25 March 1807, after intense parliamentary debate over a span of eighteen years. This represented the first major breakthrough in William Wilberforce's lifelong crusade to end both the commerce in humans and the institution of slavery itself. Despite the early and sustained support of Pitt and Fox, the abolition movement was effectively blocked in 1792 and 1796 by the West India interest. Wilberforce's dedication to his cause was finally rewarded with a general emancipation on 28 August 1833, one month after his death.

The enactment of an abolition bill in 1807 coincided with the dramatic fall of the Grenville government (see Plates 89 and 90) and was all but ignored by the caricaturists. Gillray himself was entering a period of mental instability, and an existing plate might have been thought to provide an expedient opportunity for a topical comment. The decisive debates on abolition began in the House of Lords on 2 January 1807, and concluded successfully for Wilberforce and Grenville in mid-March, at precisely the moment that the latter's administration collapsed. At some point prior to this departure (19 March) Gillray considered a satire showing Britannia on the horizon of a globe, "Lighting up ye torch of Liberty to Enlighten Africa," with the additional legend: "Grenville—Breaking off ye shackles. Vide debates on ye Slave Trade." On the reverse of this sketch (Tilden Collection, New York Public Library) there is an elaborate drawing which shows Grenville in the act of roasting John Bull (a bull) on a spit, basting him with a variety of ill-advised schemes, policies and new taxes. A second version of the same (unpublished) notion introduces a new delicacy—"Emancipation Duck Imported from ye West Indies" (Courtauld Institute Galleries, London). A third approach to the same scene shows a group of "West Indian Blacks" peering in at the kitchen window and a handbill: "Wanted for upper servants a Cargo of smart Black Lads to keep the white menials in order" (author's collection). At the very least these would imply the existence of a certain ambivalence on Gillray's part toward Grenville's motives, conceivably under the influence of Canning (cf. p. xxii), who wished to see Grenville out of power and had opposed abolition energetically the year before—on purely political grounds, against his own convictions.

In the unlikely case that the caricaturist had wanted to pay tribute to an abolition bill, he could scarcely have done so by crediting Grenville, whom he mistrusted, or Wilberforce, whom he hated. (On 1 May 1804 he caricatured the reformer as a gnomish zealot, urinating impotently in the direction of a celestial adversary. Gillray explained this image to a German journalist with the comment, "Every man uses his natural weapon . . . this skunk doesn't reject his instinct" (*London und Paris,* Weimar, 1804, vol. 13, p. 67).

If the "Powerful Arm" was intended for publication in the spring of 1807 but abandoned, it shared that distinction with a number of false starts. One satire equating the fall of Grenville with the discovery of Guy Fawkes was nursed along with amendments and alterations which kept it topical from March until early June, when it was finally abandoned in favor of another artist's version of the same idea (James Sayers' "A new Leaf for an old Book of Common Prayer," published by Mrs. Humphrey on 4 June 1807). Gillray's unfinished copperplate, "The Pillar of the Constitution," was ultimately purchased from Mrs. Humphrey's heirs by the publisher Thomas McLean on 16 July 1835, along with one other "suppressed" plate (Foster's sale catalogue *Of the Entire Stock of Mrs. Humphrey* . . . , Victoria and Albert Museum, London; McLean paid four guineas for the two items). Two weeks later (1 August) McLean issued "The Pillar" as a sort of curiosity for Gillray collectors. John Fairburn, a veteran printseller, probably acquired the "Powerful Arm" from Mrs. Humphrey's nephew George, whose business was in a pronounced decline by the end of the 1820s.

Fairburn's publication of the work as "An Allegorical Print, applicable to the Year 1831" capitalized on the wave of popular enthusiasm generated by the progress of the Reform Bill, which passed its second reading in the Commons by one vote on 22 March. Fairburn's dedication to William IV came one week after the King agreed (22 April) to a dissolution of Parliament in anticipation of a general election keyed to the issue of reform. Increasing agitation for the full emancipation of slaves helped to give the African allusion a semblance of meaning. Fairburn may have felt that the scattering of flowers was appropriate to May Day; his print appeared on Monday, 2 May. He was almost certainly responsible for the inscription "England" beneath the lady's feet.

At least three decades old at the time of publication, this tantalizing print is probably the most remarkable collection of elements in search of a purpose to be found in the history of caricature. Etching with aquatint.

[89]

THE FALL OF ICARUS. 20 April 1807

Richard Grenville, third Earl Temple, attempting a departure from office on wings of quill pens and sealing wax, is arrested in mid-flight by the stern sun of royal displeasure. Temple was alleged to have absconded with large quantities of government stationery.

The contentious Whig government that came to power on the death of Pitt was mockingly described by George Canning as "the Ministry of all the Talents," and by Gillray as "Broad-bottom'd," an earlier epithet which covered both its (unrealized) comprehensiveness and the bulky posteriors of a number of its leaders.

Lord Temple (1776–1839) held the positions of Joint Paymaster of the Forces and vice president of the Board of Trade under his uncle Lord Grenville, the Prime Minister. Temple was not celebrated for reticence; the posting of a brass plate engraved "Earl Temple" on the door of the Paymaster's office was taken as an act of singular arrogance.

In mid-March the "Broad-bottoms" committed what amounted to political suicide by refusing to promise George III that they would never again raise the hated question of political concessions for Roman Catholics. (The King took furious exception to a bill that would have opened staff ranks in the military to Catholics.) The Grenville government resigned their seals of office on 24 March, and were succeeded by a Pittite ministry which included Gillray's sometime patron Canning as Foreign Secretary.

Canning, or one of his friends, appears to have been responsible for "The Fall of Icarus," which was developed from an amateur sketch preserved in the British Museum Department of Prints and Drawings (201 c6—5, a rough horizontal composition, with the verses as published; Gillray's own preliminary drawing also survives in the Museum print room). Canning would have had a particular interest in the office of Joint Paymaster, which he held from May 1799 until Pitt left office in February 1801, and from which he departed with the greatest reluctance. The same amateur hand was responsible for the inspiration behind the "Siege de la Colonne de Pompée" (1799, Plate 62), and in all probability for a related series of *Egyptian Sketches* published the following week (see note 77, p. xxxi, and Hill, *Mr. Gillray The Caricaturist,* 1965, pp. 112–13). Interestingly enough, the "Colonne" and two of the latter *Sketches* also indicate a certain fascination with impalement.

The widely held belief that Lord Temple left office with a massive amount of government stationery provided Gillray and his collaborator an opportunity to revive a nine-year-old joke of George Tierney's. Temple was elected M.P. for Buckinghamshire in 1797 at the age of 21. In his maiden speech on 10 November he jibed at Tierney, who was then the nominal leader of the Opposition. Temple went on to support vigorous measures for national defense, observing that "from [his] connexions and situation" he had "everything to risk." On 4 December Temple supported a government move for increased taxes with the observation that he "was perfectly aware of the stake he had in the present contest."

The natural affinity of the Grenville family for profitable sinecures was something of a legend. Reporting (incorrectly) on 14 February 1798 that a new post had been awarded to Lord Grenville, the *Morning Post* commented: "Monstrous maw of the Buckinghams! when will thy thirst for sinecures be full?" This strain was revived by Tierney in parliamentary debate on 4 April 1798, after Temple pressed him for an answer he did not care to give. According to the *Parliamentary History*: "Mr. Tierney did not conceive that the noble Lord, who had so proudly boasted of his stake in the country—a stake which it now appeared had been stolen out of the public hedge—had any right to put such a question" (*The Parliamentary History of England*, 1812–20, vol. xxiii, p. 1415 and preceding). This jibe attached itself firmly to Temple's coattails in the years that followed, subject to varying accounts and elaborations.

Gillray's bulky Icarus seeks to follow the example of his father Daedalus—the Marquis of Buckingham—who soars aloft on the wings of his lucrative life sinecure, the "Tellership of the Exchequer." Temple is, however, about to fall on Tierney's wickedly pointed "Stake out of Public-Hedge!" At the rear, a "Stationary Office" cart is being loaded with supplies at the front door of the Paymaster's headquarters in Whitehall.

In Greek mythology, Daedalus was the artist-inventor who fashioned wings of feathers and wax to enable him and his son Icarus to escape from Crete. The latter came a cropper when he presumptuously flew too near the sun.

[90]

CHARON'S-BOAT.—OR—THE GHOST'S OF "ALL THE TALENTS" TAKING THEIR LAST VOYAGE. 16 July 1807

A final, belated farewell to the Grenville ministry, almost four months after their expulsion from office by George III on the issue of concessions to Roman Catholics. The role of Charon, mythical boatman of the river Styx, is filled by Charles Grey, Lord Howick, who introduced (5 March) the "fatal" bill which would have opened all military ranks to Catholics.

The "Broad-Bottom Packet" (see Plate 89) flies a standard bearing papal insignia over the motto of the Buckingham family, "Templa Quam Dilecta" (Temples How Beloved). The sail of "Catholic Emancipation" is torn and useless; its broken spar hangs by a rosary from the motto and three-feathered emblem of the Prince of Wales at the head of the mast. The motto "Ich Dien" (I serve) and the ribbon "Fitz" securing the feathers to the Catholic cause recall the Prince's former liaison with Mrs. Fitzherbert (see Plates 12 and II) and his (previous) support for Catholic concessions. Lord Moira, intimate and supporter of the Prince, stands at the mast, a crucifix pressed to his lips.

Motive power for the stricken craft is supplied by Grey, ex-First Lord of the Admiralty, who uses the "Whig Club" (Plate 35) as a punting pole. "Better to Reign in Hell!—than Serve in Heaven," he observes.

Conspicuous below and to the right of Grey are the three "Grenvilles." Temple loses hold of papers marked "Stationary Paymas[ter's] Office" and "Places, Pensions Sinecures" (see Plate 89). His father, the Duke of Buckingham, is evidently indisposed (as is Sheridan above him). Buckingham's exposed posterior, marked with a cross, is labeled "Ballast from Stow" (Stowe house was the family "seat" in Buckinghamshire). Ex-Prime Minister Grenville, wearing a cardinal's hat, extends a chalice. "Courage Brother!" he says, "take Extreme Unction: & don't despair."

At the bow of the boat, the former Chancellor of the Exchequer, 27-year-old Lord Henry Petty, tunes a tiny dancing-master's fiddle (kit). His simian foot rests on the score of a jig, "Go to the Devil & shake yourselves." Young Lord Henry's reputed fondness for dance was gleefully embraced by his detractors (". . . At balls he's so dapper a dancer,/ The misses all find him most handy;/ For tho' heavy in head/ As a plummet of lead,/ He jumps like a Jack-a-Dandy," cited in *All the Talents; A Satirical Poem*, London, 1807, p. 61, n. 1). The remainder of the passenger list consists of: Erskine, vomiting a "Catholic Emetic"; Whitbread the brewer, who sings "Wesleys Hymns," fortified by a mug of his own "Entire"; Windham, lately the Secretary at War, at work on a "Scheme for Drilling Imps in Hell"; Sir George Pretyman, Bishop of Lincoln (1750–1827), wearing a miter, grasping financial "Endowments" from Pitt and the Whigs; and Lord Lauderdale, privy councillor and Grenville peace emissary, exhibiting a decoration, "Vive Brissot" (Lauderdale returned from a visit to revolutionary France in 1792, proclaiming his friendship with the Girondist leader Jean-Pierre Brissot de Warville, 1754–93; Brissot was denounced by Robespierre and executed the following year).

Wrestling with the rudder, the Earl of St. Vincent complains, "Avast! Trim ye Boat! or these damn'd Broad bottom'd Lubber's will overset us all." St. Vincent, naval hero (see Plate 58), had just retired as commander in chief of the Channel fleet. As First Lord of the Admiralty (1801–04) he had been responsible for the inquiry which led eventually to the impeachment of Lord Melville (Plate 84)—hence his presence in this select partisan company.

Addington, now Lord Sidmouth, grips the gunwale just below the "Ballast from Stow"; to his left the wig box of Lord Chief Justice Ellenborough opens to swamp his magisterial emblem of "Loyalty" and "Opposition." The box is labeled "Lord Doublebottom his Wig—Kings Bench." (Sidmouth and his ally Ellenborough refused to act with the Grenville ministry on the Catholic Militia Relief Bill.) Gillray misrepresents the situation of Moira, the Prince's only real "representative" in the cabinet, and that of the Bishop of Lincoln, both of whom opposed the Relief Bill. The travelers are further harassed by three demonic birds overhead: the "Political Register" excretes [William] "Cobbet[t]'s Letters," the "Morning Post" follows suit with "the Protestant's Letters" and Francis Burdett, the posterior member of a double-headed Burdett–Horne Tooke radical harpy (see Plate VI) emits "Damnable Truths."

At the left-hand base of Hell's rocky proscenium, Cerberus, the three-headed watchdog of the underworld, bays at the new arrivals. Greeting them at the water's edge is Fox ("Welcome to Charley") standing between Oliver Cromwell and the headless figure of Robespierre. This trio is supported by the shades of "Quigley" (Jeremiah O'Coigley, Irish revolutionary, executed June 1798, accomplice of O'Connor; see Plates 60 and 77) and Despard (see Plate VI).

Overhead, the three witch-like "Fates" of the new administration are Canning, Castlereagh and Hawkesbury, respectively the Foreign, War and Colonial, and Home secretaries in the Duke of Portland's government. (The mythical Fates were Atropos, the inflexible, Clotho, the spinner, and Lachesis, the allotter—although their tasks were sometimes switched.) Canning holds the shears, a possible comment on the part which his failure to join the Grenvilles in March had played in their downfall.

This satire was executed by Gillray after the suggestion of another ("Js. Gillray fect."). A preliminary drawing bears the tentative inscription ". . . ye Broadbottomites on their last voyage . . . taking the dead over" (formerly in the collection of the late Minto Wilson). The insertion of the reference to ghosts in the final title is probably a tacit acknowledgment of the untimeliness of the publication date.

A broadside tribute from "G. Sidney, Printer Northumberland Street" directed to "The Author of a Print entitled Charon's Boat" (in the House of Lords Library) begins:

> Blesst hand! against corruption bent
> To whom its sharpest instrument,
> Keen satire gave in charge;
> What praise can worthily impart
> My admiration of the art
> Which Stow'd old Charon's barge.
>
> Too long that art has slept unsung;
> But now by him whose triple tongue
> Controls the Pass of hell—
> If any ink—or any brain
> Or any power of verse remain
> That verse its fame shall tell. . . .

and concludes, 21 stanzas later:

> To friends of the Broadbottom'd train
> Take warning by their fate
> Lest Satire point again its goad,
> And drive you down "the yawning road,"
> For *Charon's second freight!*

Etching with aquatint.

[91]

VERY SLIPPY-WEATHER. 10 February 1808

An assortment of loungers check the window of Hannah Humphrey's printshop at 27 St. James's Street, Gillray's home, studio and place of business after 1797. Etched after a sketch by his amateur friend, the Rev. John Sneyd.

The preliminary drawing for this, and for six other caricatures on extremes of weather, were received by Gillray in November 1807. The author, John Sneyd, described his work as "thought to be worthy of publication," and asked the caricaturist to "put them in hand" (J. Bagot, *George Canning and His Friends*, London, 1909, vol. 1, p. 226). All seven were published on 10 February.

Of the fifteen Gillray prints identifiable in the window, the entire top row, the last of the second row and the first in the third row (see Plate 36) are probably based on Sneyd's "inspirations." The top row is a single series; "Taking Physick" was published on 6 February 1801, the remainder appeared on 28 January 1804: "Gentle Emetic," "Brisk Cathartic," "Breathing a vein" and "Charming well again." The original tentative drawing for "Taking Physick," in the author's possession, indicates that Gillray had to do quite a bit with Sneyd's work "to put it in hand."

The second print in the second row is reproduced in this volume as Plate VII, the third in the third row as Plate 38 and the fourth in the third row as Plate 42. The print being studied with approval by two potential customers (dissenting clergymen?) inside the shop is the "End of the Irish Farce of Catholic-Emancipation," published 17 May 1805.

The unhappy central figure, springing his braces and losing snuffbox and small change, may have been intended by Sneyd as a self-caricature (see note to Plate 40).

Mrs. Humphrey and Gillray took up residence in St. James's Street in April 1797. The caricaturist lived there on the east side, just above the corner of Little Ryder Street, until his death in 1815. After Mrs. Humphrey's death in 1818, the business was continued by her nephew George and then by his wife until 1835. The house was finally demolished in 1963 to make room for a modern structure to house the *Economist* magazine.

On 26 February, two weeks after Gillray produced this retrospective look at his career, Honoré Daumier was born at Marseilles.

[VIII.] (color plate)

PHAETON ALARM'D! 22 March 1808

Foreign Secretary George Canning struggles to guide the sun of his mentor, Apollo-Pitt, through the menacing skies of partisan opposition. A sequel to the "Light expelling Darkness" of 1795 (Plate 35).

In Greek mythology, Phaethon, offspring of the sun

god Helios, persuaded his father to let him drive the solar chariot. When the neophyte lost control of his horses and strayed too near the earth, scorching it, he was eliminated by an emergency thunderbolt from Zeus. Phaethon was supposed to have fallen at the mouth of a northern European river, later identified with the Po.

Canning is seen as the impetuous heir of Pitt; his policies add to the general world conflagration below. A monstrous aggregation of domestic enemies attempts to extinguish, or otherwise menace, "The Sun of Anti-Jacobinism." The global holocaust ranges from America in the west (English forces withdrew ignominiously from Buenos Aires in July 1807 and Britain's Continental blockade was an increasing irritant with the United States) to the Russian Empire in the east, dominated by the omnipotent figure of Napoleon, astride a giant, servile bear ("Ursa Major"). Flames crackle from Scandinavia and the Iberian peninsula, where Englishmen had been, or were about to be, involved. The two-headed Austrian eagle, "roasted" at Austerlitz in 1805, is dwarfed by the Franco-Russian alliance.

In June 1807, shortly after Canning came to office, Napoleon destroyed the Russian army at Friedland; the peace treaty which followed included secret provisions for a naval confederation of Denmark, Sweden and Portugal directed against England. Canning anticipated Napoleon's designs on the Danish fleet and ordered a "pre-emptive raid" of sorts on Copenhagen. This resulted in a violent siege of the Danish capital on 2–5 September, its surrender, and the capture and removal by Britain of all strategic vessels and naval stores. Canning felt that his bold move had prevented a hostile Baltic alliance, a French invasion of Ireland and the closing of Russian ports. Napoleon feigned horror at the violation of the rights of a small and ostensibly neutral nation; the Foreign Secretary's opponents in Parliament raised a loud cry over the ethics of the action. Grey's maiden speech in the Lords on 27 January 1808 was a particularly bitter attack. Gillray's elaborate satire, his first of 1808, appears to hinge on the Danish venture. One of the scales of British justice (also a reference to the constellation Libra), crushed beneath the flaming wheels of Canning's vehicle, is labeled "Copenhagen." An apprehensive, craven lion—"Leo Britannicus" (both national emblem and constellation)—mean as a street dog, chases behind. Below, the shade of Apollo-Pitt gazes in horror and weeps. At the opposite corner, Pluto-Fox appears to expect the worst.

Canning is depicted as youthful, as he had been at the time of his association with the caricaturist (1797–99; see p. xxii), though by 1808 he was virtually bald. His terrified horses are fellow cabinet ministers, Hawkesbury, Perceval, Castlereagh and Eldon. Phaethon is confronted by a mythical host, primarily representative of constellations and signs of the zodiac. Clockwise, from the upper left: Pisces (a pun, of course) is Lord Henry Petty, urinating on the sun (on 9 May 1806, Gillray had

pictured Lord Henry emitting a flood of new taxes in a satire titled "A Great Stream from a Petty-Fountain"); Aquarius is the brewer Whitbread, emitting a jet of "Small Beer" (Whitbread introduced a motion condemning the Copenhagen invasion on 29 February 1808); "Sangraderius" is Addington, Lord Sidmouth, squirting an enema from a clyster pipe (on 2 May 1803, Gillray had caricatured Addington as "Doctor Sangrado curing John Bull of Repletion"; Addington's father had been court physician, and the son was accordingly nicknamed "the Doctor" by Canning; Sangrado—from Spanish *sangrar*, to bleed—was the quack healer and teacher introduced in Chapter 3 of Alain René Le Sage's novel *L'Histoire de Gil Blas de Santillane*, 1715); Astr[a]ea (Greek goddess of Justice) is Erskine, egotistical barrister and former Lord Chancellor (1806–07).

Lord Chief Justice Ellenborough, clad in a lion's skin, prepares to swing his "Herculanean Club"; Grey, Canning's most bitter adversary, is Python, after a demon of Delphi supposedly killed by Apollo; Lauderdale, in Jacobin *bonnet rouge*, is the eagle constellation Aquila (which was also the name of a Roman tribune who refused to rise for Caesar).

Phaethon's path is blocked by an Irish bull (for Taurus), enraged by the porridge pot of Catholic emancipation tied to its tail. His most fearsome attacker is a giant "Scorpio Broad-Bottomis" (see Plates 89, 90) with the head of Grenville, holding baby scorpions Temple, Spencer and Bedford on his left and Moira and Tierney on his right. On Grenville's carapace, a Communion cup is ringed by the irradiated likenesses of (from the bottom) Holland, Norfolk, Carlisle, Derby, Stanhope and (?) Grafton.

Beneath the plunging team, Sheridan is the wine demon Silenus, St. Vincent is Cancer the crab (St. Vincent, former First Lord of the Admiralty, minimized the value of the siege of Copenhagen in a speech on 8 February) and Windham is the archer Sagittarius. Just below, Neptune drops his trident, presumably in consternation at Canning's exercise of sea power.

The bitter, quarrelsome nature of public debate at this time was noted the following year by an anonymous pamphleteer: "The character of Parliament is Changed, Business drags heavily . . . [with nothing but] personalities, . . . accusations, retorts, and breaches of order" (*Public Spirit*, 1809, p. 69; quoted by Michael Roberts in *The Whig Party, 1807–1812*, London, 1939, p. 116). Etching with aquatint.

[92]

SPANISH-PATRIOTS ATTACKING THE FRENCH-BANDITTI. 15 August 1808

Napoleon's troops were considered invincible until word arrived that some eighteen thousand of them had surrendered to the Spanish general Castaños at Baylén on 23 July.

On 2 May 1808, citizens of Madrid rose in violent protest against the French occupation of Spain. The weakling Charles IV was forced to abdicate in favor of his equally spineless son Ferdinand. "Displeased" by this show of hostility, Napoleon allowed a mercenary council of regency to "persuade" him that the throne should be offered instead to his own brother Joseph. Joseph Bonaparte was proclaimed King on 15 June, shredding the illusion of Spanish rule.

Not surprisingly, the naked seizure of power by the French goaded patriots all over the Peninsula into open rebellion. Under the direction of provincial juntas, the Spanish and Portuguese fought to throw off the foreign yoke. After a series of early reverses, rebel fortunes improved as the summer wore on. The French general Dupont (Comte Pierre-Antoine, 1765–1840) was engaged at Baylén by the Army of Andalusia under Castaños from 13 to 19 July. Burdened with plunder from the sacking of Cordova and isolated by Spanish troops and enraged peasants, Dupont handed over his men on 23 July. At this moment the Imperial tide began to turn—the French were obliged to evacuate Madrid and retreat to the Ebro. Four years later, Napoleon remarked: "The capitulation of Baylén ruined everything. In order to save his wagons of booty, Dupont committed his soldiers, his own countrymen, to the disgrace of a surrender without parallel" (Caulaincourt, *Mémoires*, J. Hanoteau, ed., Paris, 1933, vol. 1, p. 475).

In England, neither government nor public were slow to grasp the significance of this reversal. Arms and equipment had been rushed to the insurgents at once. On 1 August, Sir Arthur Wellesley (the future Duke of Wellington) landed on Portuguese soil with 9000 British troops. The good news from the Peninsula came as a welcome antidote to the prevailing atmosphere of defeat; London printsellers concentrated on the topic for the remainder of the year. Gillray's salute to the "Spanish-Patriots" appeared two days before Wellesley's men first saw action. Notwithstanding the subscript "Loyal Britons lending a lift" and the heroic grenadier in the right center, there were no English soldiers at Baylén.

In the print, the Spanish attack from the left. The French, in full retreat at the upper right, carry banners inscribed "Vive le Roi Joseph," "Dupont" and "La Mort ou la Victoire." (Joseph entered Madrid on 20 July, three days before the capitulation, and he departed unceremoniously on the 29th.) At the left foreground, a cavalier, two courtesans and a monk help operate a cannon. Beyond them, a sturdy nun deals with an unhappy French officer. The three most prominent of the insurgent banners proclaim "Victoire Espagnol," "Vive le Roi Ferdinand VII" and (in the center) the figure of "la Sainte Vierge," with the Savior in one hand and a sword in the other. (The great monastic orders found their power threatened by Napoleon, and accordingly were enthusiastic supporters of the revolt.) Etching with aquatint.

[93]

THE VALLEY OF THE SHADOW OF DEATH. 24 September 1808

Napoleon, in the improbable guise of Christian from *Pilgrim's Progress*, is confronted by an aggregation of national adversaries: a grim vision of Imperial doom prompted by French difficulties in the Peninsula.

Gillray's representation of Napoleon as Bunyan's virtuous protagonist provides an ironic counterpoise to a spate of satires which showed the French ruler as rampant predator, horrific dragon (see Plate 85) or the blasphemous seven-headed, ten-crowned beast of the Book of Revelations.

Bunyan speaks of Christian setting forth "with his Sword drawn in his hand," a "deep Ditch" on one side of his narrow path, a "dangerous Quag" on the other. The "Valley of the Shadow of Death" is described as being "as dark as pitch," a place of "Hobgoblins, Satyrs, and Dragons of the Pit" . . . "and over that Valley hangs the discouraging Clouds of confusion; death also doth spread his wings over it: in a word it is every whit dreadful, being utterly without Order."

Gillray's composition was inspired by news of Wellesley's victory over Junot on 21 August at Vimeiro, Portugal. Although serviceable as long-range prophecy, it greatly exaggerates the gravity of the French situation; just as the initial accounts which Bunyan's pilgrim receives of the "Valley" tend to maximize and accentuate his peril. In actuality, the course of events in the Peninsula was turning to Napoleon's advantage; he had made peace with Prussia and his mastery of Europe appeared relatively secure. With characteristic ambivalence and complexity, Gillray evokes the chimerical quality of Bunyan's hobgoblins to suggest a lack of faith in his own optimistic predictions of French disaster.

The principal attackers in the print are Spain (Death astride a mule of "True-Royal Spanish-Breed"); the "Portuguese Wolf," broken free of its chain; "Leo Britannicus"; and its satellite "Sicilian Terrier." Beneath the mule, King Joseph (Bonaparte; see Plate 92) drowns in the "Ditch of Styx" ("Into that Quag King David once did fall . . .": Bunyan). Behind Napoleon, the captive Russian Bear seems appropriately restive. The "Lethean Ditch" in the foreground harbors, left to right, "The Rhenish Confederation of starved Rats, crawling out of the Mud" (the Confederation of the Rhine, a group of Napoleonic puppet states formed in July 1806, included Bavaria, Württemberg, Baden, Aschaffenburg, Hesse-Darmstadt and several others); "Dutch Frogs spitting out their spite"; the "American Rattle-Snake shaking his Tail" (Gillray's intimation of United States hostility to Napoleon ignores the fact that the former colonies were equally provoked at Britain, as a consequence of the latter's Continental blockade and impressments at sea; this rare American allusion harks back to the "Don't Tread on Me" banner of the Revolutionary War); and, in the right corner, the "Prussian Scare-Crow attempting to Fly" (Prussia, crippled at the battles of Jena and Auerstädt in October 1806, was eventually instrumental in the downfall of Napoleon, turning on him after the Russian debacle of 1812).

In the sky overhead, a flaming, flashing papal tiara menaces the Emperor—the "Dreadful Descent of ye Roman Meteor" (early in 1808, Napoleon had occupied Rome and absorbed the papal army; his deteriorating relations with the Vatican culminated in the arrest and imprisonment of Pius VII in July 1809). "The Turkish New-Moon, Rising in Blood" shows the shadowed area of "French Influence" superseded by the bright crescent of "British Influence" (the French had urged the Turks to resume war with Russia: bad advice which tended to turn Turkish sentiments away from France and toward Britain). "The Spirit of Charles ye XII" (soldier-king of Sweden, 1682–1718) prepares to swing a giant sword; and the Austrian double-headed eagle poises to swoop down from behind—"The Imperial Eagle emerging from a Cloud" (after some three years' recuperation following Austerlitz, Austria returned to the offensive in April 1809 and inflicted Napoleon's first actual defeat on him at Aspern, 21–22 May 1809). In the mid-distance, two ghostly French officers call, "Remember Junot" and "Remember Dupont," references to General Andoche Junot, Duc d'Abrantès, 1771–1813, defeated at Vimeiro, and to General Dupont, unsuccessful commander at Baylén (see Plate 92). Etching with aquatint.

[94]

PANDORA OPENING HER BOX. 22 February 1809

Mrs. Mary Anne Clarke, former mistress of the Duke of York, appears before the bar of the House of Commons to support charges that she had connived with the Duke, commander in chief of British forces, to sell army commissions at bargain prices. Mrs. Clarke was examined by the House on the first of February and on six subsequent days. The scandal absorbed the nation's attention for months and resulted, 20 March, in the resignation of the Duke.

Mary Anne Clarke (née Thompson, 1776–1852; married to Joseph Clarke, stonemason, 1793; established as an actress, 1794) met and captivated Frederick Augustus, Duke of York (second son of the King; see Plate 24) in 1803. She was maintained by him in a Gloucester Place mansion for the next three years, with such amenities as twenty servants, two carriages and a stable of twenty horses.

During this period she did a brisk business selling vacant commissions for personal gain, at the expense of the army's charitable "Half-Pay Fund." Mrs. Clarke was also supposed to have dealt in ecclesiastical preferments. As a result of her "pecuniary transactions," the Duke severed connections in May 1806, granting the lady an annual allowance of £400 so long as her conduct was

"correct." She failed to satisfy this condition, and by June 1808 was threatening to publish "everything which has come under my knowledge during our intimacy, with all his letters" if the stipend were not paid (from a letter produced in Parliament on 3 February; quoted by M. D. George in English Political Caricature, London, 1959, vol. ii, p. 117).

The matter was brought to a full boil in the House of Commons on 27 January 1809 by Gwyllym Lloyd Wardle (1762?–1833), M.P. for Okehampton, an ex-colonel of militia who had been refused an army commission. Wardle challenged the Duke of York, presenting a long and detailed account of Mrs. Clarke's actions, her scale of prices and records of specific transactions. His motion that a committee of the whole House look into the matter was adopted.

The inquiry commenced on the first of February with Mrs. Clarke, who was dressed, according to the Morning Post (3 February), "as if she had been going to an evening party, in a light blue silk gown and coat, edged with white fur and a white muff." She wore "a white cap or veil which was not let down" and the paper's correspondent complained of her smell, found her "not handsome, not well bred or accomplished" and spoke of "a turned-up nose" and "indifferent teeth" (quoted by John Ashton in The Dawn of the XIXth Century in England, London, 1885, p. 427). Despite this jaundiced view, Mrs. Clarke's wit, impudence and coolness under fire were a great hit with the House and the public. Wilberforce noted in his diary that she "clearly got the better in the tussle" (Wilberforce's Life, vol. iii, p. 402; quoted by Joseph Grego in The Works of James Gillray, the Caricaturist, London, 1873, p. 361). The Duke of York conceded that there had been intimacy, but denied any knowledge of, or participation in, illegal actions. On 17 March the House found him innocent of corruption or connivance by a vote of 278 to 196. He resigned three days later, but was reappointed commander in chief in 1811. In July 1809, Wardle's stature as a patriotic reformer was somewhat diminished by evidence that he too had been Mrs. Clarke's lover, and that they were apparently in collusion against the Duke. Both elected to live abroad. Mrs. Clarke was convicted of libel and eventually imprisoned (1814) before she settled in Paris (c. 1816). (Her daughter Ellen, born 1797, gave birth in 1834 to George du Maurier, noted Victorian illustrator, caricaturist and author.)

Gillray shows Mrs. Clarke lifting the "Cover of Infamy" from an "Opposition Stink Box" to release a serpentine smog of calumny, lies, ingratitude, deceit, revenge, forgery and perjury. Among the early satires on the scandal, this is one of the few to question the motives prompting the revelations and to suggest the existence of a partisan scheme to embarrass the government. The "Broad Bottom Reservoir" (toilet) at the lower left is surrounded by a heap of documents, including a prescient reference to "Love Letters from Mr. Waddle" and four other gentlemen, "Mr. Finnerty," "Gen. Clamering" (a General Clavering denied his dealings with Mrs. Clarke before the House, was found guilty of perjury and committed to Newgate), "Mr. Maltby" and "Major Hogan." Other papers refer to a "List of Mrs. Clarks Pensions," "Forged Appoint[ments]," "Forged Orders," "Forged Letters & Forged Answers from the Duke," a "Scheme to destroy the House of Bru[ns]wick," "Charges," "Commissions & Appointments for Sale to the best Bidder," "Agents to conduct the Sale—Frome Sanden Dowler Kennel Donnovan Corri" (Frome was an army commissions agent dismissed for corruption in May 1807, after a caricature print caught the eye of the King—see M. D. George, *ibid.*, p. 117—a Captain Sandon was examined by the House in 1809 and imprisoned for perjury), "Private Communications from his Excell[enc]y The Morrocco Ambassador" ("the Ambassador of Morocco" was Mrs. Clarke's nickname for one Taylor, "a ladies' shoemaker in Bond Street" who served as a conduit with the Duke after her separation from him; see Thomas Wright and R. H. Evans, *Historical and Descriptive Account of the Caricatures of James Gillray*, 1851, p. 336), and "Prices of Commissions in the Army. A. Clarke Sec."

On the Treasury Bench, Castlereagh, Canning and Perceval hold their noses. Whitbread, Petty and Burdett are visible immediately to the right of Mrs. Clarke, among the exultant Opposition. (Petty, however, did not support the inquiry.)

In Greek mythology, Pandora was the first woman, bestowed on mankind by Jupiter as punishment for Prometheus' theft of fire. Entrusted with a mysterious not-to-be-opened box (full of unimaginable evils), she lifted the lid out of curiosity and contaminated the world. Etching with aquatint.

[95]

LES INVISIBLES. 1810 (?)

A burlesque on the opportunities for self-concealment afforded by the extremes of "Empire" fashion; copied by Gillray from an anonymous French original.

The "Invisibles" would appear to have been intended as sequels to the "Incroyables" (Unbelievables), grotesquely frilled and rumpled Parisian dandies of the Directory period (1795–99).

Gillray's graceful, meticulous stipple etching is based on a preliminary drawing in the author's collection. This subject must have been "in progress" for at least three years, since an evidently earlier sketch on the reverse of the preliminary fixes the date of the first effort as no later than April 1807. In his etching, Gillray has adjusted the spatial relationships between figures and reduced the décolletage of the lady on the arm of the gentleman in the center.

Given the political situation and the French derivation, it scarcely needs to be noted that the pretentious credit lines ("Dèpose à la Bibliot Nat. Rue Montmartre N. 132 . . . et à Londres, chez H. Humphrey, St. James Street") are facetious.

[96]

A BARBERS-SHOP IN ASSIZE TIME.—FROM A PICTURE PAINTED BY H. W. BUNBURY ESQ. Dated 9 January 1811; published 15 May 1818

Rustic candidates anticipating jury duty in a county assize, or court, are made presentable for their official service. The grand assizes were periodic biannual local sittings of the high court of justice, a long-standing tradition finally abolished in 1833. Gillray's last known engraving, this plate was executed during lucid intervals after his loss of reason in 1810, and published posthumously.

Henry Bunbury (1750–1811), well born, well educated, well traveled, well connected, was easily the most popular comic artist during the transitional years between the death of Hogarth and the age of Gillray and Rowlandson. His witty tableaux, reproduced from slight but deftly modeled watercolors by a variety of engravers, enjoyed a particular vogue in the 1770s and 1780s. He retired to Keswick after the death of his wife in 1798 and died there four months after Gillray appears to have signed and dated "A Barbers-Shop."

Two Gillray preliminary drawings survive in the New York Public Library, a detail of the central pair and a careful pencil rendition of the full composition on transfer paper, more crisp and unified than the final labored plate. This project appears to have served a therapeutic function like needlework or embroidery; the modeling has been painstakingly achieved with stipple and fine roulette. A drawing dated 1 July 1811 displays a far more aggressive spirit; Gillray's line jags and veers ferociously, his inkless point gouges the paper. (George Cruikshank later recalled that the hand of the mad Gillray was always moving "as if in the act of painting.") Three weeks later he reportedly attempted suicide by trying to throw himself out of his attic window (see D. Hill, *Mr. Gillray The Caricaturist*, London, 1965, pp. 145–46).

Bunbury's fondness for tonsorial topics had surfaced on several previous occasions, notably "The Village Barber," a print of 1772, and "A Barber's Shop" (1785). The latter was a large interior view with numerous allusions to the Westminster election of 1784, similar in many respects to the plate reproduced here.

The Bunbury-Gillray "Barbers-Shop" is a riotous carnival of incidental detail. Meat and dried vegetables hang from the ceiling; the prints on the wall depict a naval battle, a "County Gaol," a public hanging, a skeleton fiddling with demons cavorting, and "A Calendar of the Prisoners to be Tried . . . Grand Assize [?]." Fishing rods and a creel are over the door; the customer beneath is treating a cut on his chin. Beneath the table a cat defecates. The magpie (center foreground) is getting into someone's wig box; the dog behind the bird reacts unhappily to the spectacle of his master's shaggy, antiquated wig. The bulbous bumpkin at the extreme left seems to be comparing his cranium to the wig block. Only the contented individual behind him appears to reflect polish and self-possession; he is probably the circuit judge, down from Westminster.

The initial impressions bore the inscription, apparently in Gillray's hand, "Publish'd January 9 1811, by H. Humphrey, St. James's Street, London," with all but the date scored out. It is conceivable that Mrs. Humphrey objected to the issuance of this plate on the grounds that it was unworthy of the caricaturist. She may have hoped, prior to his death on the first of June 1815, that he might recover and rework it. In any case, at her death—which probably occurred in March 1818—her nephew and heir lost no time in making it available. It stands as a gigantic (17 by 24 inches), poignant tailpiece to any collection of Gillray's work.